Foundation Biology

For Class X

Part-2 of 2

NOTION PRESS

NOTION PRESS

India. Singapore. Malaysia.

ISBN xxx-x-xxxxx-xx-x

Dedicated to our Beloved Prime Minister Shree Narendra Modi ji, whose life gives the Inspiration to every Individual

*If a Man **Decides** to achieve something in his life nothing is Impossible*

कर्मण्येवाधिकारस्ते मा फलेषु कदाचन।

मा कर्मफलहेतुर्भूर्मा ते सङ्गोऽस्त्वकर्मणि॥ २-४७

Karmanye vadhikaraste Ma Phaleshu Kadachana,

Ma Karmaphalaheturbhurma Te Sangostvakarmani

You have the right to work only but never to its fruits.

Let not the fruits of action be your motive, nor let your attachment be to inaction.

CONTENT

TOPIC NAME	PAGE NO.

3. HOW DO ORGANISMS REPRODUCE

TOPIC NAME	PAGE NO.

4. HEREDITY & EVOLUTION

TOPIC NAME	PAGE NO.

5. OUR ENVIRONMENT

TOPIC NAME	PAGE NO.

6. MANAGEMENT OF NATURAL RESOURCES

3 HOW DO ORGANISMS REPRODUCE

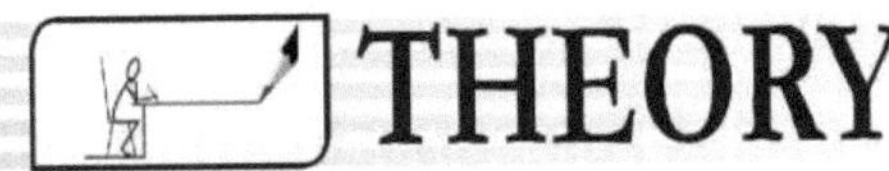

THEORY

INTRODUCTION

MEANING OF REPRODUCTION :

- Reproduction is the ability of living organisms to produce new living organisms similar to them. It is one of the important characteristic of life.

Purpose of Reproduction :

- Reproduction is aimed to multiplication and perpetuation (stability) of the species. In other words it proves group immortality by replacing the dead individuals with new ones.

Basic Features of Reproduction :

- The modes of reproduction vary in different organisms. However all of them have certain common basic features. These are -

(i) Replication of DNA
(ii) Cell division
(iii) Formation of reproductive bodies or units
(iv) Development of reproductive bodies into offspring

Significance of Reproduction :

(i) It allows perpetuation of species.
(ii) It increases the population of a species.
(iii) It plays an important role in evolution by transmitting favourable variations from one generation to another generation.

FORMS OF REPRODUCTION :

- Animals reproduce in a variety of ways, which are categorized in two categories i.e. Asexual and sexual reproduction.

1. Asexual reproduction :

- It is the process of producing new organism from a single parent without the involvement of sex cells or gametes.
- As only somatic cells are involved it is also called as **somatogenic reproduction**. Due to monoparental reproduction, it produce identical offsprings (all are clones).
  Examples : Binary fission in ***Amoeba***, Fragmentation in ***Spirogyra***, vegetative propagation in flowering plants like **Rose** and Spore formation in ***Rhizopus*** fungus.

2. Sexual reproduction :

- It is the process of producing new organism from two parents by making use of their sex cells or gametes.
  Examples : Human, fish, frogs, cats, dogs and most of the flowering plants.

ASEXUAL REPRODUCTION

Definition :

- Production of offspring by a single parent without the formation and fusion of gametes is called as **asexual reproduction**. It is more primitive type of reproduction. It ensures rapid increase in number.

Occurrence :

- Asexual reproduction occurs in protozoans and some animals such as sponges, coelentrates, certain worms and tunicates. It is absent among the higher invertebrates and all vertebrates.

Characteristics of Asexual Reproduction

(i) Only one individual of an organism is involved, i.e., opposite sexes are not involved.
(ii) Cell divisions are either amitotic or mitotic.
(iii) The new individuals produced are genetically identical to their parents.
(iv) Asexual reproduction presents a rapid mode of multiplication.

Advantages and disadvantages of Asexual Reproduction

- **Advantages**
  Asexual reproduction is simple and fast.
- **Disadvantages**

(i) Evolutionary change is not possible as no variation is produced. A species consequently cannot adapt to changes in its environment.
(ii) Asexual reproduction produces identical organisms generation after generation. In case of any defect in the parent organism, the offspring also inherits it.

TYPE OF REPRODUCTION :

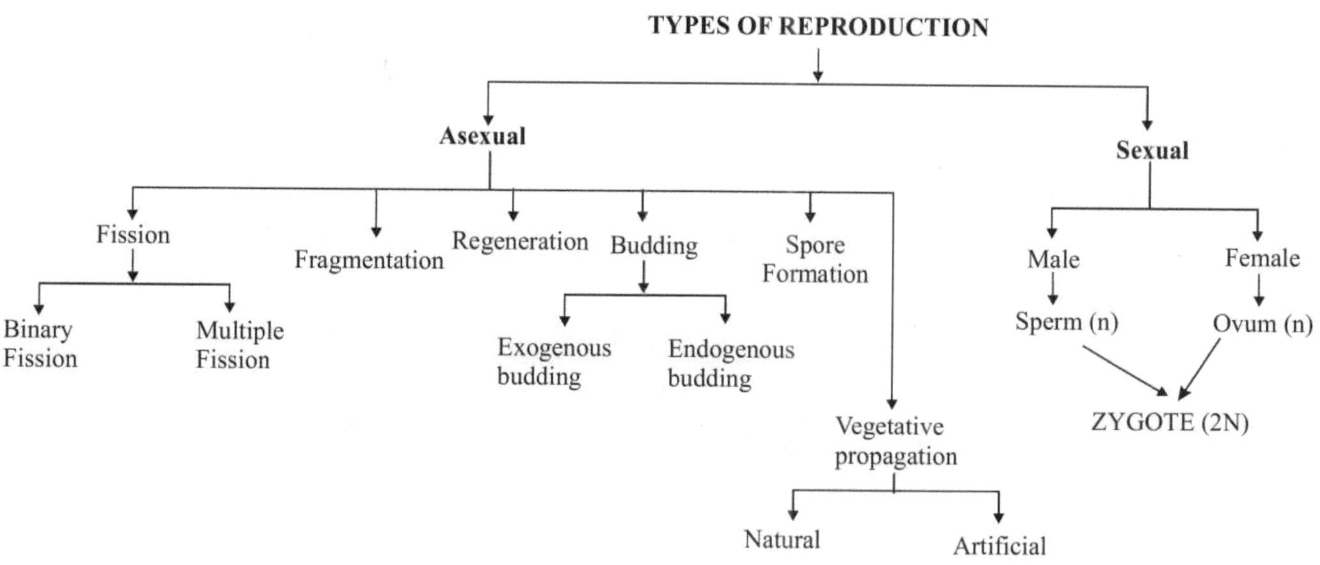

TYPE OF ASEXUAL REPRODUCTION :

- A sexual reproduction takes place in the following principal ways :

I. Fission :

- It is the simplest form of reproduction in which unicellular organism either divide into two or many organisms.
- **It is also divided into two types :**

(a) **Binary fission :** It is a type of reproduction in which nuclear division is followed by the appearance of a constriction in the cell membrane, which gradually deep inward and divides the cytoplasm into two parts, each with one nucleus. Finally two daughter cells are formed. **eg.** *Amoeba*. It may be transverse, when plane of cytoplasmic division coincides with the transverse axis of the organism, as seen in *Paramecium*; or it may be longitudinal when the cytoplasmic division coincides with the longitudinal axis of the individual, as is seen in *Euglena*.

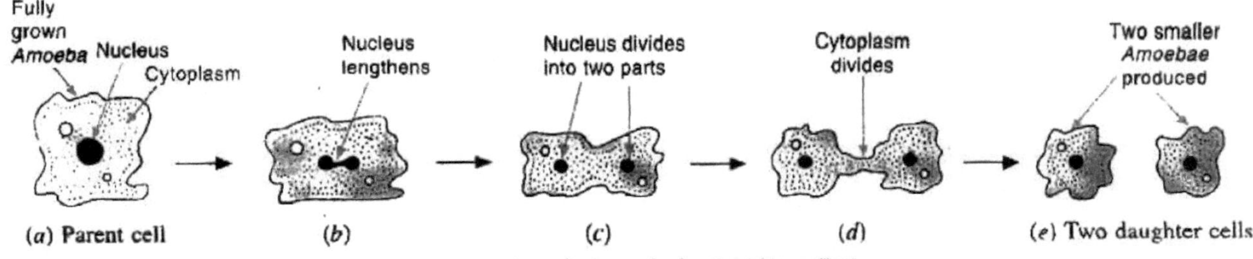

Amoeba reproducing by binary fission.

(b) **Multiple fission :** Sometimes the nucleus divides several times into many daughter nuclei. The daughter nuclei arrange at the periphery of the parent cell, and a bit of cytoplasm around each daughter nuclei is present. nucleus develops an outer membrane. Finally the multinucleated body divides into many daughter cells. **Eg.** Plasmodium.

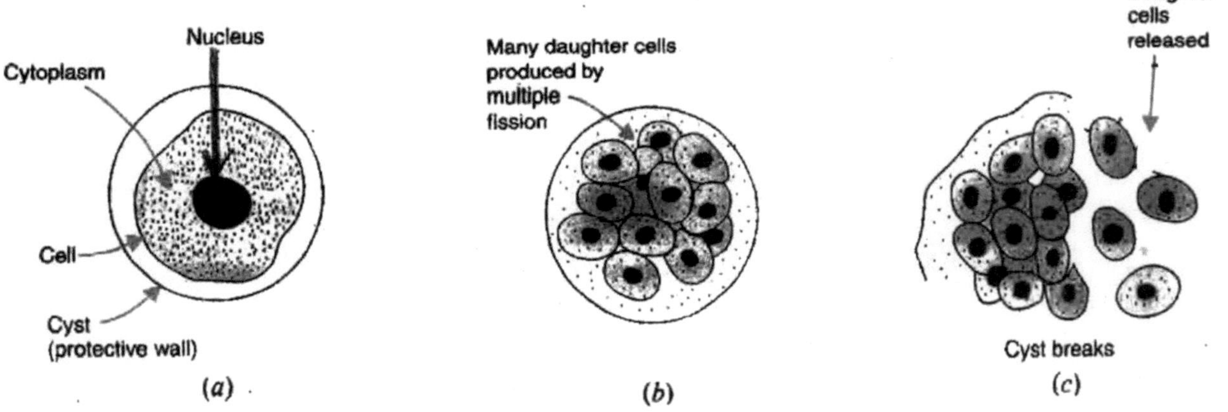

Reproduction by multiple fission.

II. Fragmentation :

In this process an entire new organism can grow from certain pieces or cells of the parent organisms. Ex. Flatworm. spirogyra.

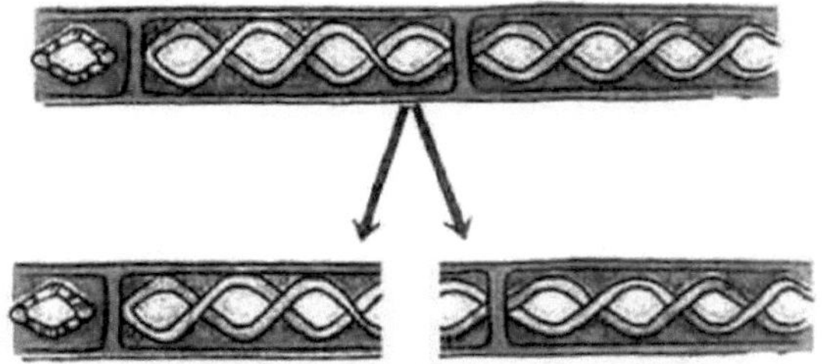

Fragmentation in spirogyra (an alga)

III. Regeneration

- The process of getting back the full organism from its body part is called **regeneration** or by autotomy (self amputation as is seen in some lizards which break off their tail). It may be described as the power to retsore lost tissues, organ or the whole body, seen in fully differentiated organism. **Eg.** *Planaria.*

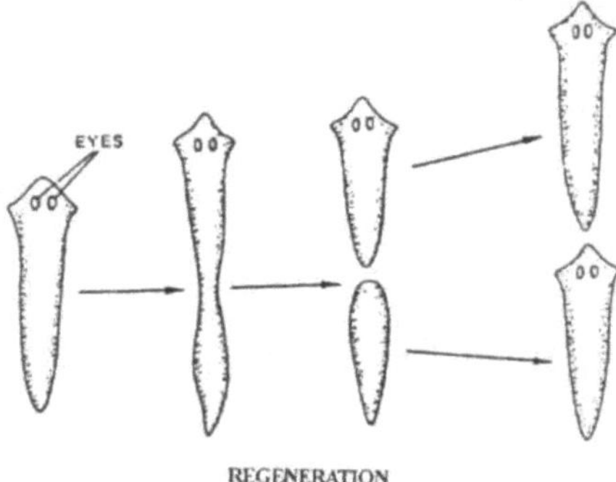

REGENERATION

IV. Budding :

- Formation of daughter individual from a small projection which is called as **bud**, arising on the parent body is called as **budding**.

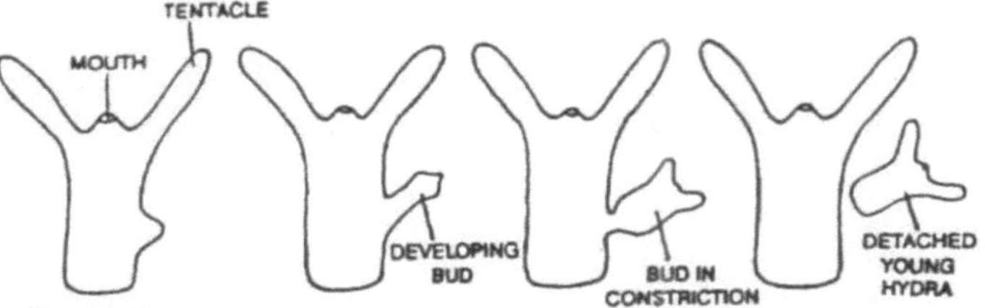

- **Budding is also of two types :**

(a) **Exogenous budding :** [External budding] In this, bud arises from the surface of parent body, **e.g.**, *Hydra.*

(b) **Endogenous budding :** [Internal budding] In this, bud arises inside or within the parent body called gammule. **e.g.**, Sponges.

> **NOTE :** During the process of budding, the bud remains attached to the parent body so as to derive it's nutrition from the parent but as it matures, it get's detached form the parent body.

V. Spore formation :

- It is a process of reproduction most commonly found in fungi, some cocci and bacillus bacteria. During this process a structure called as **sporangium** is formed. In this structure nucleus divides several times and each nucleus with a little trace of cytoplasm forms a spore. Non-motile and non-flagellated spores are called **aplanospores** while the motile and flagellated spores are called **zoospores**. These spores are then liberated out and develop into a new hypheae, **e.g.** *Rhizopus.*

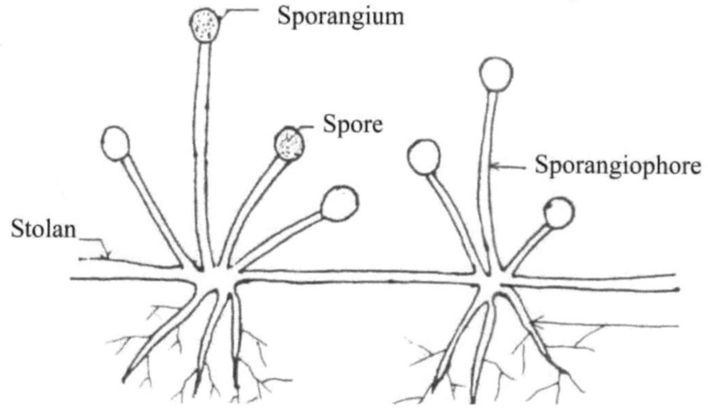

VI. Vegetative propagation :

- In vegetative propagation, new plants are obtained from the part of old plants like stems, roots and leaves, without the help of any reproductive organ.

  (a) Natural Vegetative Propagation.

  (b) Artifical Vegetative Propagation.

(a) **Natural Vegetative Propagation :** Various structures that take part in this types of reproduction are roots, stem and leaves.

(i) **Natural Vegetative Propagation by Roots :** In some plants like Dahlia, sweet potato, etc., the adventitious roots become thick, swollen and tuberous due to storage of food.

(ii) **Natural Vegetative Propagation by Leaves :** The fleshy leaves of Bryophyllum bear adventitious buds in the notches along the leaf margin.

- When the leaves fall on the soil, the buds develop into small plants under favourable conditions.
- These plantlets on being detached, develop into independent plant.

(iii) **By underground modified stems -** The node or the eye of potato tuber is used as a propagule. Rhizome of ginger, corm of banana and bulb of garlic and onion are also used as propagules.

(iv) **By runner -** The auxillary buds on the lowest leaf of the plant gives rise to modified branches known as **runners**. They give out roots at the nodes. These segments can be cut and used as propagules e.g. lawn grass.

(b) **Artificial Vegetative Propagation :** Some plant growers have developed artificial methods of vegetative propagation like cutting, layering and grafting which are used in agriculture and horticulture.

- **It is of following types :**

(i) **Cutting :** This is the very common method of vegetative propagation practised by the gardeners all over the world. It is the process in which a vegetative portion from plant is taken and is rooted in the soil to form a new plant e.g. Grapes, Sugarcane etc.

(ii) **Layering :** In this process the development of adventitious roots is induced on a stem before it gets detached from parent plant, e.g, Mango, Roses etc.

- **It is of following types :**

(a) **Mound layering :** In the process of layering the lower stem branch of plant is used. Leaves are removed from this stem. Then it is bent close to the ground, pegged and covered with the moist soil in such a way that it's growing tip remains above the solid surface. This pegged down branch is called as layer. After a few days the covered portion of stem develops roots. This stem is then detached from the parent plant and is grown separately from the parent as a result the plant develops separately into a new individual. e.g. Jasmine.

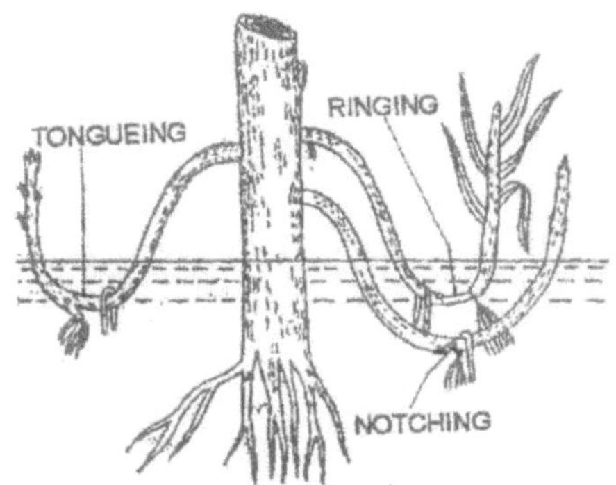

Showing vegetative propagation by layering in jasmine.

> **NOTE :** The formation of adventitious roots in a layer can be hastened by injuring the 'layer' by tonguing, ringing or notching.

(b) Air layering : It is adopted in those plants where stem cannot be bent to the ground. In this process the stem is girdled (i.e. ring of the bark is removed). then it is covered with moist moss or cotton and wrapped with a polythene sheet to preserve the moisture. After few weeks adventitious roots develop from the injured part. The branch along with roots in then separated from the parent plant and planted to grow into a new plant. **e.g.** Orange, Pomegranate etc.

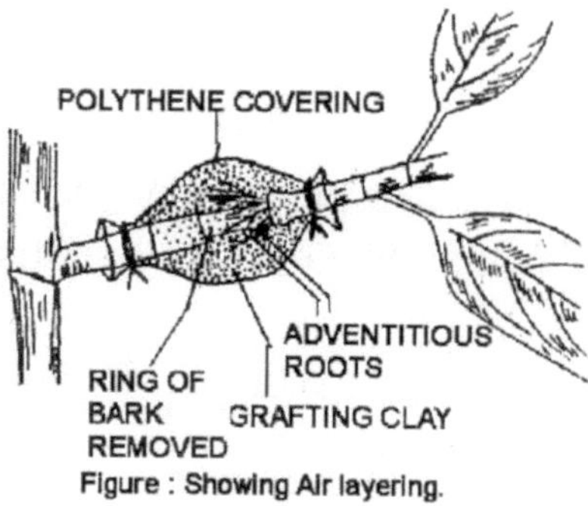

Figure : Showing Air layering.

(iii) Grafting : The process of joining together of two different plants in such a manner that they live as one plant is called as grafting. Out of the two plants one is rooted in the soil and is known as the stock. The other part consist of a small shoot bearing one or more buds, it is known as scion. Their union is carried out in such a way that their cambium must overlap each other e.g. Mango, roses etc.

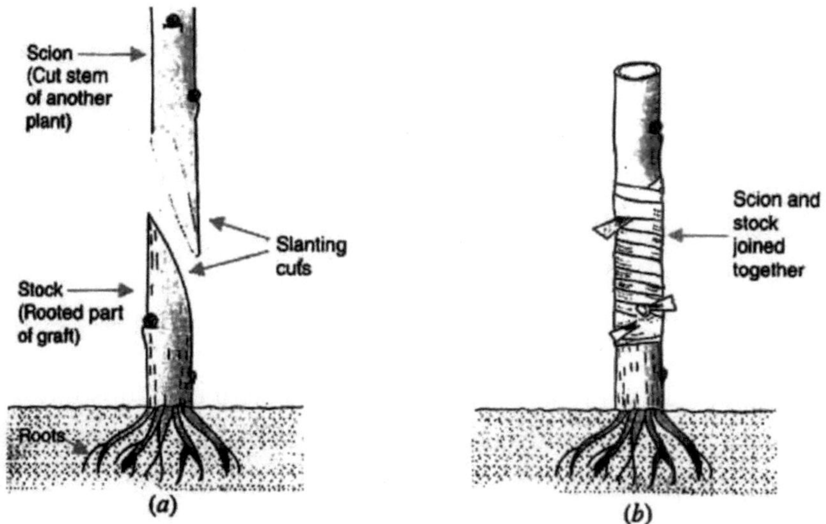

The grafting method for the artifical propagation of plants (or trees).

Advantages of Vegetative Propagation

(i) Vegetative propagation is a cheaper, easier and more rapid method of propagation in plants than growing plants from their seeds.

(ii) The traits or characters of the parent plant are preserved by vegetative propagation.

(iii) Better quality of the plants can be maintained by this method.

(iv) It results in propagation of those plants which do not produce viable seeds or produce seeds with prolonged period of dormancy.

(v) The plants generated from vegetative means require less time to grow and have the advantage of being more uniform and genetically similar to the parent stock.

Disadvantages of Vegetative Propagation

(i) Vegetative propagation induces over-crowding.

(ii) There is no genetic variation, so there is less adaptability to the environment.

(iii) The disease of the parent plant gets transferred to the offspring.

(iv) The plants lose vigour.

(v) New characters can neither be introduced nor undesirable characters be eliminated.

TISSUE CULTURE :

- It is the production or propagation of new plants from isolated plant cells or small pieces of plant tissue in a synthetic medium of culture solution. Tissue culture for producing new plants is done as follows :
  - Plants are grown by removing tissues or separating cells from the growing tip of the plant and put in an artificial medium.
  - The plant tissue divide to form small group of cells or callus.
  - The callus is transferred to another medium containing hormones for growth and differentiation, that forms plantlets.
  - The plantlets produced are transplanted into pots or soil where they can grow to form mature plants.
  - This technique is also known as invitro micropropagation because it takes place outside the body of the parent plant in a test tube using an artificial environment.
  - Micropropagation technique is being used for the production of ornamental plants like Orchids, Dahlia and Carnation.
  - It has now become possible due to recent techniques to produce a large number of plantlets from a small piece of tissue taken from the shoot tip or other suitable plant parts. This method of propagation is called as **micropropagation**. It involves the process of tissue culture. **e.g.**, Orchids, ornamental plants etc.

PARTHENOGENESIS :

- It is a modification of sexual reproduction in which an egg develops into a complete offspring without fertilization. It is monoparental (i.e. fusion of gametes does not occur, only a single parent gives rise to a new individual).

APOMIXIS

- It is the method of development of seed without fertilization.

Significance of asexual reproduction :

- It brings about multiplication of the species only. It does not play a role in evolution as no variation is introduced into the new individual formed by it.

SEXUAL REPRODUCTION :

Definition :

- Production of offspring by formation and fusion of special haploid cells called as **gametes**. These are contributed generally by two parents. *i.e.*, male gamete and female gamete is called as **sexual reproduction**.

Occurrence :

- Sexual reproduction occurs nearly in all animals including those which reproduce asexually. In most animals there are two sexes male and female, and the differences between them are genetically determined.

Types of sexual reproduction :

(i) **Syngamy :** It involves the complete and permanent fusion of two gametes to form a composite cell called as **zygote**. This is a common mode of sexual reproduction. When the two fusing gametes are morphologically and physiologically similar to each other, the process is called isogamy e.g. Monocystis. When two organism themselve act as gametes it is called **hologamy** e.g. *Yeast*.

(ii) **Conjugation :** It involve temporary pairing of two parents which exchange their pronuclei and then undergo the process of separation **.e.g.** *Paramecium* etc.

Characteristics of sexual reproduction :

(i) It is generally biparental [i.e. it involves two parents]

(ii) It involves formation and fusion of gametes.

(iii) Cell divisions are both meiotic & mitotic. Meiotic during gamete formation and mitotic during development of zygote into an offspring.

(iv) The offspring's are not genetically identical to the parents.

(v) Fertilization in case of humans is internal.

(vi) Infants can be fed on mother's milk.

(vii) Parental care is very well developed.

Significance of sexual reproduction :

(i) It results in multiplication and perpetuation of species.

(ii) It contributes to evolution of the species by introducing variation in a population much more rapidly than asexual reproduction.

SEXUAL REPRODUCTION IN PLANTS

- **A flower Consists of Following Parts :**

(i) **Calyx :** The sepals collectively are called as **calyx**. They are usually green in colour and protect the inner whorls of a flower especially during bud formation.

(ii) **Corolla :** It consists of coloured petals. They are normally large often has fragrance and bright coloured. Their primary function is to attract animals and insects for pollination.

(iii) **Androecium / stamen / male reproductive organ :** The stamens are referred to as the male reproductive organ. A typical stamen is differentiated into three parts, they are filament, connective and anther.

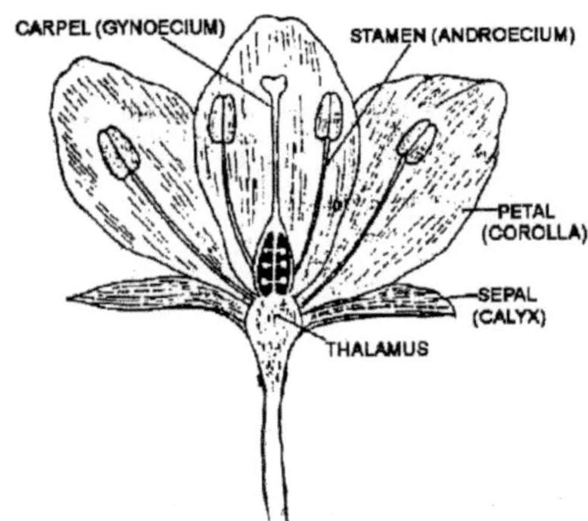

Figure. A vertical section of a typical flower

(a) **Filament :** It forms the stalk that bears more or less cylindrical or ovoid anther.

(b) **Connective :** It connects anther to filament.

(c) **Anther :** It is present on the top of filament. Each anther consists of two lobes that is why it is called as **bilobed** (Dithecous). one anther lobe has two pollen sacs called **microsporangia**, which contain millions of tiny microscopic grains, called as **microspores**. The pollen grains are like yellow dusty powder in appearance.

- A typical anther is bilobed (dithecous); a longitudinal groove separates the thecae.
- In a cross-section, the anther is a tetragonal (four-sided) structure, consisting of four microsporangia, two in each of the lobes.
- A microsporangium is more often circular in outline and is surrounded by four wall layers :

(i) The outermost is the single layer of epidermis.

(ii) The second layer is endothecium, where cells develop thickenings.

(iii) Middle layers of 2-4 layers of cells and

(iv) Tapetum, the innermost layer of large diploid/polyploid and binucleate or multinucleate cells.

- Tapetum nourishes the developing microspores or pollen grains; while the other three wall layers provide protection.

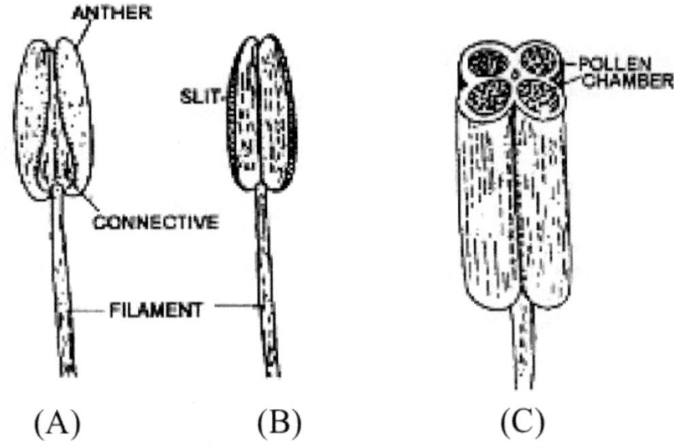

Figure: (A) Central view showing connective, (B) Dorsal view (C) T.S. of anther showing pollen chambers

- **Pollen grains** represent the male gametophyte.
- Pollen grains are generally spherical measuring about 25-50 micrometers in diameter.

- It has a two layered wall. The outer hard layer is called the **exine** which is made up of one of the most resistant organic material known as sporopollenin. It can withstand high temperatures and strong acids, alkali and enzymes.
- The exine has apertures called **germ pores**, where the sporopollenin is absent. The exine has various patterns and designs which help in identification.
- Pollen grains have been found as fossils because of the presence of sporopollein.
- The inner wall of the pollen grain is called the **intine**. It is thin and continuous layer made up of cellulose and pectin.
- The cytoplasm of the pollen grain is surrounded by a plasma membrane.
- A mature pollen grain contains two nucleus - the **vegetative nucleus** and **generative nucleus**.
- Thus hilum represents the junction between ovule and funicle. Each ovule has two protective coverings called **integuements**.
- They cover the whole ovule except at the tip where a small opening called the **micropyle** is present.
- Opposite the micropyle end is the **chalaza**, which is the basal part of the ovule.
- Enclosed within the integuments is a mass of cells called **nucellus**.
- These cells are rich in reserve food material.
- Embedded in the nucellus is the female gameotophyte called **embryo sac**.

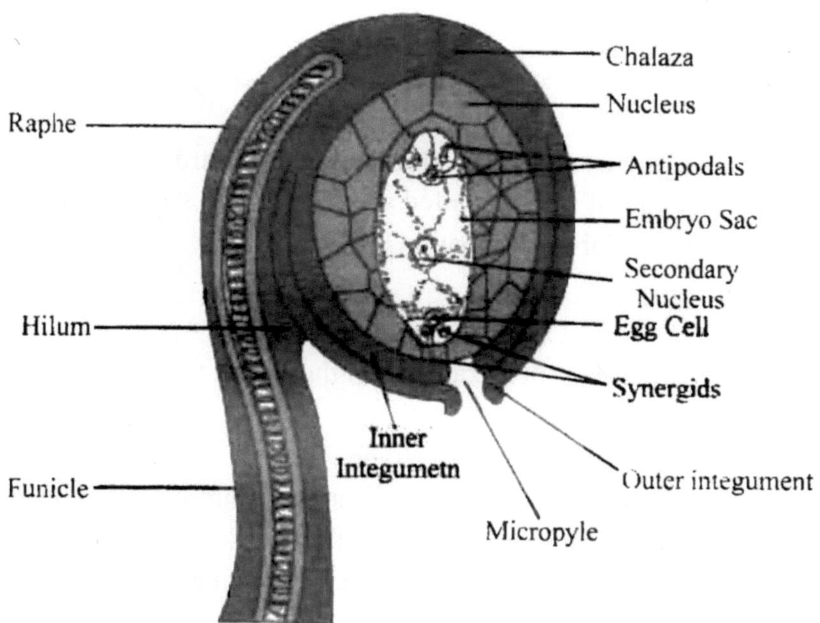

Diagrammatic representation of a mature Embryo sac.

(iv) Gynoecium / pistil / female reproductive organ :

- It is located in the center of a flower.
- It is composed of one or more carpels.
- The freely occurring units of the carpels in a flower are called pistils.
- Each pistil usually consist of three distinct parts - ovary, style and stigma.

(a) Ovary : It is a basal, swollen part of the pistil. The ovary has one or more chambers called the **loculi** which is distributed in a special cushion like parenchymatous tissue called the **placenta**, from which the ovule develops.

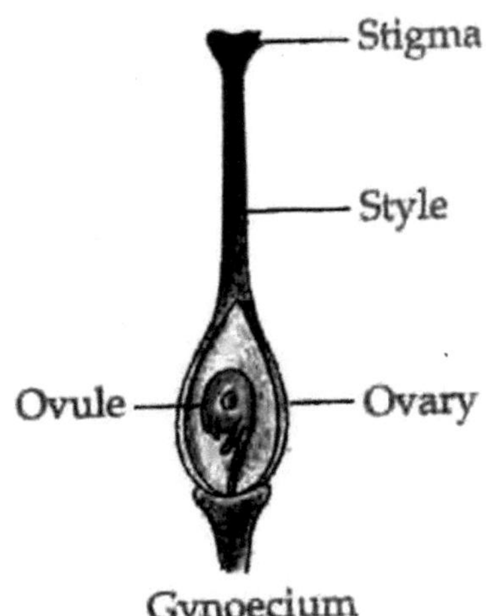

Gynoecium : Female reproductive part of a plant

Ovule:

- The ovule arises as a primordium on the placenta; it is attached to the placenta by a short stalk called **funiculus** or **funicle**.
- The junction between the funicle and the ovule is called **hilum**, which remains as a scar on the seed.

Embryo sac:

- A typical angiospermic embryo sac at maturity is eight nucleated but seven celled.

(b) **Style :** From the top of the ovary arises a long, elongated structure called as **style**.

(c) **Stigma :** The terminal end of style is called as **stigma**. The stigma is normally rough, hairy or sticky to hold pollen grains during pollination process.

POLLINATION :

◆ The transfer and deposition of pollen grains from the anther to the stigma of a flower is called as **pollination**.

◆ **Types of pollination :** Pollination is of two type :

(i) **Self pollination :** It is the process of transfer of the pollen grains from the anther to the stigma of either the same or genetically similar flower. It is further divided into two types :

(a) **Autogamy:** It is a type of self pollination in which the pollen grains are transferred from the anther to stigma of the same flower e.g. Wheat, rice pea etc.

(b) **Geitonogamy :** It is a type of self pollination in which the pollen grains are transferred from the anthers of one flower to the stigma of another flower borne either on the same plant or a genetically identical plant.

Significance of self pollination :

- It maintains purity of race.
- It also maintains the superiority of variety once developed.
- It also leads to the hybrid production.

(ii) **Cross pollination :** it is the process of transfer of the pollen grains from the anther of one flower to the stigma of another flower borne on a different plant of the same species.

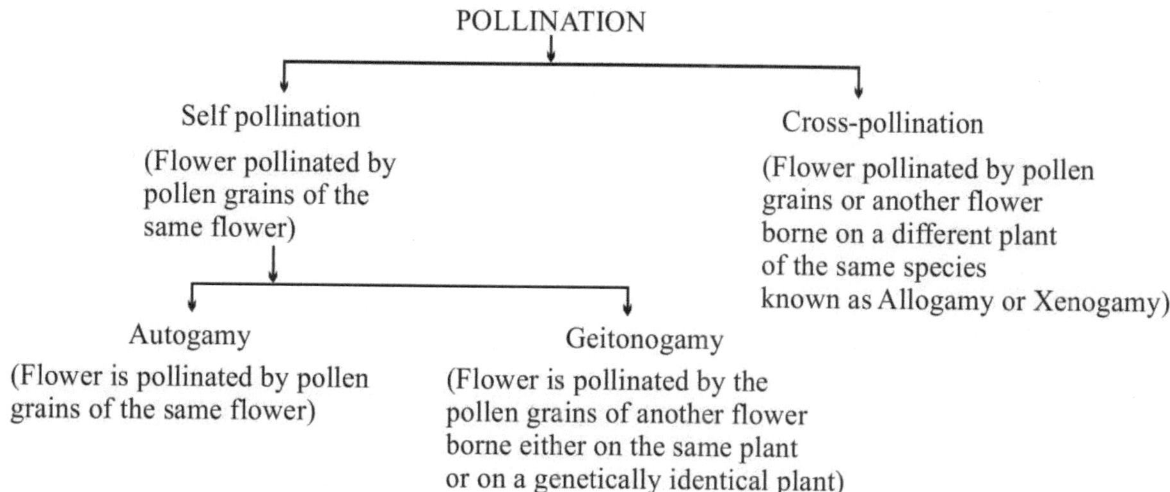

Figure : Flow diagram showing the types of pollination

- The transfer of pollen grains occurs through various ways, which may be biotic or abiotic.

		Technical terms
(i)	**Abiotic factors**	
	Wind	Anemophily
	Water	Hydrophily
(ii)	**Biotic factors**	
	Insects	Entomophily
	Birds	Ornithophily
	Bats	Chiropterophily
	Snails	Malacophily.

Significance of cross pollination :

- Increase in yield and adaptability.
- It eliminates defective traits and produces new varieties.
- It also leads to the hybrid production.

FERTILIZATION IN A FLOWERING PLANT :

- Fertilization is a process of fusion of male gamete with the female gamete.
- The process of formation of male gametophyte in case of plants is called as **microsporogenesis**.
- The process of formation of female gametophyte in case of plants is called as **megasporogenesis**.
- The process of pollination occurs, due to which the anther get stuck up to the stigma.
- After reaching to stigma pollen grains develops a pollen tube.
- This pollen tube grown through the length of style, from where it reaches to ovule.
- Pollen tube comprise of two male gametes, which is later on released in the embryo sac through an opening called as **micropyle**.
- Here one male gamete fuses with the egg to form a diploid zygote and the other male gamete fuses with the polar bodies to form a triploid nucleus which later on produces the structure called as **endosperm**.
- The process of fusion of one of the male gamete with egg and the other male gamete with polar bodies is called as **"double fertilization"**.

- The fusion of one male gamete with the two polar bodies to form endosperm is called a **"triple fusion"** (as it involves one male gamete and two polar bodies).

NOTE : The endosperm is meant to provide nourishment to the developing embryo.

- After fertilization sepals and petals fall and zygote undergoes a series of mitotic division to from a multinuclear embryo.
- At maturity wall of ovules changes to seed coat of which outer one is hard and is known as testa, while inner one is called as tegmen.
- Ovule change into seed and ovary wall change into fruit wall.

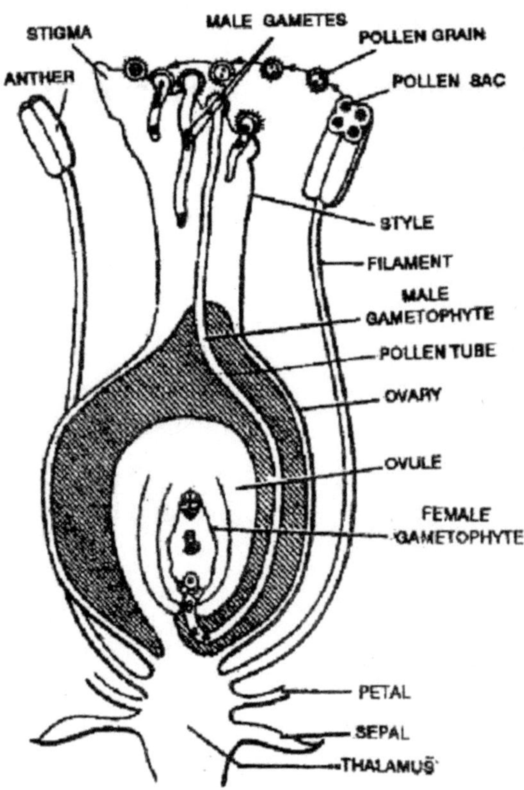

Fig. Showing Fertilization in a Flower

FRUIT

- Fruits develop from the ovary.
- The formation of seeds and fruits is simultaneous.
- Wall of the ovary develops into the wall of the fruit called **pericarp**. In fruits like guava, mango, etc. the fruits are fleshy while in fruits like mustard, groundnut, etc., they are dry.
- By the time the fruit develops the other floral parts degenerate and fall off. However, in some fruits such as apple, strawberry, etc. the thalamus contributes to fruit formation.
- Such fruits are called **false fruits**.
- Fruits that develop only from the ovary are called **true fruits**. Fruits are normally formed as a result of fertilisation but some fruits like banana develop without the act of fertilisation.
- Such fruits are called **parthenocarpic fruits**.

SEED

- Seed has three parts : **cotyledon** (store food), **plumule** (future shoot), **radicle** (future root).

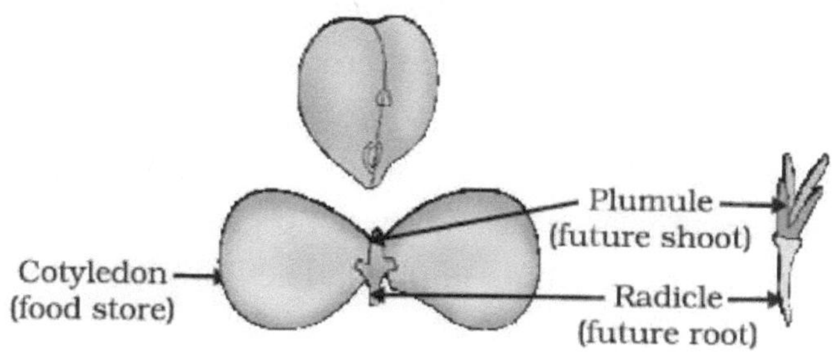

Fig.: Structrure of Seed

Differences between Self pollination and Cross pollination		
S.No.	**Self Pollination**	**Cross Pollination**
1.	Pollen grains are transferred from the anther to the stigma of the same flower (autogamy) or another flower on the same plant (geitonogamy)	Pollen grains are transferred from the anther of one flower to the stigma of another flower borne on a different plant of the same species (allogamy).
2.	Both the anther and stigma mature at the same time.	The anther and stigma of a flower generally mature at different times.
3.	It can occur even when the flowers are closed	It occurs only when the flowers are open.
4.	External agent is not required for self-pollination.	An external agent abiotic or biotic, is essential for cross-pollination
5.	It is economical for the plant.	Cross-pollination is not economical at the plant has to produce a lot of pollen grains, nectar, scent and bright-coloured corollas etc.
6.	Self-pollination ultimately results in progenies which are pure lines i.e. homozygous.	Cross-pollination produces the offspring which as hybrids i.e., heterozygous. They show variations in characteristics.
7.	In cannot eliminate useless or harmful characters.	It can eliminate useless or harmful characters.
8.	Highly useful characters get preserved in the race.	Useful characters cannot be preserved in the progenies.
9.	Self-pollination does not introduce any variations and hence the offspring are unable to adapt to the changed environment.	Cross-pollination introduce variations in the offsprings. These variations make these plants to adapt better to the changed environment for the struggle for existence.
10.	Immunity of the race towards disease falls in the succeeding progenies.	Immunity of the race towards disease is usually maintained in the succeeding progenies.
11.	Yield of the plant gradually falls with time.	Yield of the plant usually does not fall.
12.	Self-pollination never helps in the production of new varieties and species.	Cross-pollination is a mechanism of producing new varieties and species among plants.

REPRODUCTION IN HUMAN BEINGS :

- The reproductive organs of human beings, i.e., testis in male and ovary in female become functional only after attaining sexual maturity.

- In males, sexual maturity is attained at the age of 13-14 years, while in females at the age of 10-12 years. This is known as the age of puberty.
- The testes and ovary produce viable gametes and also secrete hormones like testosterone (male hormone from testes) and estrogen and progesterone (female hormones from ovary).
- Mammals are unisexual.
- Reproductive system of each organism consists of many reproductive organs.
- These can be primary sex organs or secondary sex organs.
- The primary sex organs are called as **gonads**. They produce sex cells or gametes and also secrete sex hormones.
- The gonads of males are called a **testis**, which produce sperms.
- The gonads of females are called as **ovaries**, which produce ova or female gametes.
- Secondary sex organs include the reproductive ducts which transport gametes and reproductive glands which help in process of reproduction.
- These organs do not produce gametes. **e.g., In males :** Vasa efferentia, epididymis, seminal vesicles, ejaculatory duct, urethra etc. **In females :** Fallopian tube, uterus, vagina, mammary glands etc.
- Accessory or external secondary characters help to distinguish the two sexes of a species externally. **e.g., In male :** Muscular body, more height, low pitched voice, moustaches etc. **In female :** High pitched voice, breast development, lateral pubic hairs etc.
- Puberty : Beginning of sexual maturity is known as puberty.
- At this stage primary sex organs start functioning.
- Secondary sex organs develop dully under the influence of sex hormones produced by primary sex organs.
- In the stage of puberty body growth is very rapid.

MALE REPRODUCTIVE SYSTEM :

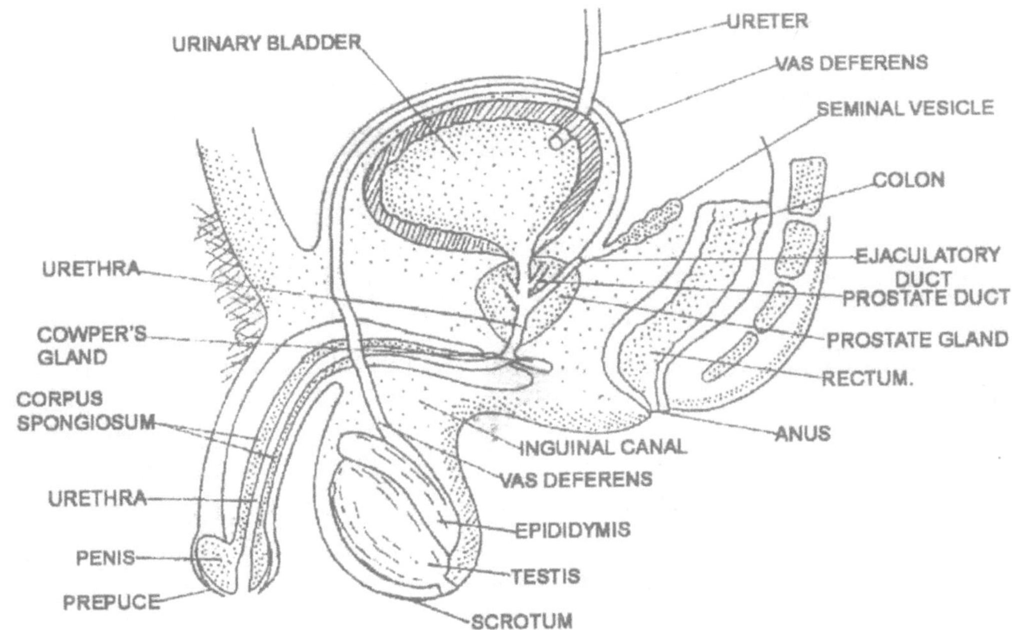

Fig. Male reproductive system

- **Male reproductive system comprises of following parts :**

(i) Testis	(ii) Scrotum	(iii) Vasa efferentia
(iv) Epididymis	(v) Vas deference	(vi) Ejaculatory duct
(vii) Urethra	(viii) Accessory sex glands	(ix) Penis

I. Testis :

- They are soft, smooth, pinkish, oval organs. They are housed [present] in a sac like structure called as **scrotum**. Outer covering is called as **tunicavaginalis**.
- It's inner covering is called as **tunica albuginea**.
- Ingrowths of tunica albuginea are called as septa, that divide the testis into 200-300 lobules.

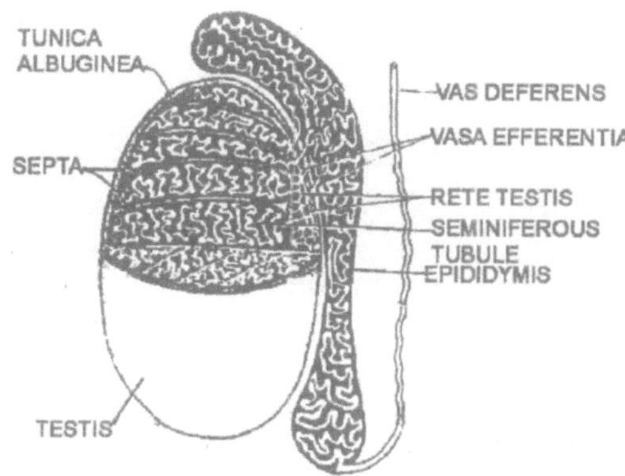

Figure. Longitudinal section of mammalian testis.

- Each lobe has a network of seminiferous tubules and interstitial cells.
- The germinal epithelium lining of the seminiferous tubule consists of two types of cells:
  • **Spermatogenic cells** or spermatogonia.
  • **Sertoli cells** or supporting cells.
  The most numerous are the smaller spermatogenic cells which undergo spermatogenesis to produce sperms. A few larger tall, columnar **Sertoli cells** nourish spermatozoa.
- In between seminiferous tubules, there are interstitial cells known as **Leydig cells** which secrete male hormone called as **testosterone**. This hormone helps in the growth and development of male sex hormone.
- These seminiferous tubules at one end join to form tubules which open into a network of irregular cavities known as rete testis.
- This rete testis comes out from a dorsal surface of the testis with the help of vasa efferentia. This vasa efferentia combines to form a single tube which becomes highly coiled and from epididymis.
- Epididymis open into a narrow tube vas deferens.
- Seminiferous tubules form the spermatogenic tissue of the testis.
- It consists of a germinal epithelial layer at the periphery. Spermatogenesis occurs at the center.
- It forms spermatogonia which grows and form spermatocytes which further grow to form primary spematocytes, which undergo meiosis to form secondary spermatocytes and then spermatids.
- The later (i.e. spermatids) metamorphose into spermatozoa.

- This process of formation of spermatozoa from spermatogonia is called as **spermatogenesis**.
- These spermatozoa are nourished during the development by nurse cells.

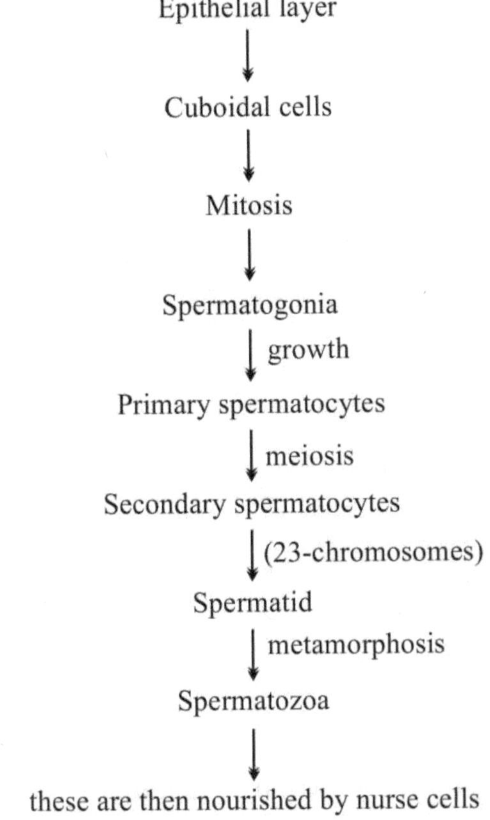

Flow chart showing the process of Spermatogenesis

II. Scrotum :

- It is a pouch of pigmented skin arising from the lower abdominal wall and hanging between the legs.
- It is divided internally into two compartments by a muscular partition called as septum scroti.
- Scrotum possesses smooth involuntary dortus muscles.
- Scrotum sac is connected to the abdominal cavity through inguinal canal.
- Function of dortus muscle is to change the position of testis to keep them at proper temperature.
- Scrotum has temperature 1 - 3 lower than body temperature which favours the formation of sperms.

III. Vasa efferentia :

- Rete testis is connected to epididymis through a fine tubule called as **vasa efferentia**. They help in conduction of sperms.

IV. Epididymis :

- They are long tubules which lie compacted along the testis from their upper ends to lower back side.
- Its walls are muscular and glandular to provide or secrete nutritive fluid which provides nourishment to the sperms.

V. Vas deference :

- Vasa efferentia from epididymal duct finally opens into vas deferens.
- It comes out through inguinal canal passing over urinary bladder to receive ducts from seminal vesicles.
- They are thick walled and muscular and conduct sperms.

VI. Ejaculatory duct :

- They are short, straight, muscular tubes, each formed by the union of vas deferens and duct of seminal vesicles.

VII. Urethra :

- It arises from urinary bladder forming a urinogenital canal. It carries urine, sperm and secretion of seminal vesicles, prostrate and cowper's gland.

VIII. Accessory glands :

- They consist of prostrate gland, a pair of seminal vesicles, and a pair of cowper's gland.
  - **Prostrate gland :** It is a large pyramidal gland that encloses a part of urethra including it's junction with the ejaculatory duct. It contains 30 - 40 alveoli which open separately into urethra by fine ducts. Secretion is thick, milky and alkaline which continue 20 - 30% semen.
  - **Cowper's glands :** These are a pair of small glands, present below the prostrate and consist of separate opening. Their secretion provide lubrication to the reproductive track.
  - **Seminal vesicle :** It is paired and present between urinary bladder and rectum. It's secretion from a major part of semen (60-70%). It is thick, viscous, alkaline having proteins, fructose and prostaglandins.

IX. Penis :

- It is a male copulatory organ which also passes urine. It consists of highly sensitive covering of skin called **prepuce**.
  - **Semen :** It is milky, viscous and alkaline fluid, ejaculated by reproductive system of males during copulation.
  - It's quantity is 2.5 - 4.0 ml at a time having about 40 million sperms.
  - Semen has chemical for nourishment of sperms neutralizing the acidity of urethra and vagina, stimulating their movement in female tract.
  - Spermatogenesis starts at puberty under the influence of gonadotropin secreted from anterior pituitary gland.

STRUCTURE OF SPERM :

- Each sperm consists of following parts :

  (i) Head **(ii) Neck** **(iii) Middle piece** **(iv) Tail**

(i) **Head :** It is oval in structure. It is composed of a large nucleus and a small acrosome. The nucleus is compact. It consists of DNA and basic proteins. Acrosome lies at the tip of nucleus. It is formed of golgi complex. It consist of hydrolytic enzymes and is used to contact and penetrate the egg during fertilization.

(ii) **Middle piece:** It is cylindrical in human sperms. It consists of ATP and mitochondria in a thin layer of cytoplasm. Mitochondria is coiled round the axial filament, it provided energy and it is said to be the power house of the sperm.

(iii) **Neck :** It is very short and contains two centrioles. These play an important role during the first cleavage of the zygote.

(iv) **Tail :** It is very long, slender and tapering. It is formed of cytoplasm. It's main function is to provide mobility to the sperm. End piece consists of the exposed axial sheath, which forms a fine filament.

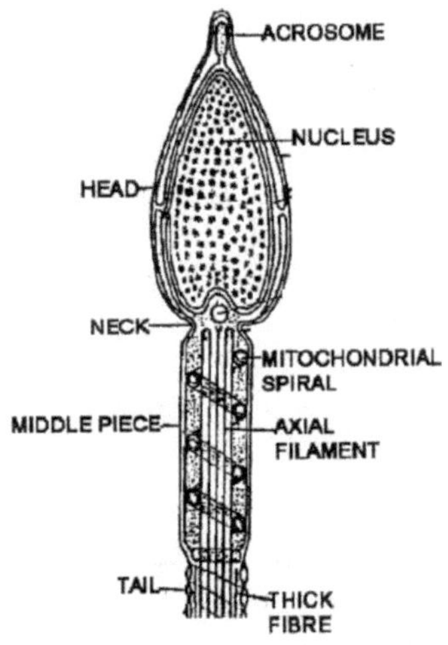

Figure : Mammalian sperm

FEMALE REPRODUCTIVE SYSTEM :

- Female reproductive system comprises of following parts :
  (i) Ovaries **(ii) Fallopian tube** **(iii) Uterus** **(iv) Vagina** **(v) Glands**

I. Ovaries :

- These are oval shaped lying near the kidney.
- Ovary is covered by two layers outer is made up of germinal epithelial cells.
- Inner layer is called as **tunica albuginea** which is made up of fibrous connective tissues.
- The ovary consists of inner part called as **stroma**.
- It's outer peripheral part is called as **cortex** while inner part is called a **medulla**.
- Medulla consists of connective tissues containing numerous blood vessels, lymphatic vessels and nerves.

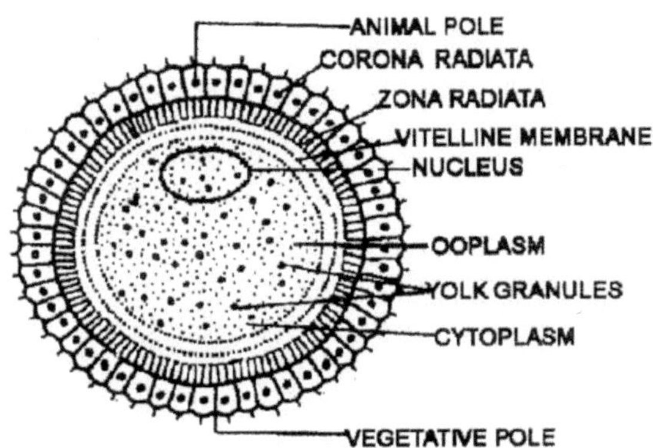

Figure : Structure of Ovum.

- Cortex also consists of large mass of yellow cells termed as corpus luteum, formed in an empty graffian follicle after the release of it's ovum.

- The cells of corpus luteum secrete the hormones
  (A) Progesterone during pregnancy. (B) Relaxing at the end of pregnancy.
- Oestrongen is secreted by graffian follicle and intestinal cells. It's secretion is maximum during ovulation. It is also secreted during pregnancy.

II. Fallopian tube :

- It is about 10 cm. long muscular tube. It shows 4 regions :

(A) **Infundibulum :** It is the broad, funnel shaped proximal part of fallopian tube. It's margin bears finger like processes called as fimbriae. This is meant to carry ovum by ciliary movement to the uterus.

(B) **Ampulla :** It is a long, wide part of the fallopian tube next to the Infundibulum.

(C) **Isthmus :** it is the narrow part that follows ampulla.

(D) **Uterine part :** It is also narrow and passes through the uterine wall.

III. Uterus :

- It is large, highly elastic sac specialized for the development of the embryo.
- It is situated in a pelvic cavity.
- It is attached to the fallopian tube from the sides and below it opens into vagina through cervix.
- This uterus undergoes cyclic changes during phases of menstrual cycle.
  The body of the uterus consists of three layers of tissue, the outer thin membranous **perimetrium**, middle thick layer of smooth muscle **myometrium** and inner glandular layer called **endometrium** that lines the uterine cavity. The endometrium plays an important role in reproduction. Its secretion nourishes the blastocyst for few days before implantation.
- **Cervix :** Lower narrow cervix that projects into the vagina. The cervix communicates above with the body of the uterus and below with the vagina.

IV. Vagina :

- It is a large, median, elastic, muscular tube. This canal opens externally into labia minora and labia majora. It's folds consist of stratified squamous epithelium which has mucous lining It secretes a lubricant fluid. Labia majora is the innermost, thin, moist fold. Labia minora is outer large and hair covered. pH of vagina is 4.3 It is also called a **"Birth canal"**.

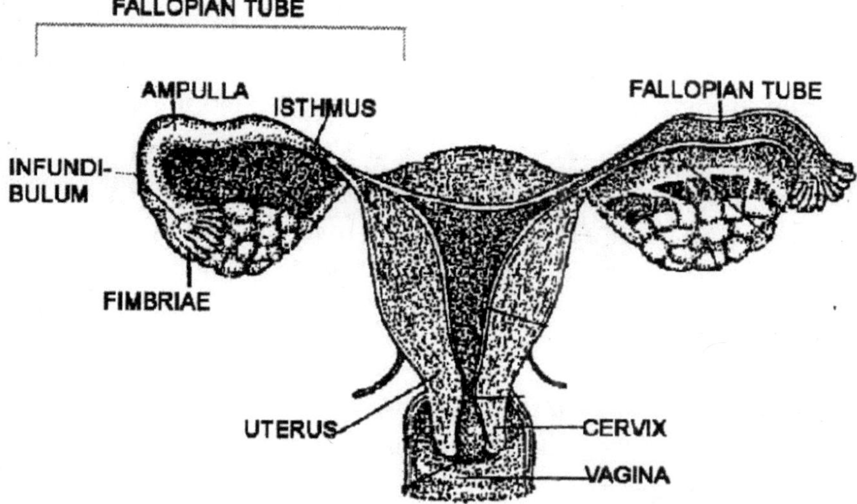

Figure : Female reproductive system.

V. Gland :

- Bartholin's gland : it secretes a clear, viscous fluid under sexual excitement.
- The fluid serves as a lubricant during copulation or mating.

SEXUAL CYCLE IN HUMAN FEMALE :

- In ovaries of female 1000 of immature ova are present which are contained in immature follicles.
- When girls reaches puberty, then one follicle develops at a time to form a mature ovum.
- On maturation, the follicle bursts and the ovum shoots out of the ovary. This is called OVULATION or in other words the release of an ovum (or egg) from an ovary is called **ovulation**.
- Ovulation takes place on 14 days of the begining of MENSTRUAL CYCLE of 28 days.
- In human females the ovaries start realising ovum or egg once in every 28 days from the age of puberty.

MENSTRUATION :

- Menstruation occurs in anthropoid primates that has flat face, mobile eyes forward. e.g. Monkey, Human beings and Apes.
- The break down and removal of the inner, thick and soft lining of the uterus along with its blood vessels in the form of a vaginal bleeding is called **MENSTRUAL** cycle or **MENSTRUATION**.
- It is a cyclic phase of the flow of blood with mucus and tissues etc. from the uterus of a woman at monthly interval.
- It occurs on average of 28 days interval.
- It starts at the age of 12-14 years and stops at 45-50 years of life.
- This cycle stops during pregnancy.
- The menstrual cycle consists of following phases :
  - (i) **Bleeding or menstrual phase**
  - (ii) **Proliferative phase**
  - (iii) **Ovulation phase**
  - (iv) **Secretory phase**
- The commencement of menstruation of puberty is called as **menarche**.
- It's stoppage around the age of 50 years is called as **menopause**.
- The period between menarche and menopause is the reproductive phase in human female.
- Mammals other than primates do not menstruate and their sexual cycle is called **estrous cycle**. This cycle run only during the breeding season. The estrogen level in blood increases at the time of ovulation resulting strong sex urge in the female called **"period of heat"**.

Oogenesis :

- Oogenesis is a process of formation of ovum. the ovum is a rounded, non-motile cell. It's size varies in different animals depending upon the amount of yolk in it.

FERTILIZATION :

- It included release of ovum from the ovary, where it remains viable for 12 - 24 hours.
- At the time of sexual intercourse the sperm enters in to the vagina.
- The rate of movement of sperm is 1.5 to 3.0 mm/min.
- Only one sperm is required for fertilization of the ovum.

- The head of the sperm penetrates the corona radiata layer of ovum and then the zona pellucida layer.
- This process is facilitated by acrosome and proteolytic enzymes.
- After penetration the tail and body of the sperm is lost, only head remains inside the ovum.
- It's head begins to swell and forms male pronucleus.
- Here the pronuclei of sperm and ovum fuse to form a new resultant nucleus each contributing 23 chromosome, so that the resultant may have 46 chromosomes.
- Fusion of male & female gametes is called as **fertilization**. Zygote starts developing in fallopian tube and forms embryo, this later on moves to uterus. It gets attached to uterine walls and the whole process is called as **implantation**.

ARTIFICIAL INSEMINATION :

- It is a technique to make a female pregnant by artificially introduction of semen into vagina.
- In this process semen from a good quality male is collected, preserved by freezing and used when required.
- In case of humans it is also being used for improving the chances of fertility.
- A man may be infertile due to insufficient number of sperms, weak or premature ejaculation, inability of penis to undergo and enter the vagina or nonmotile sperms.
- In this case husband's semen is collected, concentrated and introduced artificially into the wife's vagina. this is called as artificial insemination.
- If the husband's sperms are faulty, some donors sperm can be used. This is called as artificial insemination.
- Artificial insemination has following two advantages.

(i) Semen of good quality male animal is used to inseminate a number of females.

(ii) Preserved semen can be transported to distant places, excluding the need for sending the male animal there.

Differences between asexual and sexual reproduction

Asexual reproduction	**Sexual reproduction**
1. It is always uniparental	It is generally biparental.
2. Gametes are not formed.	Gamete are formed
3. There is no fertilization.	Fertilization occurs in it.
4. In involves mitotic cell division.	It involves meiotic cell division.
5. Daughter individual are genetically identical to the parent	Daughter individual are different from the parents.
6. It does not contribute to the evolution.	It contributes to the evolution by introduction variation in the offspring

REPRODUCTIVE HEALTH :

- Reproductive health is all those aspects of general health which help a person to lead a normal, safe and satisfying reproductive life.
- **Sexually Transmitted Diseases (STDs)** are the diseases which are spread by sexual contact from an infected person to a healthy person.
- They are caused by various micro-organisms that live in warm and moist environments of the vagina, urethra, anus and mouth.

- Some of the common sexually transmitted diseases are :

(i) **Gonorrhoea :** It is caused by bacterium ***Neisseria gonorrhoea***. It is characterised by inflammation of urinogenital tract and the patient feels burning sensation during urination. This bacteria infects the ureter in men and the cervix in women.

(ii) **Syphilis :** It is caused by bacterium ***Treponema pallidium***. It is characterised by lesions in the mucous membrane of urinogenital tract and ulcers on genitalia.

(iii) **Trichomoniasis :** It is caused by protozoan ***Trichomonas vaginalis***. It is characterised by some vaginal discharge at the urinogential tract of the female.

(iv) **AIDS (Acquired Immune Deficiency Syndrome) :** It is caused by a virus called HIV (Human Immunodeficiency Virus) which suppresses the body's immune mechanism and thereby making it susceptible to any disease.

(v) **Wart :** It is caused by human papillona virus (HPV).

Mode of transmission of AIDS is as follows :

- By having sexual contact with an infected person.
- By the transfusion of blood from an infected person.
- Through infected needles used for injection.
- Through the placenta from the mother to child during pregnancy.

POPULATION GROWTH :

- The term population refers to the total number of individuals of a species occupying particular geographical area at a given time.
- The scientific study of human population is called as "***demography***".
- Factors that lead to increase in population are :
  (i) Increase in protection from risk
  (ii) Illiteracy
  (iii) Desire of son
  (iv) Decline in death rate
  (v) Desire for more earning hands
  (vi) Unawareness of various birth control measures

SEX RATIO

- The number of females in a population for thousand males is called sex ratio.

$$\text{sex ratio} = \frac{\text{No. of females}}{\text{1000 males}}$$

METHODS ADOPTED FOR POPULATION CONTROL :

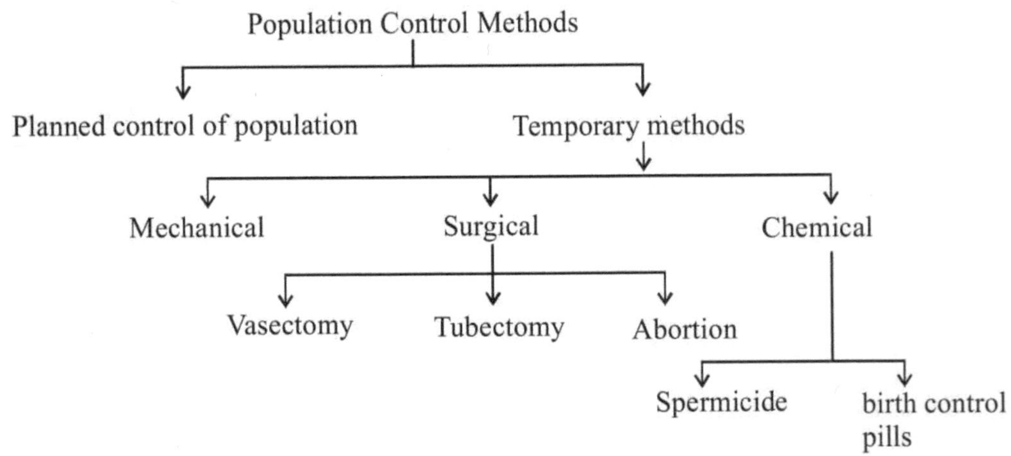

Planned control of population :

(A) By educating people about the advantages of small family.

(B) Raising the age of marriage can help in reducing population growth.

(C) By family planning.

Temporary methods :

(A) **Safe period :** A week before and after the menstrual cycle is considered to be infertile and fertilization, does not occur during this period.

(B) **Chemical means :** These includes certain jellies, paste, tablets which when intro duced into vagina cause immobilization of sperms and kill them. They also include con traceptive pills which inhibit secretion of F.S.H. and L.H. ovulation is inhibited.

(C) **Mechanical means :**

- They involve use of condoms.
- Use of cervical or diaphragm cap which is fitted in the vagina that checks the entry of sperms.
- IUD (intrauterine device) called as copper-T is also fitted in the uterus which prevents fertilization.

(D) **Surgical methods:** It involves tubectomy in females which involves cutting of fallopian tube, and vasectomy in males which involves cutting of vas deference from both the sides. However, surgical removal of ovaries also occurs which is called as ovariectomy and in males removal of testis called as castration.

(E) **Abortion :** Medical termination of pregnancy is called as abortion.

POINTS TO REMEMBER

General Terms :

(i) **Fertilization :** It is the process of fusion of gametes.

(ii) **Unisexual organism :** In case of humans male and female sex organs are separate and therefore called as **unisexual**.

(iii) **Bisexual :** In plants and some organisms like tapeworm, earthworm etc. both male and female organs are present in the same individual and therefore called as **bisexual**.

(iv) **Gonads:** Organs which are involved in the formation of gametes are called as **gonads**.

(v) **Copulation or mating :** The process of transfer of male gametes into female body.

- In angiosperms, the male gametes are carried to the egg through pollen tube. It is called siphonogamy.
- During fertilization, one male gamete fuses with the egg and the other male gamete fuses with the diploid secondary nucleus (or two polar nuclei). The process is called double fertilization.
- As a result of double fertilization, a diploid zygote and a triploid primary endosperm nucleus are formed inside the mature embryo sac.
- After fertilization, the ovule develops into a seed. The diploid zygote develops an embryo and the triploid primary endosperm nucleus form an endosperm. The ovary is transformed into a fruit.

2-3 ml semen → 300 million of sperm is discharged into vagina by penis.
sperm fuse with ovum
↓
Zygote $\xrightarrow{\text{Mitosis}}$ *Foetus (implants in Utreus)*
(1) Stopage of Menstrual cycle after implantation
(2) formation of Placenta

- Placental formation occurs between uterine wall and the foetus, which provides nourishment to the foetus.
- The time period for which a developing fetus remains inside the mother's womb is called as gestation period. It extends for about 9 months or 40 weeks or 280 days.
- The process of giving birth to baby is called as parturition.

Parturition → process of giving birth
Placenta → Relaxin $\xrightarrow{\text{hormone}}$ ***[Relax Pubic symphysis]***
Pitutary → Oxytocin (contraction and Relaxation in Uterus)
It occurs in 3 stages
(a) Dilation (b) Expulsion (c) Final contraction

- **Accessory organs :** Organs that have supportive function.
- **Acrosome :** A small granule-like structure at the top of the head of the sperm, which produces lysosomal enzyme.

- **After-birth :** Shedding of placenta from the uterus of the mother after the birth of a baby.
- **Agamospermy :** The phenomenon of formation of seed through asexual reproductive process without the formation and fusion of male gametes.
- **Artificial vegetative propagation :** Man made methods (cutting, grafting, layering and tissue culture) for the vegetative propagation of plants, from detached parts without the formation and fusion of gametes.
- **Foetus :** Developing embryo in human being.
- **Implantation :** Attachment of developing embryo with the uterine wall of mother.
- **Ovulation :** Release of egg of ovum by the Graafian follicle.
- Reproduction is the biological process by which new individuals of the same kind are produced.
- Reproduction is not essential for the survival of an organism, but is vital for the survival of a species.
- Reproduction produces identical copies of the body design.
- DNA is the informational macromolecule of our body. It provides information for protein synthesis.
- During cellular reproduction, DNA duplication occurs followed by creation of an additional cellular apparatus.
- The process of DNA copying is not accurate, resulting in variations arising during reproduction, which is the basis for evolution.
- Variations may or may not be beneficial for the individual, but help in the survival of the species during adverse conditions.
- Depending on their body design, the modes of reproduction differ in different organisms.
- Reproduction is broadly divided into asexual and sexual reproduction.
- Fission, fragmentation, regeneration, budding, vegetative propagation and spore formation are various modes of asexual reproduction.
- Fission occurs in unicellular organisms like bacteria and protozoa through simple cell division. Depending on the number of individuals formed, fission may be binary or multiple fission.
- On maturation, certain multi-cellular organisms (with simple body makeup) break up into smaller fragments, each of which develops into new individual. This reproductive method is called fragmentation.
- Simple reproductive methods cannot occur in higher multi-cellular organisms, since they have a complex and carefully organized body structure.
- In complex multi-cellular organism, reproduction is brought about by a single, specialized cell type that is capable of proliferating and forming all other cell types of the body. Get the Power of Visual Impact on your side
- Regeneration is found in many completely differentiated simple organisms, like Hydra and Planaria. If such an organism is split into several parts, most of the parts will develop into complete organisms.
- Regeneration involves specialized totipotent cells which proliferate and differentiate to form the complete body.
- Certain organisms like Hydra produce buds on their body surface, which mature into new individuals and separate from parent body.
- Vegetative propagation is used by many plants, especially those incapable of producing seeds. Here, new plants are produced from roots, stems or leaves of parent plant. This reproductive method is widely used by plant breeders.
- Spore formation is an asexual mode of reproduction found in certain multicellular organisms like Rhizopus. The thick walled spores have the capacity to develop into new individuals under suitable conditions.

- Sexual reproduction requires both male and female sexes to produce the offspring.
- Sexual reproduction creates large number of novel variations.
- In comparison to the non-reproductive body cells, the germ cells contain only half the chromosome number.
- The male gamete is smaller and motile whereas the female gamete is larger and stores food.
- When the offspring is produced by the union of the male and female gametes, its specific chromosome number and DNA content is reestablished.
- In angiosperms, flower is the reproductive organ of the plant.
- Stamen, the male reproductive part of flower, is made up of anther and filament. Carpel is the female reproductive part and is composed of stigma, style and ovary.
- The pollen grain is present in the anther whereas the egg cell is enclosed in the ovary.
- Pollination and fertilization are two essential events in reproduction of angiosperms.
- Pollination is the transfer of pollen grains from anther to stigma. It may be either self-pollination or cross-pollination.
- Pollen tube carries the male gamete from stigma to the female gamete in ovary.
- Fertilization of male and female gametes produces the zygote, which then forms the embryo.
- Following fertilization, the ovule develops into seed whereas the ovary forms the fruit. On germination, the seed develops into a seedling.
- In humans, reproduction occurs sexually.
- Puberty is the time when the juvenile body of a person starts sexual maturation.
- Before puberty, the body resources are used mainly to grow and develop the organism to its adult size. Once this is achieved, puberty sets in.
- Some changes occurring during puberty are common to boys and girls, whereas other changes are specific to boys and girls.
- Changes such as appearance of pimples on face, growth of thick hair in armpits and genital areas occur in both boys and girls.
- Increase in breast size, darkening of nipples and occurrence of menstruation are puberty associated changes in girls. In boys, facial hair growth, cracking of voices and occasional enlargement of penis occur during puberty.
- Changes associated with puberty are slow and gradual and does not occur uniformly in everyone.
- The changes taking place during puberty, signals the occurrence of sexual maturation in an individual to other members of the same population.
- In humans, the male reproductive system is composed of testes, vas deferens, seminal vesicles, prostate gland, urethra and penis.
- Testis is situated outside the abdominal cavity. It produces sperms and secretes testosterone.
- Sperm shows a small head containing the genetic material and a long tail, which helps in motility.
- Vas deferens and urethra are the thin tubes through which sperms are transported from testes to outside. The sperms are nourished in the seminal fluid.
- The female reproductive system is made up of ovaries, fallopian tubes, uterus, cervix and vagina.
- Ovaries are responsible for production of ova/egg as well as for secreting the hormones, estrogen and progesterone.
- On reaching puberty, ovulation occurs once a month in females, where in one immature egg present in any one of the ovaries becomes mature and is released. This egg is carried by the fallopian tube.

- Sperms which are introduced into the vagina of females during intercourse, may encounter the egg on reaching the fallopian tube, resulting in fertilization.
- The zygote gets implanted in the uterus and develops into the embryo.
- The placenta provides nourishment and oxygen to the embryo and removes the waste generated by the embryo.
- Gestation period is nine months in humans after which the child is born due to uterine contractions.
- In case fertilization does not occur, the released egg along with the thickened lining of the uterus is shed out through the vagina in a process called menstruation.
- Engaging in unprotected sexual intercourse can cause pregnancy as well as spreading of sexually transmitted diseases like gonorrhea, syphilis and AIDS.
- Condoms help to control the spread of sexually transmitted diseases.
- Unwanted pregnancies can be avoided through several contraceptive methods.
- Mechanical barrier methods prevent sperm from reaching the egg, e.g. condom.
- Oral contraceptive pills alter the hormonal balance, thereby preventing the egg from being released.
- Surgical blocking of vas deferens in male or fallopian tube in female can also prevent pregnancy.
- Abortions remove unwanted pregnancies, but this method is being misused to carry out female foeticide.
- Birth control methods are essential to keep the human population in check and thereby improve the standard of living for everyone.

CONCEPT APPLICATION LEVEL - I [NCERT Questions]

Q.1 What is the importance of DNA copying in reproduction?

Ans. DNA (Deoxyribonucleic acid) is the genetic material found in the chromosomes, which are present in the nucleus of a cell. The DNA is the information present for making proteins and each specific type of protein leads to a specific type of body design.

Thus, it is the DNA molecule that determines the body design of an individual. Therefore, it can be concluded that it is the DNA that gets transferred from parents to offsprings and makes them look similar.

Q.2 Why is variation beneficial to the species but not necessarily for the individual?

Ans. Variations are beneficial to the species as compare to individual because sometimes for the species, the environmental conditions change so drastically that their survival becomes difficult. For example, if the temperature of water increases suddenly, then most of the bacteria living in that water would die. Only few variants that are resistant to heat would be able to survive. However, if these variants were not there, then the entire species of bacteria would have been destroyed. Thus, these variants help in the survival of the species. However, all variations are not necessarily beneficial for the individual organisms.

Q.3 How does binary fission differ from multiple fission?

Ans. In binary fission, a single cell divides into two equal halves. Amoeba and Bacteria divide by binary fission.

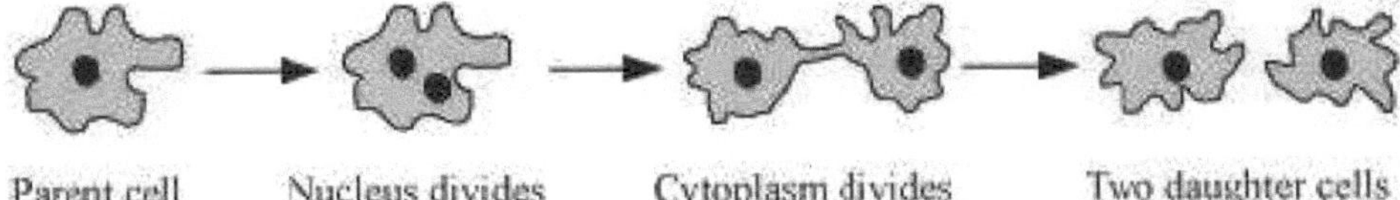

Binary fission in Amoeba

In multiple fission, a single cell divides into many daughter cells simultaneously. Amoeba and Plasmodium divides by multiple fission.

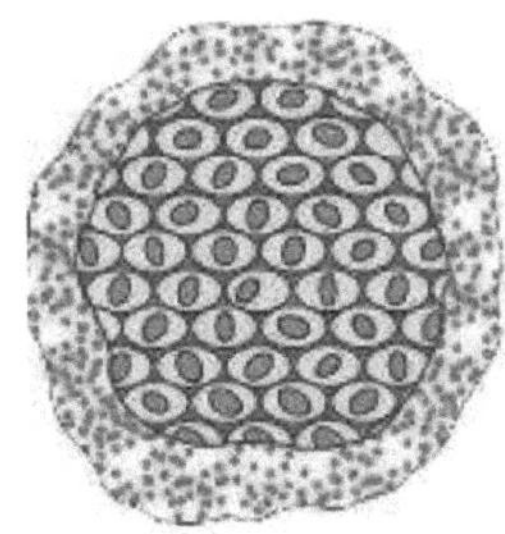

Multiple fission in Plasmodium

Q.4 How will an organism be benefited if it reproduces through spores?

Ans. There are many advantages, if an organism reproduces through spores.

Advantages of spore formation :

- Large numbers of spores are produced in one sporangium.
- Spores are distributed easily by air to far-off places to avoid competition at one place.
- Spores are covered by thick walls to prevent dehydration under unfavourable conditions.

Q.5 Can you think of reasons why more complex organisms cannot give rise to new individuals through regeneration?

Ans. Simple organisms such as Hydra and Planaria are capable of producing new individuals through the process of regeneration. The process of regeneration involves the formation of new organisms from its body parts. Simple organisms can utilize this method of reproduction as their entire body is made of similiar kind of cells in which any part of their body can be formed by growth and development.
However, complex organisms have specialised organ-system level of organization. All the organ systems of their body work together as an interconnected unit. They can regenerate their lost body parts such as skin, muscles, blood, etc. However, they cannot give rise to whole new individuals through regeneration.

Q.6 Why is DNA copying an essential part of the process of reproduction?

Ans. DNA (Deoxyribonucleic acid) copying is an essential part of reproduction as it passes genetic information from parents to offspring. It determines the body design of an individual. The reproducing cells produce a copy of their DNA through some chemical reactions and result in two copies of DNA. The copying of DNA always takes place along with the creation of additional cellular structure. This process is then followed by division of a cell to form two cells.

Q.7 How is the process of pollination different from fertilization?

Ans. Pollination is the process of transfer of pollens from anther to stigma. It occurs with the help of certain pollinators such as air, water, birds, or some insects.
Fertilization, on the other hand, is the fusion of the male and female gametes. It occurs inside the ovule and leads to the formation of zygote.

Q.8 What is the role of the seminal vesicles and the prostate gland?

Ans. The secretions from seminal vesicles and prostate glands lubricate the sperms and provide a fluid medium for easy transport of sperms. Their secretion also provides nutrient in the form of fructose, calcium, and some enzymes.

Q.9 What are the changes seen in girls at the time of puberty?

Ans. Secondary sexual characteristics in girls :

- Increase in breast size and darkening of skin of the nipples present at the tips of the breasts.
- Appearance of hair in the genital area.
- Appearance of hair in other areas of skin like underarms, face, hands, and legs.
- Increase in the size of uterus and ovary.
- Beginning of menstrual cycle.
- More secretion of oil from the skin (sebaceous gland) which results in the appearance of pimples.

Q.10 How does the embryo get nourishment inside the mother's body?

Ans. The embryo develops inside the mother's body for about nine months. Inside the uterus, the outer tissue surrounding the embryo develops finger-like projections called villi.
These villi are surrounded by uterine tissue and maternal blood. They provide a large surface area for exchange of oxygen and nutrients. Also, there is a special tissue called placenta, which is embedded in the uterine wall. The embryo receives the oxygen and nutrients from the mother's blood via the placenta. The waste materials produced by the embryo are also removed through the placenta.

Q.11 If a woman is using a copper.T, will it help in protecting her from sexually transmitted diseases?

Ans. No. Using a copper-T will not provide a protection from sexually transmitted diseases, as it does not prevent the entry of semen. It only prevents the implantation of the embryo in the uterus.

Q.12 What are the advantages of sexual reproduction over asexual reproduction?

Ans. Advantages of sexual reproduction :

- In sexual reproduction, more variations are produced. Thus, it ensures survival of species in a population.
- The newly formed individual has characteristics of both the parents.
- Variations are more viable in sexual mode than in asexual one. This is because in asexual reproduction, DNA has to function inside the inherited cellular apparatus.

Q.13 What are the functions performed by the testes in human beings?

Ans. The testes are the male reproductive organs that are located outside the abdominal cavity within a pouch called scrotum.

Functions of testes :

- Produce sperms
- Produce a hormone called testosterone, which brings about secondary sexual characters in boys.

Q.14 Why does menstruation occur?

Ans. Menstruation is a process in which blood and mucous flows out every month through the vagina. This process occurs every month because one egg is released from the ovary every month and at the same time, the uterus (womb) prepares itself to receive the fertilized egg. Thus, the inner lining of the uterus gets thickened and is supplied with blood to nourish the embryo. If the egg does not get fertilised, then the lining of the uterus breaks down slowly and gets released in the form of blood and mucous from the vagina.

Q.15 What are the different methods of contraception?

Ans. The contraceptive methods can be broadly divided into the following types:

- **Natural method :** It involves avoiding the chances of meeting of sperms and ovum. In this method, the sexual act is avoided from day 10th to 17th of the menstrual cycle because during this period, ovulation is expected and therefore, the chances of fertilization are very high.
- **Barrier method :** In this method, the fertilization of ovum and sperm is prevented with the help of barriers. Barriers are available for both males and females. Condoms are barriers made of thin rubber that are used to cover penis in males and vagina in females.
- **Oral contraceptives :**In this method, tablets or drugs are taken orally. These contain small doses of hormones that prevent the release of eggs and thus fertilization cannot occur.
- **Implants and surgical methods** :Contraceptive devices such as the loop or Copper-T are placed in uterus to prevent pregnancy. Some surgical methods can also be used to block the gamete transfer. It includes the blocking of vas deferens to prevent the transfer of sperms known as vasectomy. Similarly, fallopian tubes of the female can be blocked so that the egg will not reach the uterus known as tubectomy.

Q.16 How are the modes for reproduction different in unicellular and multicellular organisms?

Ans. In unicellular organisms, reproduction occurs by the division of the entire cell. The modes of reproduction in unicellular organisms can be fission, budding, etc. whereas in multicellular organisms, specialised reproductive organs are present. Therefore, they can reproduce by complex reproductive methods such as vegetative propagation, spore formation, etc. In more complex multicellular organisms such as human beings and plants, the mode of reproduction is sexual reproduction.

Q.17 How does reproduction help in providing stability to populations of species?

Ans. Living organisms reproduce for the continuation of a particular species. It helps in providing stability to the population of species by producing a new individual that resembles the parents. This is the reason why cats give birth to only cats or dogs give birth to only dogs. Therefore, reproduction provides stability to populations of dogs or cats or any other species.

Q.18 What could be the reasons for adopting contraceptive methods?

Ans. Contraceptive methods are mainly adopted because of the following reasons:

(i) To prevent unwanted pregnancies.

(ii) To control population rise or birth rate.

(iii) To prevent the transfer of sexually transmitted diseases.

CONCEPT APPLICATION LEVEL - II

SECTION – A

Q.1 What is a clone? Why do offspring formed by asexual reproduction exhibit remarkable similarity?

Ans. Clone is an exact genetic replica of another individual. All the offspring formed from a parent through asexual reproduction are clones of one another as well as their parent. The remarkable similarity of asexually produced daughter individuals is due to genetic similarity as they possess exact copies of DNA of their parent.

Q.2 Explain how, offspring and parents of organisms reproducing sexually have the same number of chromosomes.

Ans. The patents are diploid (2n) as each of them has two sets of chromosomes. They form haploid (1n) male and female gametes through the process of meiosis. The haploid gametes have one set of chromosomes. During fertilization, one male gamete fuses with one female gamete. It restores the diploid (2n) chromosome number in the offspring that is formed from fusion product or zygote (2n).

Q.3 Colonies of yeast fail to multiply in water but multiply in sugar solution. Give one reason for this.

Ans. Yeast is heterotrophic. It obtains its nourishment from outside. Plain water cannot provide nourishment to yeast while sugar solution can do so. Therefore, Yeast multiplies in sugar solution and not in plain water.

Q.4 Give two reasons for the appearance of variations among the progeny formed by sexual reproduction.

Ans. Variations appear in the progeny of sexually reproducing organisms due to (i) Random separation and coming together of chromosomes during gamete formation and gamete fusion (ii) Crossing over and mutations.

Q.5 Where is the zygote located in the flower after fertilization?

Ans. Zygote is the fertilized oosphere which occurs in the embryo sac present inside an ovule located in the ovary part of the pistil.

Q.6 Trace the path of sperm during ejaculation and mention the glands and their function associated with the male reproductive system.

Ans. Ejaculated sperms are the ones which are stored in epididymis. They are formed regularly in seminiferous tubules from where they pass through vasa efferentia into epididymis. At the time of ejaculation, the sperms are first pushed through vasa deferentia, enter ejaculatory duct where receive secretion of seminal vesicles and then urinogenital duct where they receive secretion of prostate gland to form semen. The urinogenital duct is lubricated by secretion of a pair of Cowper's glands (bulbourethral glands).

Secretion of Seminal Vesicles provides nourishment, activation and providing fluid medium for sperm transport.

Secretion of Prostates Gland provide motility of sperms.

Q.7 What would be the ratio of chromosome number between an egg and its zygote ? How is the sperm genetically different from the egg ?

Ans. Chromosome Number in Egg and Zygote. 1 : 2

Genetic Difference between Sperm and Egg. Sperms are genetically of two types, X-containing and Y-containing. Eggs are always of one type, X-containing .

Q.8 What is placenta ? Mention its role during pregnancy.

Ans. **Placenta.** It is a special double layered, spongy tissue connection between the foetus and uterine wall found in pregnant females. It has finger-like out growths or **Villi** which are in contact with blood sinuses present in the uterine wall.

Role :

(i) Attachment. Placenta attaches the foetus to uterine wall.

(ii) Villi. Placenta has finger-like outgrowths or villi which develop a large surface area for fixation and absorption.

(iii) Nutrients. Placenta picks up nutrients from mother's blood and passes it to the blood of the foetus.

(iv) Waste Products. Waste products produced by the foetus passes out through the placenta into mother's blood.

(v) Gases. Foetus obtains oxygen supply from mother's blood and eliminates carbon dioxide through placenta.

Q.9 Reproduction is essentially a phenomenon that is not for survival of individual but for the stability of a species. Justify.

Ans. Reproduction is not essential for survival of the individual. Survival of the individual depends upon input of nutrients and energy and eliminarion of wastes. Reproduction has no role in these. It is, however, essential for the stability and survival of the species. Reproduction takes part in

(a) Perpetuation of Species. **(b) Replacement.** **(c) Population Characteristics.**
(d) Variations. **(e) Transfer of Variations.**

Q.10 Define fertilization.

Ans. The process of fusion of male gamete with the female gamete of the same species that is the sperm with the ovum, known as fertilization.

After fertilization the product obtained with the zygote, which eventualy develops into a complete organs.

Q.11 Mention any two function of human ovary.

Ans. The two functions are

(i) It is responsible for production of female gametes, ovum.

(ii) It secretes hormone likes estrogen & progesterone.

Q.12 Define menopause.

Ans. At the age of around 45 to 50 years. The ovaries of female stop producing ova. The stopage of menstrual flow and other events like the changes in the hormonal composition is known as menopause.

Q.13 Define double fiertilization in plants.

Ans. In the case of plants, the pollen grain releases two male gametes. One fuses with the egg and forms the zygote. The other male gamete fuses with the two pollen nuclei. This fusion is said to be triple fusion. Thus inside an embryo sac two fusion syngamy be triple fusion takes place, this mechanism of two fusion in embryo sac is known as double fertilization.

Q.14 What is Ovulation?

Ans. The ovarian follicle present inside ovary, develope into mature follicles. Usually one mature ovary follicle durlops into mature ovum.

It pinches off from the surface of the ovary be enter fallopian tube. This process is termed as **ovulation**.

Q.15 Write the full forms of

(i) IUCD (ii) AIDS (iii) HIV (iv) OC

Ans. **IUCD** – Intra Uterine Contraceptive Devices

AIDS – Acquired Immuno Deficiency Syndrome

HIV – Human Immuno Virus

OC – Oral Contraceptives

Q.16 Mention the reproductive parts of flower.

Ans. (i) Male reproductive part – Stamen

(ii) Female reproductive part – Pistil, Carpel

Q.17 Write the name of various methods of vegetative propagation.

Ans. Cutting, layering, grafting, parthenogenesis, tissue culture.

SECTION – B
(Previous Years Questions)

Q.1 If the migration of testes does not take place in man, from abdominal cavity to scrotal sac, then **[NTSE Stage-I_2005]**

(A) man will die
(B) the development of male secondary sex character will not take place
(C) the development of male reproductive system will not take place
(D) the formation of sperms will not take place

Q.2 Viviparous germination is found in **[NTSE Stage-I_2006]**

(A) Hydrophytes (B) Xerophytes (C) Halophytes (D) Mesophytes

Q.3 The plants in which vegetative propagation is found, are **[NTSE Stage-I_2013]**

(A) Bryophyllum (B) Sugarcane (C) Rose (D) All of the above

Q.4 The endosperm of angiosperms is **[NTSE Stage-I_2014]**

(A) haploid (B) diploid (C) triploid (D) polyploid

Q.5 Which of the following diseases is not related with sexual transmission? **[NTSE Stage-I_2014]**

(A) Syphilis (B) Gonorrhoea (C) Allergy (D) AIDS

Q.6 The method of mechanical barrier to avoid pregnancy is **[NTSE Stage-I_2015]**
(A) condoms (B) contraceptive pills (C) surgical methods (D) abortion

Q.7 Seed is modification of : **[NTSE Stage-I_2016]**
(A) ovary (B) ovule (C) thalamus (D) all of these

Q.8 Regeneration is found in **[NTSE Stage-I_2016]**
(A) tapeworm (B) leech (C) hydra (D) ascaris

Q.9 In flowers which one of the following conditions will increase chances of self-pollination ? **[NTSE Stage-II_2013]**
(A) Pistil is longer than stamens in a flower
(B) Stamens are just above the stigma of pistil in a flower
(C) In all flowers of the plant only pistil is present
(D) In all flowers of the plant only stamens are present.

Q.10 Which one of the following is correct route for passage of sperms ? **[NTSE Stage-II_2014]**
(A) Testes — scrotum — vasdeferens — urethra — penis
(B) Scrotum — testes — urethra — vasdeferends — penis
(C) Tetes — vasdeferens — urethra — seminal vesicles
(D) Testes — vasdeferens — urethra — penis

Q.11 In human female, immature eggs are for the first time seen in ovary **[NTSE Stage-II_2015]**
(A) at puberty (B) before birth, at the foetus stage
(C) during the first menstrual cycle (D) after the first year birth

Q.12 The human embryo gets nutrition from the mother blood with the help of a special organ called **[NTSE Stage-II_2016]**
(A) Zygote (B) Ovary (C) Oviduct (D) Placenta

Q.13 At every 20 minutes, one bacterium divides into two. How many bacteria will be produced after two hours, if one starts with 10 bacteria? **[NTSE Stage-II_2017]**
(A) $2^5 \times 10$ (B) $2^5 \times 10^5$ (C) $2^6 \times 10$ (D) $2^6 \times 10^6$

Q.14 Testes descend down the scrotum through **[NSEJS Stage-I_2009]**
(A) outurator canal (B) inguinal canal (C) vertebral canal (D) vertebra arterial canal

Q.15 Ripened follicle in the ovary is called **[NSEJS Stage-I_2009]**
(A) corpus albicans (B) corpus luteum (C) mature follicle (D) Graafian follicle

Q.16 Which one of the following is a true fruit? **[NSEJS Stage-I_2010]**
(A) Pear (B) Coconut (C) Apple (D) Cashewnut

Q.17 Plants with inferior ovary always bear **[NSEJS Stage-I_2012]**
(A) pseudocarps (B) berries (C) aggregate fruits (D) seedles fruits

Q.18 The combination of the following structures possessing a single set of genome is **[NSEJS Stage-I_2013]**

(i) Ovary (ii) anther (iii) Egg (iv) Zygote (v) Sepal (vi) Petal (vii) Pollen

(A) i, ii, iv and vi (B) ii, iii, iv and vii (C) only iii and vii (D) only ii, iii and vii

Q.19 Of the following the combination of processes related to sexual reproduction are **[NSEJS Stage-I_2013]**

(i) Conjugation (ii) Fragmentation (iii) Gamete formation (iv) Zygote

(A) i, iii and iv (B) i, ii and iv (C) ii, iii and iv (D) only iii and iv

Q.20 In pregnant women, foetus's physiological functions like nourishment, respiration and excretion are taken up by **[NSEJS Stage-I_2014]**

(A) Stomach of mother (B) Placenta (C) Umbilical cord (D) Uterus

Q.21 In some societies, "Women were solely held responsible for giving birth to female baby" assuming no role for men. But scientific advancement has proved men equally responsible for the birth of either sex. Armed with this information which of the following would be the most appropriate scenario for the birth of female child? **[NSEJS Stage-I_2014]**

(A) Ovum with X chromosome and Sperm with Y chromosome is Female

(B) Ovum with Y chromosome amd Sperm with Y chromosome is Male

(C) Ovum with X chromosome and Sperm with X

(D) Ovum with X chromosome and Sperm without chromosome is Female

Q.22 In plant, 30 megaspore mother cells are generated. If all the ovules are fertilised, how many sees are expected to be formed? **[NSEJS Stage-I_2015]**

(A) 60 (B) 30 (C) 90 (D) 120

Q.23 Most of the insects have egg, larva, pupa and adult stages in the life cycle. This is primarily due to : **[NSEJS Stage-I_2015]**

(A) relatively short adult phase (B) terrestrial habitat they have adapted to

(C) flying mode of locomotion majority have (D) eggs storing little reserved food

Q.24 A number of bacteria are placed in a glass. 1 second later each bacterium divides in three, the next second each of the resulting bacteria divides in three again, and so on. After one minute the glass is full. When was $1/9^{th}$ of the glass full? **[NSEJS Stage-I_2015]**

(A) 15 sec (B) 45 sec (C) 58 sec (D) 38 sec

Q.25 The testes of men lie in a small muscular pouch called scrotum located outside the abdominal cavity; choose the correct reason. **[NSEJS Stage-I_2016]**

(A) Sperm formation in testes requires a higher temperature than the normal body temperature.

(B) Seminal vesicles requires lower temperature to produce nutrients for sperm.

(C) Sperm formation in testes requires a lower temperature than the normal body temperature.

(D) Sperm produced in scrotum is easily released out without going into abdominal cavity.

Q.26 In honey bee the drones (males) are produced from **[NSO 2010]**
(A) Unfertilized eggs
(B) Fertilized eggs
(C) Larvae from unfertilized eggs, which are fed on royal jelly
(D) Lavae from unfertilized eggs, which are not cared by the workers at all

Q.27 Which of the following is / are true / false regarding the development of an embryo? **[NSO 2011]**
(i) An embryo is made up of many cells.
(ii) The stage of development in which all the body parts can be identified is called the foetus.
(iii) The stage of development in which the cell begin to form groups that develop into different tissues and organs of the body is called the embryo.
(iv) The embryo gets nutrition from uterus.
(A) (i), (ii) & (iii) are true; (iv) is false (B) (i), (ii), (iii) & (iv) are true
(C) (i) & (iv) are true; (ii) & (iii) are false (D) (ii) & (iii) are true; (i) & (iv) are false

Q.28 Given below are four statements regarding external fertilization.
(i) The male and female gametes are formed and released simultaneously.
(ii) Only a few gametes are released into the medium.
(iii) Water is the medium of fertilization in majority of organisms exhibiting external fertilization.
(iv) Offsprings developed from external fertilization have better chances of survival than those developed from internal fertilization.
Which of the given statements are correct? **[NSO 2012]**
(A) (i), (ii) and (iii) (B) (i), (iii) and (iv) (C) (iii) and (iv) (D) (i) and (iii)

Q.29 Select the incorrect statement regarding AIDS. **[NSO 2012]**
(A) It is an immunodeficiency disease,
(B) HIV has RNA as its genetic material.
(C) AIDS can be transmitted to an infant from the infected mother through her milk.
(D) The time-lag between the infection and appearance of AIDS symptoms may vary from week to month.

Q.30 The menstrual period of a woman, having regular 28 days, started on March 1st. When is she most likely to ovulate and when will her next menstrual period start? **[NSO 2012]**

	Ovulation	**Menstrual Period**
(A)	March 7th	March 21st
(B)	March 14th	March 29th
(C)	March 10th	March 26th
(D)	March 14th	April 4th

Q.31 The given Venn diagram represents the changes that occur at puberty in adolescents. Which of the following options is correct regarding this? **[NSO 2012]**

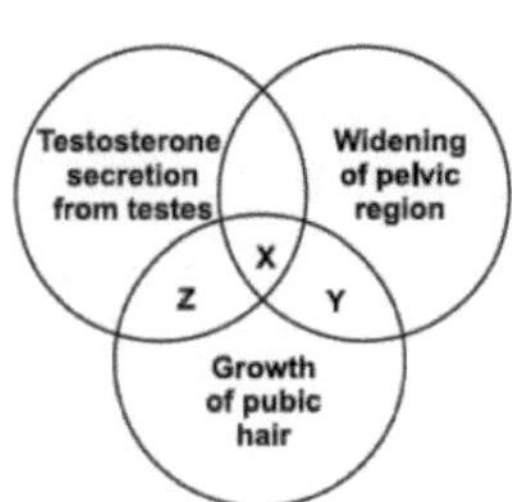

(A) X represents male and Z represents female.
(B) Z represents male and X represents female.
(C) Y represents male and Z represents female.
(D) Z represents male and Y represents female.

Q.32 Mrs. Mehra, who is 32 years old, underwent a surgery to get her oviducts removed after having girl. Now she wants to have another baby. Do you think she can have another baby? **[NSO 2013]**

(A) Yes, she can have another baby as her ovaries are still functional to produce eggs.

(B) No, she cannot have another baby because fertilization of egg takes place in the oviduct.

(C) Yes, she can have another baby because the surgery can be reversed.

(D) No, she cannot have another baby as the hormones associated with the oviduct will not be present.

Q.33 Which of the following statements is incorrect about Dolly, the clone? **[NSO 2013]**

(A) Dolly was developed from a cell taken from mammary gland of Scottish blackface ewe and an unfertilised egg obtained from Finn Dorsett sheep.

(B) The egg produced by the fusion was implanted into Scottish blackface ewe.

(C) Dolly was identical to Fin dorsett sheep and was called its clone.

(D) None of the above

Q.34

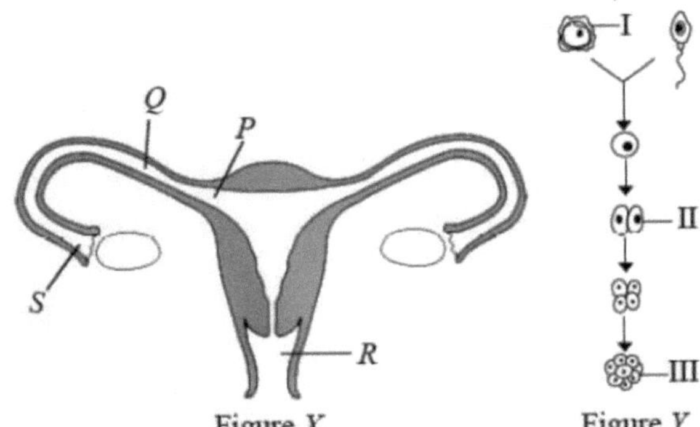

Figure X Figure Y

Figure X shows the female reproductive system and figure Y shows the development of a fertilized egg cell. In which labelled pans of tile female reproductive system will the stages I, II and III occur? **[NSO 2014]**

(A) I-S, II-P, III-P (B) I-S, II-Q, III-P (C) I-S, II-Q, III-Q (D) I-S, II-Q, III-R

Q.35 Read the following statements regarding female reproductive system and select the correct option.

(i) If the ovum released from the ovaries is not fertilized, then it is shed alongwith blood during menstruation.

(ii) Menopause occurs in the females at an age of 45-50 years.

(iii) Vagina of female reproductive system is primary sex organ.

(iv) Development of breasts in females is the accessory sex character. **[NSO 2014]**

(A) Statements (i), (ii) and (iii) are true; while statement (iv) is false.

(B) Statements (i), (ii) and (iv) are true; while statement (iii) is false.

(C) Statements (ii), (iii) and (iv) are true; while statement (i) is false.

(D) Statements (i) and (ii) are true; while statements (iii) and (iv) are false.

CONCEPT APPLICATION LEVEL - III

SECTION-A

- **Fill in the blanks**

Q.1 In ___________ a bud develops as an outgrowth due to repeated cell division at one specific site.

Q.2 After fertilisation the ___________ divides several times to form an embryo within the ovule.

Q.3 The sperm formed in tests are delivered through the ___________ which unites with a tube coming from urinary bladder.

Q.4 Child sex ratio is declining at an alarming rate in some sections of our society, due to female ___________.

Q.5 Chromosomes in the nucleus of a cell contain information for inheritance of features from parents to next generation in the form of ___________.

SECTION-B

- **Multiple choice questions with one correct answer**

Q.1 Area of embryo axis between cotyledonary mode and plumule is called
(A) Tigellum (B) Epicotyl (C) Hypocotyl (D) Chalaza

Q.2 Fruit develops from
(A) Pistil (B) Stigma (C) Style (D) Ovary

Q.3 Egg apparatus is
(A) 8-nucleate (B) 4-celled (C) 3-celled (D) 2-celled

Q.4 Frog is
(A) Oviparous (B) Viviparous (C) Hermaphrodite (D) Both B and C

Q.5 In horticulture, graft is
(A) Scion (B) Stock (C) Gootee (D) Layer

Q.6 Sugarcane is propagated through
(A) Leaf cutting (B) Stem cutting (C) Root cutting (D) Layering

Q.7 Sporulation occurs in
(A) Hydra (B) Rhizopus (C) Planaria (D) *Bryophyllum*

Q.8 Yeast multiplies by
(A) Binary fission (B) Multiple fission (C) Budding (D) Fragmentation

Q.9 Genital warts are caused by
(A) Bacterium (B) Protozoan (C) Virus (D) Worm

Q.10 ***Neisseria*** is causal agent of
(A) Syphilis (B) Gonorrhoea (C) Trichomaniasis (D) AIDS

Q.11 Vasa deferentia are blocked in
(A) Vasectomy (B) Tubectomy (C) IUD (D) Implants

Q.12 Which one is a mechanical barrier method of contraception?
(A) Copper–T (B) Diaphragm (C) Tubectomy (D) Implant

Q.13 Ovum rests in the ampulla part of fallopian tube for
(A) 1–2 hours (B) 6–12 hours (C) 12–24 hours (D) 1–2 days

Q.14 Gestation period in humans is
(A) 360 days (B) 300 days (C) 285 days (D) 270 days

Q.15 Implantation occurs in which state of embryo development?
(A) Blastocyst (B) Morula (C) Gastrula (D) Zygote

Q.16 Glands associated with the female reproductive system are
(A) Bulbourethral glands (B) Seminal vesicles
(C) Bartholin's glands (D) Prostate

Q.17 Shape of Amoeba is :
(A) Irregular (B) Every changing (C) Both A and B (D) Oval

Q.18 In binary fission a unicellular :
(A) Divides into two equal daughters
(B) Forms on large parent cell and a small daughter
(C) Divides into two unequal daughters
(D) All the above.

Q.19 In the process of binary fission :
(A) Cytoplasm divides first followed by division of nucleus
(B) Nucleus divides first followed by division of cytoplasm
(C) Both nucleus and cytoplasm divide simultaneously
(D) Cell protrudes followed by division of nucleus.

Q.20 Binary fission begins in Amoeba with :
(A) Construction of the body (B) Elongation of the body
(C) Constriction of the nucleus (D) Elongation of the nucleus

Q.21 In Amoeba the common mode of multiplication is :
(A) Binary fission (B) Multiple fission (C) Sporulation (D) Budding

Q.22 The slide of Amoeba showing binary fission is characterised by :
(A) Rounded Amoeba with elongated nucleus
(B) Amoeba having pseudopodia and rounded nucleus
(C) Amoeba constricted in the middle with round nucleus
(D) Amoeba constricted in the middle with elongated nucleus.

Q.23 Plane of binary fission in Amoeba is :
(A) Transverse (B) Oblique (C) Any (D) Longitudnal

Q.24 Binary fission in Amoeba is a mode of :
(A) Vegetative multiplication (B) Asexual reproduction
(C) Sexual reproduction (D) Perennation.

Q.25 Becuase of binary fission, Amoeba is :
(A) Immortal (B) Shows senescence (C) Gets revitalized (D) None of the above

Q.26 In which mode of reproduction, the identity of the parent is lost :
(A) Budding (B) Binary fission (C) Multiple fission (D) Both B and C.

Q.27 Yeast is a :
(A) Bacterium (B) Protozoan (C) Fungus (D) Alga

Q.28 Yeast multiplies by :
(A) Binary fission (B) Multiple fission (C) Cyst formation (D) Budding

Q.29 Budding is a mode of :
(A) Asexual reproduction (B) Sexual reproduction
(C) Vegetative reproduction (D) Perennation.

Q.30 In budding a new individual develops as a :
(A) Part of the parent (B) Outgrowth of the parent
(C) Spore (D) Both (A) and (B)

Q.31 In budding :
(A) Outgrowth develops earlier than nuclear division
(B) Nucleus divides earlier than development of outgrowth
(C) Both occur simultaneously
(D) There is no fixed sequence.

Q.32 In yeast budding occurs in :
(A) Unfavourable conditions (B) Favourable coniditions
(C) During perennation (D) Overgrown individuals

Q.33 Fertilization in angiosperms is the :
(A) fusion of two dissimilar flowers (B) union of stamens of unequal length
(C) fusion of dissimilar gametes (D) fusion of two similar spores.

Q.34 Syngamy refers to :
(A) fusion of one of the sperms with secondary nucleus
(B) fusion of one of the sperms with the egg cell
(C) fusion of one of the sperms with the egg and other with the secondary nucleus
(D) fusion of one of the sperms with synergids.

Q.35 Cowper's glands are present in :
(A) female mammals (B) male mammals (C) both (A) and (B) (D) none of the above

Q.36 When a mature egg leaves the ovary, it enters the :
(A) follicle (B) endometrium (C) interstitial cells (D) oviduct

SECTION-C

- **Assertion & Reason**

  Instructions: In the following questions as Assertion (A) is given followed by a Reason (R). Mark your responses from the following options.

  (A) Both Assertion and Reason are true and Reason is the correct explanation of 'Assertion'.
  (B) Both Assertion and Reason are true and Reason is not the correct explanation of 'Assertion'.
  (C) Assertion is true but Reason is false.
  (D) Assertion is false but Reason is true.

Q.1 **Assertion:** Bryophyllum show vegetative propogation
Reason: Propagation may be artificial or natural.

Q.2 **Assertion:** If each new generation is to be the combination of the DNA copies from two pre-existing individual, then each new generation will end up having twice the amount of DNA.
Reason: DNA is a genetic material in humans.

SECTION-D

- **Match the following (one to one)**

Q.1

Column I	Column II
(A) Rhizobium	(P) Multiple fission
(B) Rhizopus	(Q) Roots
(C) Rhizoid	(R) Bread mould
(D) Plasmodium	(S) N_2 fixing bacteria

Q.2

Column I	Column II
(A) Testis	(P) Female gamete
(B) Ovary	(Q) Male gonad
(C) Egg	(R) Male gamete
(D) Sperm	(S) Female gonad

Q.3

Column I	Column II
(A) Sugar cane	(P) Binary fission
(B) Rose	(Q) Endospore formation
(C) Bacteria	(R) Vegetative propagation
(D) Plasmodium	(S) Multiple fission

Q.4

Column I	Column II
(A) Amoeba	(P) Binary fission
(B) Plasmodium	(Q) Multiple fission
(C) Angiosperm	(R) Triple fusion
(D) Ovulation	(S) Menstrual cycle

ACTIVITY / PRACTICAL BASED QUESTIONS

Q.1 Under exceptionally favourable conditions, yeast
(A) Develops buds over buds (B) Forms a chain or pseudomycelium
(C) Both A and B (D) Produces vinegar.

Q.2 Yeast has

(A) Everchanging shape (B) Rounded body

(C) Oval body (D) Both B and C.

Q.3 The diagram illusrates

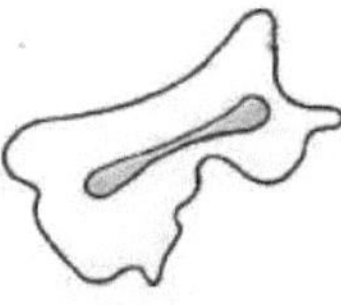

(A) Bud formation in Yeast (B) Binary fission in Amoeba

(C) Formation of daughter cells in Yeast (D) Fseudopodia formation in Amoeba

Q.4 Out of the four slides I, II, III, IV whose details are shown, which one should be focussed under the microscope for showing budding in yeast ? **[CBSE Delhi 2007]**

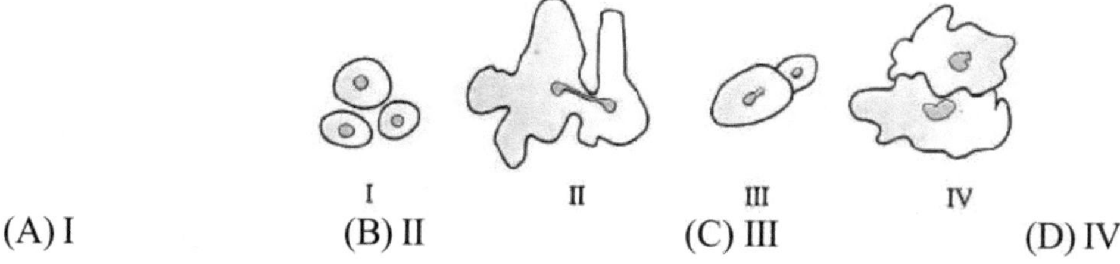

(A) I (B) II (C) III (D) IV

Q.5 Given below are stages of binary fission in Amoeba. Which one out of the following would you select as correct sequence of these stages. **[CBSE AI 2007]**

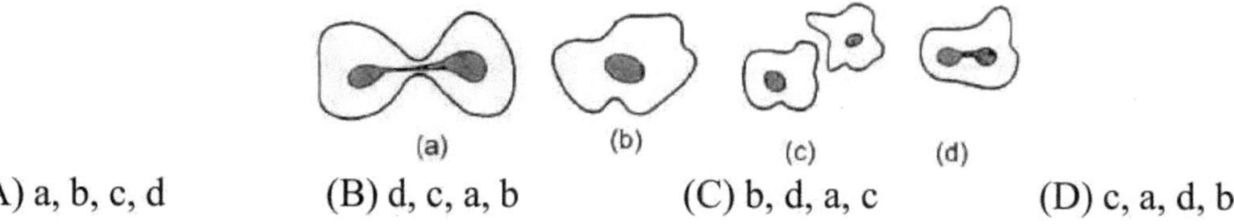

(A) a, b, c, d (B) d, c, a, b (C) b, d, a, c (D) c, a, d, b

Q.6 Which one out of the following sets of diagrams correctly depicts reproduction in Amoeba and yeast.

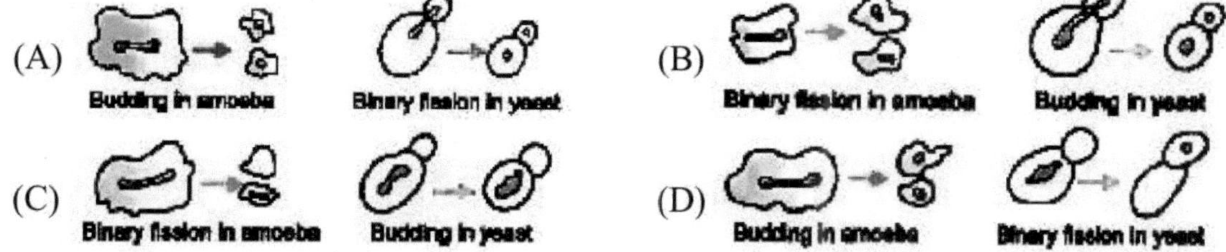

Q.7 In the slides showing binary fission in Amoeba and budding in yeast, the correct observations are **[CBSE Delhi 2007 C]**

(A) The daughter cells of Amoeba and the bud of yeast are smaller than their respective parental cells.

(B) The daughter cells of Amoeba and the bud of yeast are of the same size as their respective parental cells.

(C) The daughter cells of Amoeba are bigger than parent cells but bud of yeast in smaller than the parent.

(D) The daughter cells of Amoeba are smaller than parent but of yeast is larger than the parent.

Q.8 In the figure of budding in yeast, structures a, b, c and d should be labelled respectively as

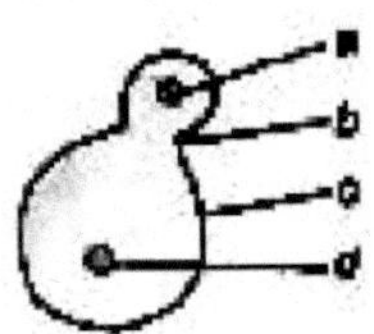

(A) Nucleus of bud, bud, Yeast, nucleus
(B) Dividing nucleus of bud, bud, Yeast, nucleus
(C) Nucleus of bud, bud, Yeast, dividing nucleus of Yeast
(D) Dividing nucleus of Yeast, yeast, bud, nucleus of bud. **[CBSE Delhi 2007 C]**

Q.9 Which one of the following sketches does not illustrate budding in yeast. **[CBSE AI 2007 C]**

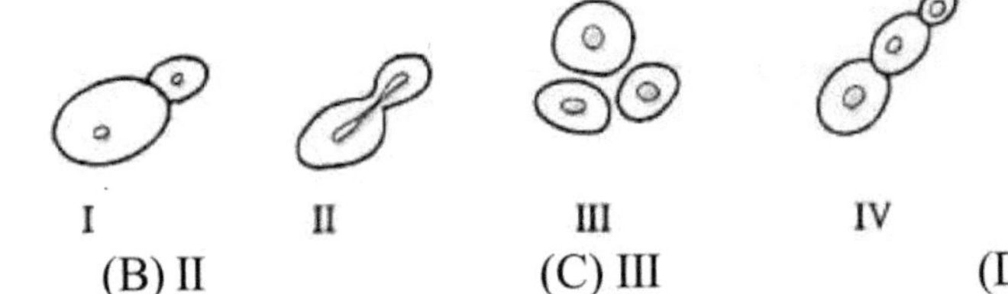

(A) I (B) II (C) III (D) IV

Q.10 The given slides a and b were identified by four students I, II, III and IV

	Slide A	Slide B
I.	Binary fission of Amoeba	Daughter cells of Amoeba
II.	Budding in Yeast	Buds of Yeast
III.	Binary fission in Amoeba	Buds of Yeast
IV.	Budding in Yeast	Daughter cells of Amoeba

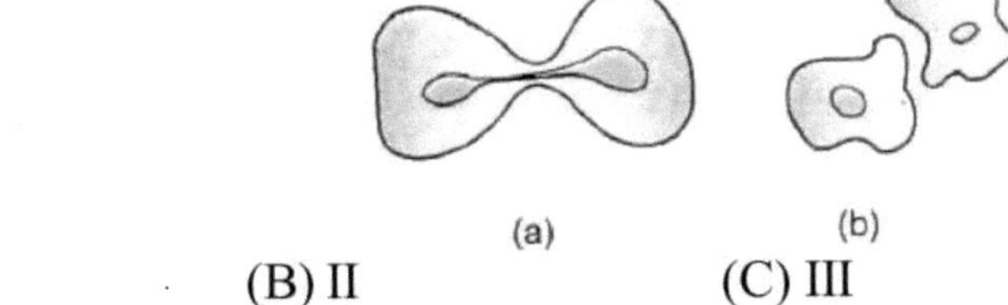

(A) I (B) II (C) III (D) IV **[CBSE Delhi 2008]**

Q.11 The correct diagram showing an Amoeba undergoing binary fission is **[CBSE AI 2008 C]**

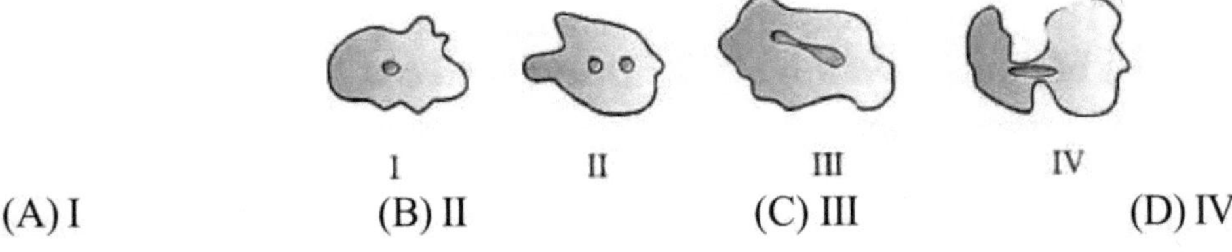

(A) I (B) II (C) III (D) IV

Q.12 The figure given here shows **[CBSE AI 2008]**

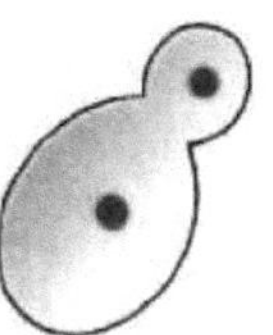

(A) Amoeba undergoing binary fission (B) Yeast undergoing binary fission
(C) Yeast undergoing budding (D) Amoeba undergoing budding

Q.13 Which of the following diagrams shows yeast cell undergoing budding. **[CBSE 2008 C]**

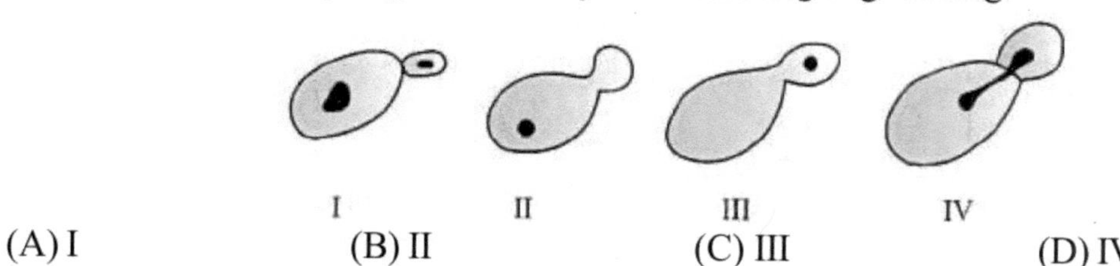

(A) I (B) II (C) III (D) IV

Q.14 Four stages of binary fission in Amoeba are shown. The stage at which nuclear fisson and cytokinesis are observed is **[CBSE Delhi 2009]**

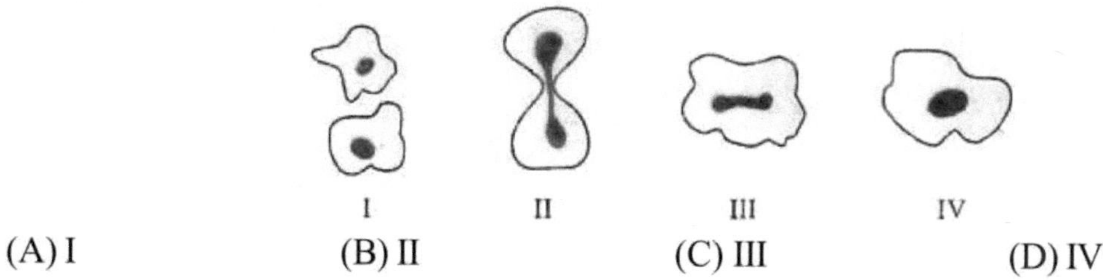

(A) I (B) II (C) III (D) IV

Q.15 Out of the given diagrams, the correctly labelled diagram showin budding in Yeast is **[CBSE AI 2009]**

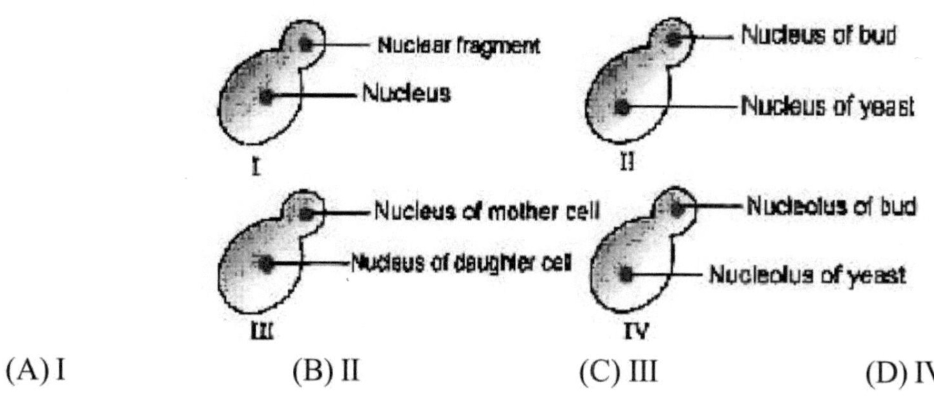

(A) I (B) II (C) III (D) IV

Q.16 The diagram showing daughter Amoeba formed after binary fission is **[CBSE 2009 C]**

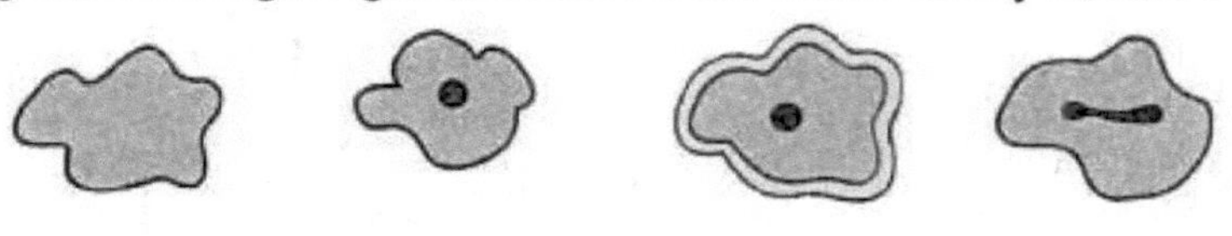

I II III IV

(A) I (B) II (C) III (D) IV

Q.17 Multiple fission is found in :
(A) Amoeba (B) Plasmodium (C) Both (D) None

Q.18 Synergids are :
(A) haploid (B) diploid (C) triploid (D) tetraploid

Q.19 The endometrium is the lining of :
(A) bladder (B) vagina (C) uterus (D) oviduct

Q.20 Progesterone hormone is produced by :
(A) germinal epithelium of ovary (B) follicular cells
(C) corpus luteum (D) none of the above

Q.21 After ovulation, endocrine part of the ovary is :
(A) corpus callosum (B) corpus albicans (C) corpus spongiosum (D) corpus luteum

Q.22 Inner lining of uterus is
(A) Myometrium (B) Perimetrium (C) Endometrium (D) All of these

Q.23 Which of the following is the correct sequence of hormonal increase beginning from menstruation?
(A) Estrogen, progestrone, FSH (B) FSH, progesterone, estrogen
(C) FSH, estrogen, progesterone (D) estrogen, FSH. progesterone.

ANSWERS

CONCEPT APPLICATION LEVEL - II

SECTION-B

Q.1	D	Q.2	C	Q.3	D	Q.4	C	Q.5	C	Q.6	A	Q.7	B
Q.8	C	Q.9	B	Q.10	D	Q.11	B	Q.12	D	Q.13	C	Q.14	B
Q.15	D	Q.16	B	Q.17	A	Q.18	C	Q.19	A	Q.20	B	Q.21	C
Q.22	B	Q.23	A	Q.24	C	Q.25	C	Q.26	A	Q.27	A	Q.28	D
Q.29	D	Q.30	B	Q.31	D	Q.32	B	Q.33	A	Q.34	B	Q.35	B

CONCEPT APPLICATION LEVEL - III

SECTION-A

1. Hydra 2. zygote 3. Vas deferens 4. Foeticides 5. DNA

SECTION-B

Q.1	B	Q.2	D	Q.3	A	Q.4	A	Q.5	A	Q.6	B	Q.7	B
Q.8	C	Q.9	C	Q.10	B	Q.11	A	Q.12	B	Q.13	D	Q.14	D
Q.15	A	Q.16	C	Q.17	C	Q.18	A	Q.19	B	Q.20	D	Q.21	A
Q.22	D	Q.23	C	Q.24	B	Q.25	A	Q.26	D	Q.27	C	Q.28	D
Q.29	A	Q.30	D	Q.31	A	Q.32	B	Q.33	C	Q.34	B	Q.35	B
Q.36	D												

SECTION-C

1. A 2. B

SECTION-D

1. (A) S, (B) R, (C) Q, (D) P
2. (A) Q, (B) S, (C) P, (D) R
3. (A) R, (B) R, (C) PQ, (D) S
4. (A) P, (B) Q, (C) R, (D) S.

ACTIVITY / PRACTICAL BASED QUESTIONS

1.	C	2.	D	3.	B	4.	C	5.	C	6.	B	7.	A
8.	A	9.	C	10.	A	11.	C	12.	C	13.	D	14.	B
15.	B	16.	B	17.	C	18.	A	19.	C	20.	C	21.	D
22.	C	23.	A										

4 HEREDITY & EVOLUTION

INTRODUCTION

- **Genetics** (Gk. *genesis* – descent) is the branch of biology that deals with study of heredity and variations. The term was given by Bateson in 1906.
- **Variation** (L. *variare* – to change) are differences present in morphological, physiological and other traits found among individuals belonging to the same family, race and species.
- **Heredity** (L. *hereditas* – heirship or inheritance) is the transmission of genetic characters from parents to offspiring.

VARIATIONS

- The differences in the characters of the individuals of a species are called variations.
- Whatever the magnitude of variation may be one thing is clear 'like begets like'. It means a human being produces human babies, a cow produces calves, a cat produces kittens, a bitch produces puppies and a mango tree produce mango.
- The transmission of characters from parents to their offsprings is called **heredity**.

Accumulation of Variation :

- Variations produced during asexual reproduction are minor, not easily detectable. They are produced due to occasional DNA copying errors.
- In sexually reproducing organisms there are many opportunities for the creation of variations.
- It means that variations are not only created by copying errors of DNA but by many other factors also.
- They may appear during gamete formation, random fusion of gametes etc.
- These variations produced during successive generations get accumulated in the organisms.

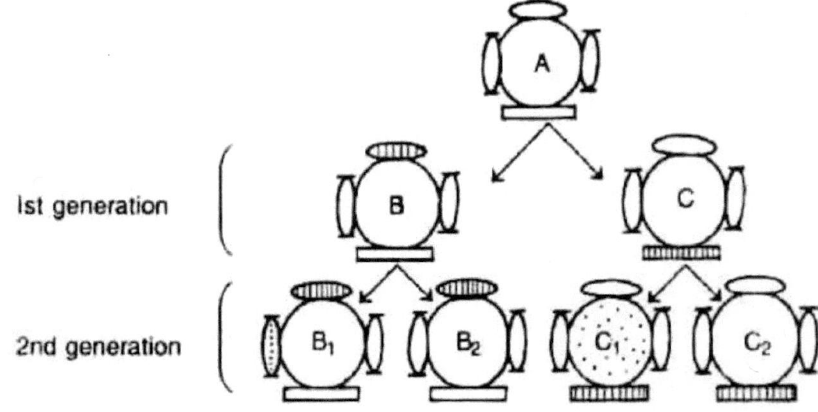

Fig. Creation of diversity over succeeding generations.

Significance of Variations :

- Variations of organisms increase the chances of survival of the species as a whole. For example, suppose a variation of heat tolerance or antibiotic resistance appears in a bacterium.
- If the temperature of the place where it lives rises permanently or an antibiotic is added in its environment, all the normal bacteria would die.
- The bacterium which had a variation of heat tolerance and antibiotic resistance will survive and reproduce.
- In nature, large number of variations get accumulated in living organisms in time and space.
- Ultimately, a great diversity develops specially in sexually reproducing organisms.
- These variations form the foundation of organic evolution.

TYPES OF VAIRATIONS

- Variation could be of two types :
  (I) Somatic Variation
  (II) Germinal Variation

I. Somatic Variation

Somatic variation affects the somatic cells of an organism. It is neither inherited from parents nor transmitted to next generation. It is acquired by individual during it's own life and is lost with it's death. It is therefore also called as **acquired variation**.

- Somatic variations are due to :

(A) **Environment :** This includes the factors that affect the organisms such as food, air pressure, humidity, water etc.

- **Light :** Strong sunlight affects the human skin by increasing the dark pigment melanin in the epidermal cells. Melanin protects the underlying cells by absorbing the ultra violet rays of the sun.
- **Habitat :** It also affects the genetic makeup of an individual and leads to variations.
- **Nutrition :** It is also one of the various factors that cause variations.

(B) **Use and disuse of organs :** Continuous use of an organ makes it better developed whereas constant disuse makes it reduced.

(C) **Conscious efforts :** Consious efforts by man produce somatic variations in humans themselves, in domestic animals and plants.

II. Germinal Variation

This variation affects the germ cells of an organism and is consequently inheritable. It is received by the individual from the parents and is transmitted to the next generation.

Significance of Variation :

- Variation enables the organisms to adapt themselves to the changing environment.
- It forms raw material for evolution.
- It enables the organisms to face the struggle for existence in a better way.
- It helps men in improving the races of useful animals and plants.
- It is the basis of heredity.
- It also leads to the existence of new traits.

MENDEL'S CONTRIBUTION

- Gregor Johann Mendel (1822–1884) in silisian (Austria) now a part of Czechoslovakia. He is known as the **Father of genetics**.
- He conducted his experiments on garden pea (*Pisum sativum*).
- Mendel presented his experiments data conclusions before **Brunn Natural Society** in 1865 and was published in Annual Proceedings of the **Natural History Society** in 1866.
- His work was recognized in 1900 after his death (1884). Mendel's conclusions (laws) were rediscovered simultaneously by Hugo de vries a Dutch biologist, Carl Correns a German botanist and Erich von Tschermak as Austrian botanist.

SOME GENERAL TERMS (Termonolgy)

(i) **Gene :** It is a hereditary unit which carries character from one generation to another generation.

(ii) **Allele :** Term allele refers to each of the members of a genetic pair or alternate trait of a gene pair.

(iii) **Homozygous traits :** They have similar alleles for specific trait (TT or tt). They produce only one type of gametes.

(iv) **Heterozygous traits :** They have dissimilar alleles for a specific trait (Tt). They produce two types of gametes.

(v) **Dominant trait :** The trait which appears in F_1 generation is called as dominant trait. It is denoted by capital letter. e.g. TT (tall)

(vi) **Recessive trait :** The trait which does not appear in F_1 generation is called as recessive trait. It is denoted by small leter. e.g. tt (dwarf)

(vii) **Genotype :** It is the genetic representation of a trait. e.g. TT or Tt for a tall plant.

(viii) **Phenotype :** It is the expression (physical appearance) of a trait e.g. Tall pea plant. It can be noted by direct observation of an individual.

(ix) **Monohybrid cross :** It involves the study of inheritance of one pair of contrasting characters. e.g. Inheritance of tall and dwarf characters.

(x) **Dihybrid cross :** It is the inheritance of two pairs of contrasting characters.

(xi) **Trihybrid cross :** It is the inheritance of three pairs of contrasting characters.

(xii) **Back cross :** The cross between F_1 generation with any of the parents is known as back cross.

(xiii) **Test cross :** The cross between F_1 generation and the recessive parent is called as test cross.

(xiv) **Emasculation :** The removal of anther from a flower for the cross pollination.

MENDEL'S EXPERIMENT

- Mendel chose garden pea as plant material for his experiments, since it has following advantages:
  - Well defined characters
  - Bisexual flowers
  - Predominantly self – fertilization
  - Easy hybridization
  - Cross fertilization is possible
- **Traits chosen by Mendel for his experiments –**

S.No.	Characteristics	Dominant	Recessive
1.	Stem height	Tall	Short
2.	Flower Colour	Voilet	White

3.	Flower position	Axial	Terminal
4.	Pod shape	inflated	constricted
5.	Pod colour	green	yellow
6.	Seed shape	round	wrinkled
7.	Seed colour	yellow	green

- **Mendel performed experiments in three stages :**
  - He made sure that, the plant which he had selected must be a true breeding plant, by letting the plant to undergo self – fertilization.
  - He performed the process of cross pollination of alternate forms of traits. The resultant generation obtained was termed as hybrid, and these hybrids formed are called as F_1 generation i.e. First filial generation.
  - He allowed the hybrid to self pollinate upto five generations and these generations are subsequently termed as F_2, F_3, F_4 and so on.
- **Reason of Mendel's Success :**

  (a) He selected true breeding (pure) pea plants for his experiments.

  (b) He studied single trait at a time.

  (c) He kept an accurate mathematical record of his breeding experiments.

  (d) He was lucky enough to select to seven traits they were located on four different chromosomes.

MONOHYBRID CROSS

- When the F_1 generation was obtained, it was found that the resultant generation would express only one of the trait and not the other.
- The trait which is being expressed is called as **dominant**, whereas the one which is not expressed is called as **recessive trait**.
- The F_2 generation is obtained by self pollination, the dominant and the recessive traits obtained were in the ratio of 3 : 1 i.e. 75% of the offsprings which appeared in F_2 generation had dominant trait, while 25% had recessive trait. This ratio of 3 : 1 is also said to be known as Mendelian monohybrid ratio. In F_2 we will get 3 : 1 ratio.

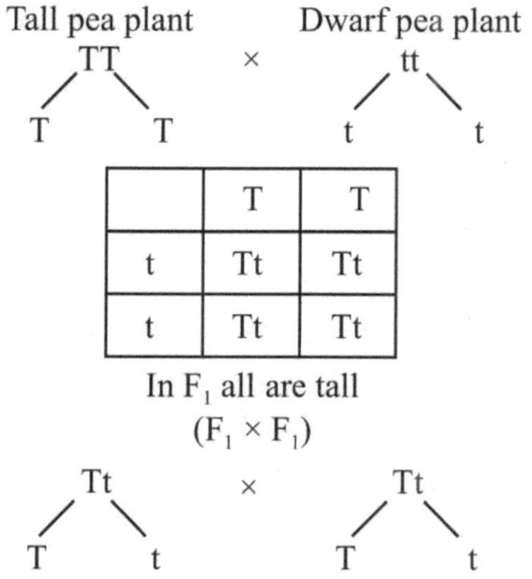

	T	T
t	Tt	Tt
t	Tt	Tt

In F_1 all are tall

($F_1 \times F_1$)

♀ \ ♂	T	t
T	TT	Tt
t	Tt	tt

In F_2 we will get 3 : 1 ratio.

TT → Homozygous tall ⎤ Tall [3]
Tt → Heterozygous tall ⎦
tt → Homozygous dwarf → Dwarf [1]

Homozygous tall : Heterozygous tall : Homozygous dwarf

1 : 2 : 1

- Mendel further found that the phenotypic ratio of 3 : 1 of dominant to recessive form of a trait was actually a genotypic ratio of 1 : 2 : 1 of pure dominant, hybrid and pure recessive forms.
- The traits which remain hidden in F_1 generation got expressed in F_2 generation. This was later on proved in F_3 generation.

DIHYBRID CROSS

- In dihybrid cross Mendel crossed genetically pure yellow round seeded (YYRR) pea plant with green wrinkled (yyrr) pea plant.
- All the plants of F_1 were yellow and round seeded (YyRr).
- In F_2 generation four types of plants appeared as :

Yellow rounded - 9 Yellow wrinkled - 3

Green round - 3 Green wrinkled - 1

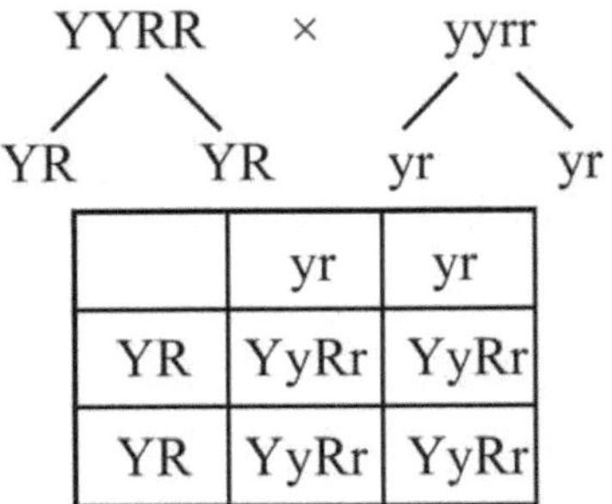

	yr	yr
YR	YyRr	YyRr
YR	YyRr	YyRr

All F_1 Plants are yellow and round seeded

YyRr × YyRr

YR Yr yR yr YR Yr yR yr

	YR	Yr	yR	yr
YR	YYRR	YYRr	YyRR	YyRr
Yr	YYRr	YYrr	YyRr	Yyrr
yR	YyRR	YyRr	yyRR	yyRr
yr	YyRr	Yyrr	yyRr	yyrr

So here phenotypic ratio is 9 : 3 : 3 : 1

MENDEL'S LAWS OF INHERITANCE

- **The Principle of Paired Factors :**
  - Each character in an individual is governed by two factors called as **gene**.
  - The alternatives form of gene is called as **alleles** or **allelomorphs**.
  - If an individual consists of similar types of alleles, they are called as **homozygous** e.g. TT, tt while those having different types of allels are called as **heterozygous** e.g. Tt etc.

- **The Principle of Dominance or Law of Dominance :**
  - When two homozygous individuals with one or more sets of contrasting characters are crossed the characters that appear in the F_1 hybrids are dominant characters and those which do not appear in F_1 are recessive characters.

- **The Principle of Segregation or Law of Segregation :**
  - (Law of purity of gametes) The law of segregation states that when a pair of contrasting factors or genes or alleles are brought together in a heterozygous condition, the two remains together without being contaminated but when gametes are formed from them the two separate out from each other.
  - This is also known as Mendel's first law of heredity.

- **The Principle of Independent Assortment or Law of Independent Assortment :**
  - If the inheritance of more than one pair of characters is studied simultaneously, the factors or genes for each pair of characters assort out independently. It is called as **Mendel's second law of heredity**.

GENES

The term Gene was introduced by Johanssen for Mendalian factor. Gene determines the physical as well as physiological characterestics. Mendel called them factors.

Chromosomal Theory of Inheritance

Sutton and **Boveri** in 1902 postulated a **chromosomal theory of inheritance**. It states that **the factors or genes are located on the chromosomes are found in the form of homologous pairs which segregate and assort independently during gametogenesis**.

Co-Dominance

In co-dominance, both the genes of an allelomorphic pairs express themeselves equally in F_1 hybrids. It means a heterozygote for codominant genes exhibits both the characters side by side. **e.g.** Codominance of blood group alleles in man.

Incomplete Dominance

It was dicovered by **Correns**, 1903. It is a post Mendelian discovery. Incomplete dominance is the phenomenon of neither of the two alleles being dominant so that expression in the hybrid is a fine mixture or some what intermediate between the expressions of two alleles in their homozygous states. Incomplete dominance is not blending inheritance because parental characters reappear in F_2 generation. In Snapdragon (Dog flower, *Antrrhinum majus*) and Four O'clock (*Mirabilis jalapa*; **Correns**, 1903) there are two types of pure breeding plants, red flowered and white flowered. On crossing the two,

F_1 plants or hybrids possess pink flowers. On selfing them F_2 generation has 1 red : 2 pink : 1 white flowered plants with phenotypic ratio beings similar to genotypic ratio. Pink flower colour is due to incomplete dominance of red flower trait over white flower trait.

Linkage : Linkage is the phenomenon of certain genes (present on the same chromosome) to remain together and get inherited in block (as a single unit) through generations. It was discovered by **Morgan** (1910). Linkage is an exception to the principle of independent assortment. The genes which remain together on the same chromosome are called **linked genes**. Bateson, Punnett, Saunders discovered its on sweet pea.

HOW DO THESE TRAITS GET EXPRESSED ?

- Cellular DNA is the information source for making proteins in the cell. A part of DNA that provides information for one protein is called the **gene** for that protein.
- Let us take the example of tallness as a characteristic.
- We know that plants have hormones that can trigger growth.
- Plant height thus depends on the amount of a particular plant hormone.
- The amount of the plant hormone made will depend on the efficiency of the process for making it.
- Consider now a protein that is important for this process.
- If this protein works efficiently, a lot of hormone will be made, and the plant will be tall.
- If the gene for that protein has an alteration that makes the protein less efficient, the amount of hormone will be less, and the plant will be short.
- Thus, genes control characteristics, or traits.

SEX DETERMINATION

- Establishment of male and female individuals or male and female organs of an individual is called sex determination.
- Different species use different strategies for this. Some rely entirely on environmentalcues. For instance:

(a) Marine mollusc crepidula becomes female if reared alone. But in the company of female it develops into male.

(b) Marine worm Bonellia develops into female if larva settles down in an isolated space. But it grows into male if it comes in close contact to female.

(c) In crocodiles high temperature induces maleness. But in some turtles high temperature induces femaleness.

- However, in most of the higher organisms including human beings, the sex of the individual is largely determined by the genetic constitution.
- In other words the genes inherited from our parents decide whether we will be boys or girls.
- The human species has 23 pairs of chromosomes.
- The figure shows that each of the chromosome pairs numbered 1-22 have identical chromosomes and these are categorized as autosomes. But the 23rd pair is different.
- It is called **sex chromosomes** which are designated as X and Y.
- XX pair with similar partners is found in females whereas XY pair with dissimilar partners is found in males.
- All the eggs produced by the mother carry 'X' chromosome. But half of the sperms produced by the father carry 'X' chromosome and the half carry 'Y' chromosome.

- During fertilization there are equal chances that an ovum will be fertilized by an X bearing sperm or Y bearing sperm.

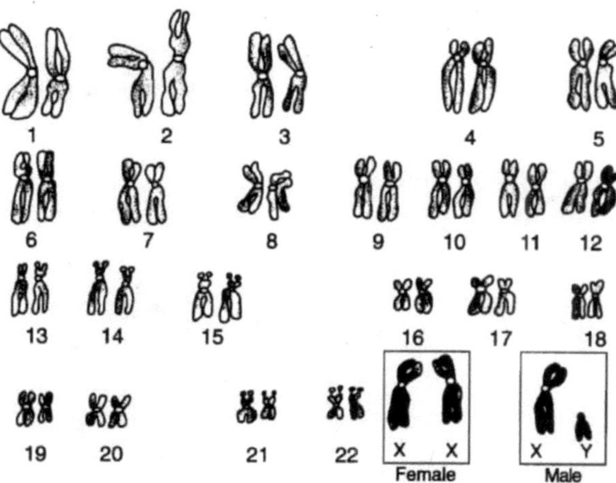

- If the egg is fertilized by 'X' bearing sperm (XX), the child will be a girl.
- If the egg is fertilized by 'Y' bearing sperm (XY), the child will be a boy.

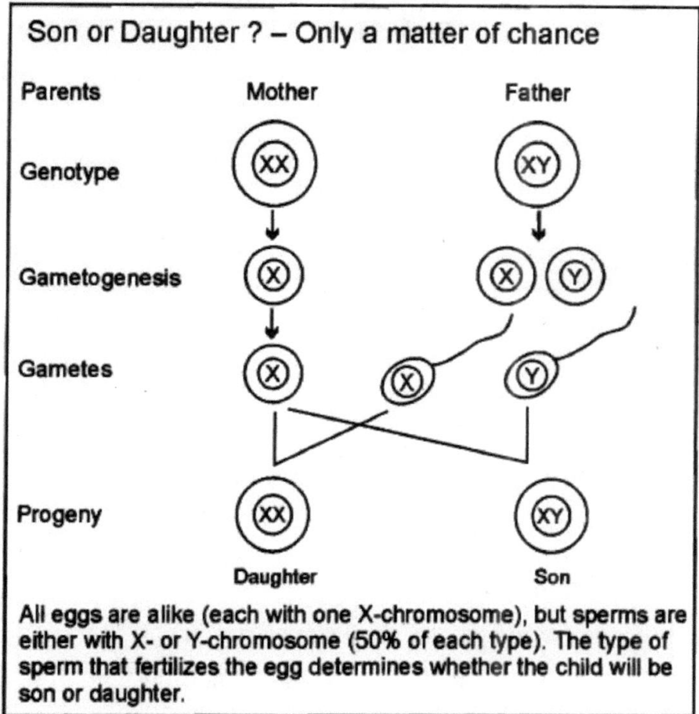

EVOLUTION

- **Evolution** (L. *evolvere* - to unfold) or **organic evolution** (Spencer, 1852) is the development of newer types of organisms from the pre-existing ones through modification.
- Darwin (1859) has called evolution to be descent with modifications.
- Modifications occur due to accumulation of variations.
- Variations develop during reproduction due to errors in DNA copying or mutations, chance separation of chromosomes during gametogenesis, crossing over and chance pairing of chromosomes.
- Variations taking part in evolution are genetic variations.
- Certain variations develop during life time of an organism. They are called acquired variations. Acquired variations have no role in evolution.

Case I.

- The process of sexual reproduction results in the formation of few green beetles instead of red beetles.
- These green beetles will be able to pass the colour on to its progeny, so that all its progeny beetles are green.
- These green beetles cannot be seen by crows. So, they are not eaten.
- Increased feeding of red beetles by crows will result in drastic reduction of red beetles and increased number of green beetles in the population.
- In this case, **natural selection** is directing evolution in the beetle population. The natural selection is **exerted by the crows**.

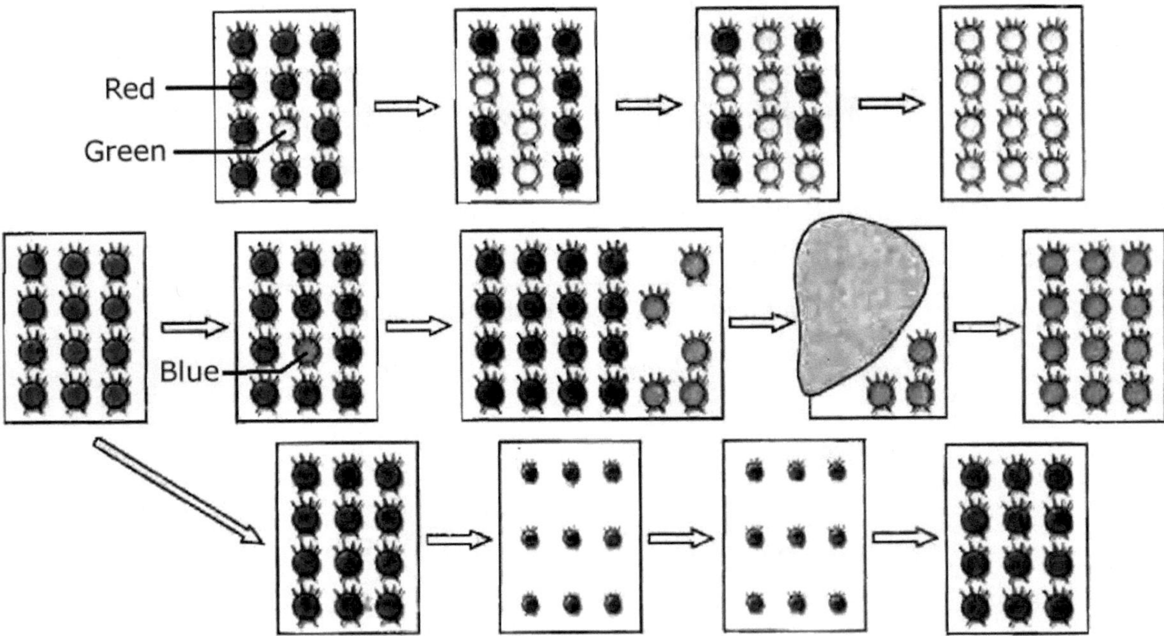

Case II.

- The process of reproduction again result in the formation of another colour variant i.e., blue colour beetles.
- These beetles are also able to pass the colour on to its progeny, so that all its progeny beetles are blue.
- These beetles can be seen by crows, so they are eaten.
- In initial stages there are more number of red beetles in comparison to blue beetles in a population. But at this point, an elephant comes by and stamps on the bushes where the beetles live.
- This kills most of the beetles. But by chance, the few beetles that have survived are mostly blue. These beetles (blue) will now slowly increase their number.
- In this case, the colour change gave no **survival advantage**.
- It is simply a matter of **accidental survival of beetles** of one colour that changed the common characteristics of the resultant population.
- The elephant would not have caused such major havoc in the beetle population if the beetle population had been very large.
- *This random change in the gene frequency occurring by chance irrespective of its being beneficial or harmful is called* ***genetic drift****.*
- For this reason, in small populations, some unfavourable characters may also be fixed or beneficial characters may be lost.

Case III.

- Beetle population begins to increase. Suddenly, the bushes are attacked by a plant disease.
- The amount of leaf material is reduced.
- The average weight of adult beetles decreases because of scarcity of food.
- Their number also decreases. Decrease in number and weight of beetles due to reduction in food is an **acquired trait**.
- After a few years, when bushes once again become healthy, the average weight of beetles should once again increase, due to adequate availability of food.
- If there is good amount of food and the predators are few, the beetle population will also grow in size.

ACQUIRED AND INHERITED TRAITS

- Some traits are acquired by an organism during its life time. For example, a person can develop his muscles by exercise, but this bodily change is not transferred to his children.
- Changes which take place in body cells are not transmitted to next generation.
- In other words, the change in non-reproductive tissue cannot be passed on to the DNA of the germ cells.
- Germ cells are produced in specialised reproductive tissues.
- These are the testes and the ovaries.
- Therefore, the skills and experiences of an individual during its lifetime cannot be transferred to next generation.
- The traits of an organism can be grouped into following two categories :
  Acquired traits and inherited traits

(a) **Acquired Traits.** These traits are acquired by organisms in their life. For example, weight gain or weight loss, development of muscles, learning, driving etc.

(b) **Inherited Traits.** These traits are controlled by specific genes and therefore, passed on from one generation to the next. Eye colour, and colour of hair of human beings are inherited traits. Colour of flower in plants is also an inherited trait.

ORIGIN OF LIFE

- The widely accepted hypothesis is that inorganic molecules of primitive earth combined to produce organic molecules and eventually from these molecules first cell arose.
- This idea was first of all proposed by **J.B.S. Haldane** a British scientist (who became a citizen of India later.) and **A.I. Oparin**, a Russian biochemist independently.
- The main points of this idea are :
  - The environment of primitive earth was entirely different from the present day environment.
  - There was no oxygen in the atmosphere and the temperature was high.
  - Life arose in sea water.
  - Simple substances of the atmosphere combined to form complex organic substances. The energy for this combination was provided by lightning, thundering and high temperature etc.
  - By the accumulation and further chemical synthesis of these organic molecules the first cell like structure evolved.
  - These findings were proved experimentally by **Stanley L. Miller** and **Harold C. Urey** in 1953.

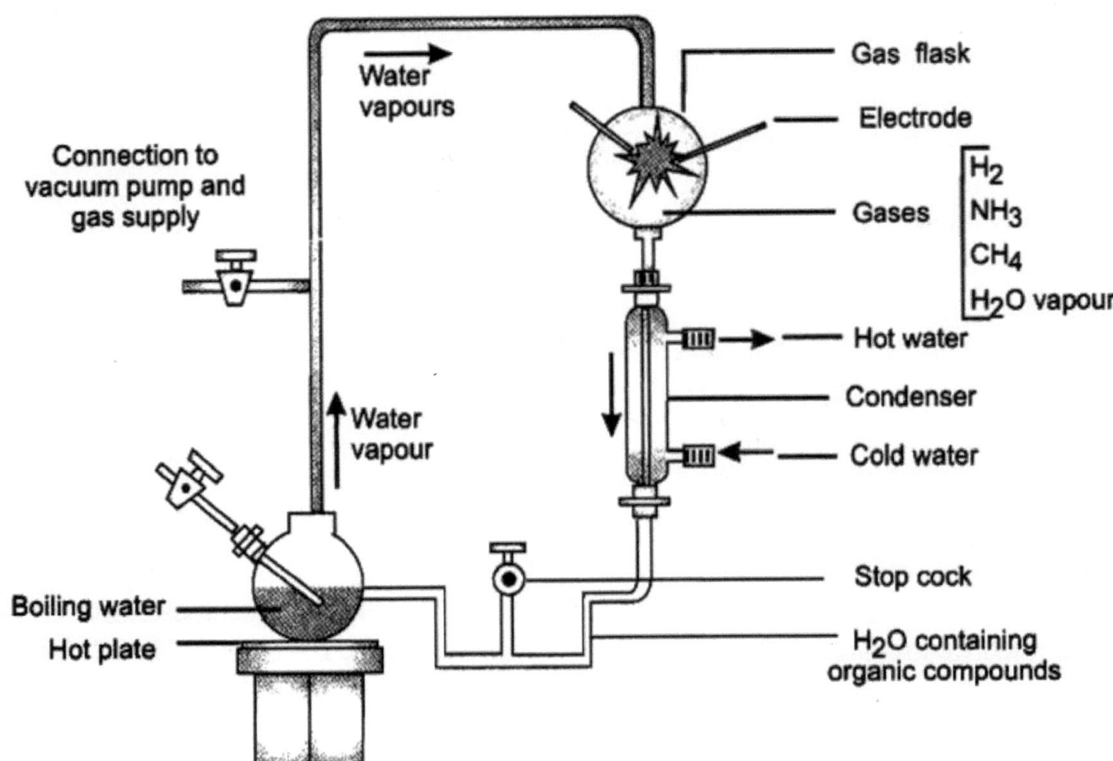

Fig. Origin of Life : Miller and Urey's experiment

- They took gases which were present in the environment of primitive earth, like ammonia, methane and hydrogen sulphide in a flask and stimulated the atmosphere of primitive earth. (Artificially created the atmosphere of primitive earth.)
- As oxygen was not there in primitive earth's atmosphere, it was not taken in experimental flask, spark chamber.
- A temperature just about 100°C was maintained and electric sparks were passed through the mixture of gases to simulate lightning.
- After a week they noticed the presence of simple organic substances, like amino acids. Amino acids are building blocks of proteins. About 15% carbon of methane converted into organic form.
  This process of formation of living cell from simple inorganic substances is called **chemical evolution**.

SPECIATION

- The transformation of one species into a new species over time is called **speciation.**
- Splitting of one species into two or more species is also speciation. In simple words, this is creation of a new species from existing ones.
- **Micro-evolution :** Creation of a green variant or a blue variant in the population of red beetles are examples of micro-evolution. Development of heat tolerant and antibiotic resistant bacteria are also examples of micro-evolution. Therefore, the term micro-evolution means origin of new variants due to appearance of small but significant variations. These variations change the common characteristics of a particular species only.

OR

- Variations at sub-species level are called micro-evolution.
- **Macro-evolution.** Macro-evolution refers to any evolutionary change at or above the level of species. It means the origin of a new species and higher categories.

How does speciation occur (Mechanism of Speciation) ?

- A population of a species may get **geographically isolated** from other populations of that species.
- It means that there appears a geographical barrier like river or mountain etc. between two populations.
- Now in isolated populations variations keep on accumulating by directional selection, or genetic drift etc.
- Ultimately, due to large geographical barrier the **Gene flow** between two sub populations would stop.
- The two isolated populations will become more and more different from each other.
- Eventually, the members of these two groups will be incapable of reproducing with each other.
- Now even if they meet they will not be able to breed with each other.
- These reproductively isolated individuals will form a new species.
  [The gene flow is also called **gene migration**. It is the movement of genes between populations by breeding individual.]

OTHER METHOD OF SPECIATION

- A new species may also develop if the DNA changes are severe enough.
- A change in the number of chromosomes can lead to formation of a new species.
- Due to changed number of chromosomes the germ cells of two groups would not be able to fuse with each other.
- **Common wheat plants have emerged as new species by this method**. Any other big change in genetic material may also lead to reproductive isolation of a species.

EVOLUTION AND CLASSIFICATION

- Classification refers to grouping of organisms on the basis of their similarities.
- It means that organisms having same characteristics are classified or grouped together.
- Characteristics are details of appearance or behaviour, in other words, a particular form or particular function.
- Presence of wings is a characteristic of birds and primitive nucleus is a characteristic of prokaryotes like bacteria.
- Knowledge of evolution helps in grouping of organisms also.
- Evolution is often called **descent with modifications**, It is actually a sort of going backwards in time.
- For this we have to identify the hierarchies of characteristics between species.
- Based on evolution the next characteristics are
  - Cell design
  - Unicellular or multicellular organisms
  - Organisms make their own food by photosynthesis or take readymade food.
  - Skeleton is inside the body or around the body.

  Due to this a hierarchy develops which allow us to classify organisms.
- The more characteristics two species will have in common, the more closely they are related.
- All animals which have hair on body, external ears and mammary glands are more closely related than the animals which do not have these characteristics.
- It means that more recently all these have had a common ancestor.
- **Classification of species is therefore, reflection of their evolutionary relationship.**

EVIDENCES IN FAVOUR OF EVOLUTION

- There are many evidences on the basis of which we can trace the evolutionary relationship between organisms. The characteristics in different organisms would be similar if they are inherited from a common ancestor. Evidences of different characteristics have been gathered for this purpose like homologous organs, analogous organs and fossils.

MORPHOLOGICAL EVIDENCE

Homologous Organs :

- Those organs which have the similar basic structure but different functions are known as **homologous organs**.
- The forelimbs of vertebrate animals, like forelimb of a human being, forelimb of a bird, flipper of a whale, forelimb of a horse are very good example of homologous organs.
- The basic structure of the limbs is similar though they are modified to perform different functions.
- Even in vertebrates like amphibians, reptiles, birds and mammals the basic design of forelimbs is strikingly similar. These are called **homologous organs**.
- In human being the hand is used to hold things and for grasping, in birds it helps in flying, in whales it helps in swimming etc.
- It mean they perform different functions, but their structure is same.
- The homologous forelimbs indicate that all these animals have evolved from common ancestor.

Analogous Organs

- The organs which have different basic structural design but perform similar functions are called **analogous organs**.
- The wings of birds and bat (both vertebrate animal) present another example of analogous organs.
- The wings of bat are simply folds of skin stretched between elongated fingers. But the wings of birds are modified forelimb.
- They are made of a feathery covering extended all along the arm.
- Their design appears to be similar but their origins are not common.

EVIDENCE FROM FOSSILS

- *The remains or remnants of organisms of remote past are known as fossils.* They may be in the form of dead mineralised part or an impression etc. The fossils provide good evidence for establishing evolutionary relationships.

Determination of the Age of the Fossils :

- Two approaches are generally used to know how old the fossils are. The first one is **relative**.
- The rocks are present in the form of concentric layers.
- The layer closer to the surface are more recent than the deeper layers.
- It is, therefore, reasonable to suppose that the fossils we find closer to the surface are more recent than the fossils we find in deeper layers.
- It means that as we dig deeper, we will find older and older fossils.
- For example, near the surface of earth we will find fossils of horse, if we dig deeper then there will be fossils of dinosaur. In still deeper layers there will be fossils of invertebrate animals.

- In second approach, **dating of rocks** is done. For dating purpose radioactive isotopes are used. In this method ratios of different isotopes like ^{14}C etc., are calculated.

Important Fossils :

- **Ammonite :** The ammonites represent fossils of mollusc in the form of tight spiral shell. (Marine)
- **Trilobite :** Trilobites are fossils of marine arthropods, Knightia fish.
- **Dinosaur Skull (Rajasaurus) :** These terrible lizards roamed the earth 250–65 millions years ago. It was obtained from Narmada valley.

EVOLUTION BY STAGES

A. Evolution of Eyes:

- The very well developed eyes of human beings, vertebrate animals, insects and octopus have developed in stages.
- These complex structures cannot be developed by a single DNA change.
- Actually, the positive changes for the betterment of the eyes have developed gradually in stages, bit by bit over generations.
- Ability to sense light was a useful variation, therefore, it was selected generation over generation.
- Even the intermediate forms of eye gave certain advantage to the animals.
- In very primitive organisms there is an eye spot to sense the light.
- From this eye spot, evolved the primitive eye like structures of flatworm Planaria.
- It proved to be a fitness advantage.
- The eyes of insects, octopus and vertebrate animals are altogether different, very well adapted to their mode of life.
- They have developed through different lines of evolution.

B. Evolution of Feathers :

- Presence of feathers in some non flying dinosaurs clearly indicates that feathers were developed in these animals for insulation in cold weather.
- Later on they became useful for flight.
- It is clear that a change that is useful for one property can become useful later for quite a different function.
- Birds, used the feather, basically developed for thermal insulation, for flight.
- It is an evidence in favour of organic evolution because birds have evolved from reptiles.
- *Archaeopteryx* is a fossil which represents a link between reptiles and birds.

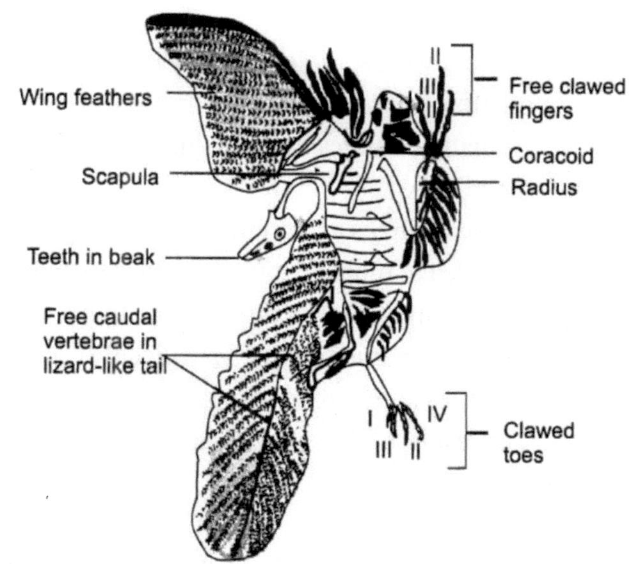

C. Artificial Selection

- Artificial selection is a process by which man selects traits of organisms (plants and animal) useful for him.

- Artificial selection has led to domestication of many plants and animals.
- The wild cabbage plant is a good example.
- Cabbage, Kohlrabi, cauliflower, broccoli, kale etc. have been developed from a common wild ancester.
- Different breeds of pigeon like ponter, fantail, jocobin have been produced by artificial selection from wild rock pigeon.
- The basic difference between natural selection and artificial selection is that in artificial selection the traits selected are beneficial to man while in natural selection traits best suited to the species are selected by nature.

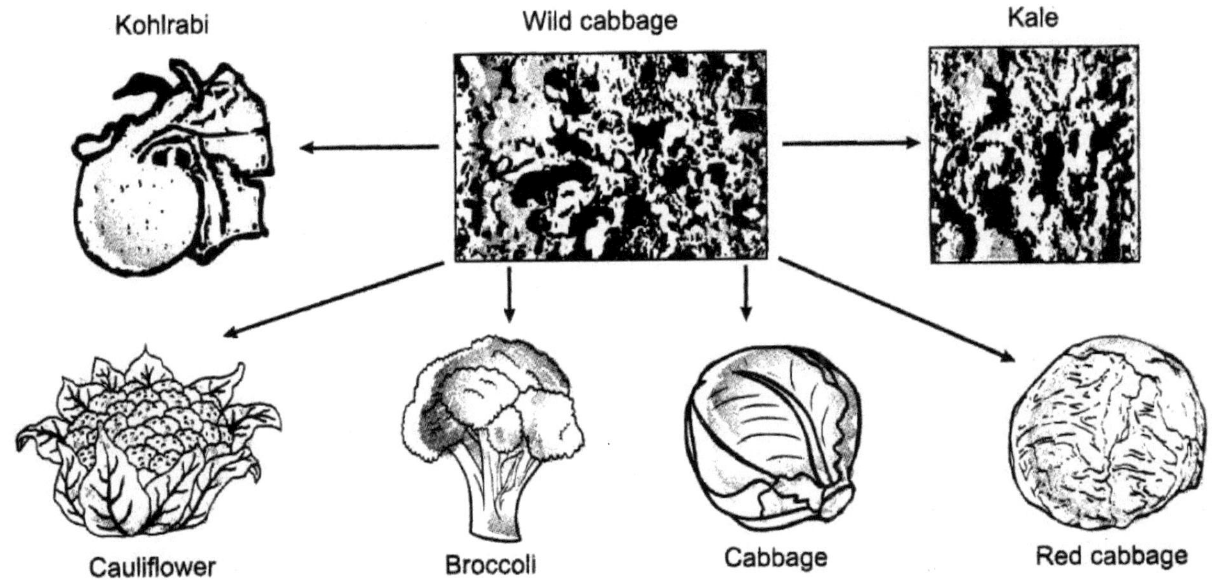

MOLECULAR PHYLOGENY

- Evolutionary history of a group of organisms based on molecules of the cell is known as molecular phylogeny.
- In other words, molecular phylogeny traces the evolutionary relationship among group of organisms on molecular bases.
- Actually, changes in DNA during cell division lead to changes in the proteins that are made from this new DNA.
- These changes accumulate from one generation to the next.
- The idea of molecular phylogeny is to trace the changes in DNA backwards in time and find out where each change diverged from the other.
- Similar organisms which are closely related show similarities in their DNA.
- While distantly related organisms have greater number of differences in their DNA.
- The results of the study of molecular phylogeny of organisms match the classification scheme you have studied earlier.

EVOLUTION SHOULD NOT BE EQUATED WITH PROGRESS

- The diversity of organisms which we see around us have evolved from simple common ancestor.
- Evolution is simply the shaping of the diversity by environmental selection.
- There is no real progress in the idea of evolution.

- Of course, the organisms which evolved initially were simple in design and structure and from these more and more complex body designs have emerged overtime.
- The idea of evolution becomes very clear when we trace the family tree of species.
- That is why it is called a tree.
- It has many branches.
- Actually, multiple or many branches are possible at each and every stage of this process.
- It is not as if one species is eliminated to give rise to new one.
- When a new species is generated, the old one is not disappeared all the times.
- The old one may split into two populations. It all depends on environment.
- The newly emerged species are in no way better than the older one.
- It simply means that natural selection and genetic drift have together led to the formation of a population that cannot reproduce with the original one.

HUMAN EVOLUION

- Like any other species, human beings came into being as an accident of evolution.
- To study human evolution the same tools are used which are used to trace evolutionary relationship of any other animal.
- We have gathered information about human evolution on the basis of excavations, time dating, study of fossils and by determining DNA sequence.
- All humans inhabiting this planet belong to the single species *Homo sapiens*. There is no biological basis to the notion of human races. The so called races which show variations of skin colour etc. developed due to different environment.
- Human beings originated in Africa. We all, wherever we live on this planet, come from Africa. Our genetic footprints can be traced back to our African roots.
- Some of our ancestors left Africa and spread to all parts of the world, while some stayed back in Africa.
- There is continuous 'gene flow' among different populations of human beings. Man has the ability to cross any geographical barrier.

POINTS TO REMEMBER

1. Variations arise during the process of reproduction. They may be few in asexual reproduction, but many in case of sexual reproduction.
2. The minor variations arising during asexual reproduction are caused by slight inaccuracies in DNA copying. In sexual reproduction, variations are also caused by crossing over process of meiosis.
3. Beneficial variations help the species to survive better in the environment.
4. Nature selects the beneficial variations thereby leading to evolution.
5. Reproduction produces offsprings with similar body design of the parents. However the offspring are not identical, but show a great deal of variation from the parents.
6. Sexually reproducing organisms like humans have 2 (or more) versions of genes for each trait, called alleles.
7. Gregor Johann Mendel carried out several experiments on pea plants. He carried out large number of monohybrid and dihybrid crosses using many contrasting characteristics and put forward several important conclusions.
8. In case of monohybrid cross with pure variety of plants, the phenotypic ratio obtained in F_2 generation is 3:1.
9. In case of dihybrid cross involving 2 pairs of contrasting characters, the phenotypic ratio obtained in F_2 generation is 9:3:3:1.
10. Mendel concluded that out of any pair of contrasting characters, one is dominant and the other recessive.
11. The homozygous dominant trait is denoted by two capital letters whereas the homozygous recessive trait is denoted by two small letters.
12. The factors or genes controlling a particular trait separate from each other during gamete formation. Hence gamete is always pure as far as contrasting characters are considered. Each gamete will possess only one gene set.
13. In crossing if two or more traits are involved, their genes assort independently, irrespective of the combinations present in the parents.
14. Genes carry information for producing proteins, which in turn control the various body characteristics.
15. For a particular trait, the offspring receives one allele from the father and one allele from the mother.
16. The combination of the male and female germ cells gives a diploid zygote. Thus the normal diploid number of chromosomes in the offspring is restored.
17. Different mechanisms are used for sex determination in different species.
18. The sex of human offspring is genetically determined.
19. Humans have 22 pairs of autosomes and one pair of sex chromosomes.
20. Females have similar sex chromosomes XX, whereas males have an imperfect pair i.e. XY. All eggs carry X chromosome.
21. The sex of the child depends on whether the egg fuses with the sperm carrying X chromosome (resulting in a girl) or with the sperm carrying Y chromosome (resulting in a boy).
22. Variations beneficial to a species have a greater chance of flourishing in the species than the harmful or neutral variations.
23. Genetic drift can alter gene frequencies in small population and provide diversity without any survival benefits.
24. Several factors like environment, mutations, reproduction etc can cause alterations in gene frequencies in a population over generations, leading to evolution.
25. Changes occurring in the DNA of germ cells are heritable whereas changes taking place in the non-reproductive tissues are not inherited.

26. Charles Darwin proposed that evolution of species occurred by natural selection, but he did not know the underlying mechanism.
27. Natural selection, genetic drift, variations and geographical isolation can lead to speciation in sexually reproducing organisms.
28. Gene flow between the members of a population prevents speciation.
29. The fundamental characteristics used to classify organisms are:
    - presence of prokaryotic or eukaryotic cells.
    - whether the organism is unicellular or multicellular.
    - ability to perform photosynthesis.
    - presence of endoskeleton or exoskeleton in heterotrophic organisms.
30. Classification of living organisms is closely related to their evolution.
31. As we go back in time to trace common ancestors, we find that all organisms must have arisen and radiated from a single species, which in turn originated from non-living material. Thus life arose from non-living matter.
32. Study of homologous organs, e.g. hand of man and wing of bird, helps in tracing the evolutionary relationship between different species.
33. Analogous organs, e.g. wing of insect and wing of bird, do not have common origins, but arose in different species to fulfill similar functions.
34. Fossils help in tracing evolutionary pathways.
35. The age of fossils can be determined by using the relative method or the isotope dating method.
36. Evolution is not a one-step process, but a continuous process occurring in several stages.
37. Complex organs are formed slowly over many generations, sometimes with intermediate forms playing an important role.
38. Sometimes the use of certain features gets modified with time. For example, feathers may have provided insulation initially but later became associated with flight.
39. Evolutionary studies have shown that birds are closely related to reptiles.
40. Humans have carried out artificial selection for various features of cabbage and produced different vegetables.

Vegetable produced	Selected feature
Broccoli	Arrested flower development
Cauliflower	Sterile flowers
Kohlrabi	Swollen parts
Kale	Larger leaves

41. Molecular phylogeny can also be used to trace evolutionary relationships. Here the DNA of different species is compared. Greater the differences in DNA, more distantly related are the species.
42. Disappearance of the existing species is not a requirement for formation of new species.
43. The new species formed are better adapted to the environment, but they need not be superior to the existing species.
44. The common ancestor of humans and chimpanzees evolved in different ways to produce the present forms.
45. Evolution produces more diverse and complex body forms over time, but the newly formed species are not more progressive than the already existing ones. So it is wrong to say that evolution produces progressive higher forms from lower ones.
46. All human beings, whether fair skinned or dark skinned, belong to the same species i.e. Homo sapiens that originated in Africa.
47. The human ancestors gradually migrated from Africa to various parts of the world like Asia, Europe, Australia and America. Thus, they spread to different parts of the Earth and adapted as best as they could to their environmental conditions.

CONCEPT APPLICATION LEVEL - I [NCERT Questions]

Q.1 Does genetic combination of mother play a significant role in determining the sex of a new born ?

Ans. No. Mothers have no role in determining the sex of the new born. Mothers are **homogametic**, that is, they produce only one type of ova (22 + X). Fathers are heterogametic, that is, they produce two types of sperms, **gynosperms** (22 + X) and **andosperms** (22 + Y). If gynosperm (22 + X) fertilises the ovum (22 + X), the sex of new born will be female (44 + 2X). If androsperm (22 + Y) fuses with ovum (22 + X), the new born will be boy (44 + XY).

Q.2 Why do all the gametes formed in human females have an X-chromosome ?

Ans. Human females are **homogametic**. Their genetic constitution is 44 + XX. The two sex chromosomes are similar. Their ova which are provided after meiosis carries a gametic constitution of 22 + X. No other combination is possible.

Q.3 In human beings the satistical possibility of getting either a male or female child is 50 : 50. Give suitable explanation.

Ans. Human females (44 + XX) are **homogametic**, that is, they produce only one type of ova (22 + X). Human males are **heterogametic**. They produce two types of sperms (22 + X and 22 + Y) in equal proportion, that is, 50 : 50 ratio. The chance of male or female child is also 50 : 50, as there is equal chance of androsperm (22 + Y) or gynosperm (22 + X) fertilizing an ovum.

Q.4 What are homologous structures? Give an example. Is it necessary that homologous structures always have a common ancestor?

Ans. **Homologous structures** or **organs** are those structures which have similar origin, similar development, similar internal structure and similar basic plan but show different external form and function, e.g., forelimbs of amphibians, reptiles, mammals and birds.

Homologous structures always have a common ancestry because there cannot be any similarity in basic plan, internal structure, development or origin. Modifications have occurred in them due to varied adaptations.

Q.5 Does the occurrence of diversity of animals on earth suggest their diverse ancestry also ? Discuss this point in the light of evolution.

Ans. Diversity of animals does not mean that they have diverse ancestry. Animals can be grouped into distinct lineages (*e.g.*, mammals, birds, reptiles, annelids). Many of the lineages further show some similarities in basic traits indicating a common ancestry. *e.g.*, vertebrates. Therefore, animals having a common ancestor in the remote past have successively developed newer traits forming various groups of animals.

Q.6 A woman has only daughters. Analyse the situation genetically and provide a suitable explanation.

Ans. A woman produces only one type of ova (22 + X) while her husband produces two types of sperms, gynosperms (22 + X) and androsperms (22 + Y) in equal proportion. It is a chance that each time the woman conceived, only the gynosperm fertilised the egg so that only daughters were born.

Q.7 Does geographical isolation of individuals of a species lead to formation of a new species? Provide a suitable explanation.

Ans. Yes. Geographical isolation of a population will lead to **genetic drift** as there will be no gene flow between it and the parent species. Inbreeding in small population will result in fixation of certain alleles and elimination of others. There will be change in gene frequency. Mutations will produce new alleles and hence a new gene pool. Accumulation of new alleles and hence new variations over several generations will ultimately lead to the formation of new species.

Q.8 Bacteria have a simpler body plan when compared with human beings. Does it mean that human beings are more evolved than bacteria. Provide a suitable explanation.

Ans. Both bacteria and human beings perform all the activities of life and live comfortably in their environments. They, therefore, seem to be equally evolved. However, human beings have a far more complex organisation and differentiation which are absent in bacteria. Since complex organisation and differentiation develop only through evolution, humans are far more evolved than bacteria.

Q.9 All the human races like Africans, Asians, Europeans, Americans and others might have evolved from a common ancestor. Provide a few evidences in support of this view.

Ans. All the human races have evolved from a common ancestor because they possess (i) Common body plan (ii) Common structure (iii) Similar physiology (iv) Similar metabolism (v) Similar chromosome number (vi) Common genes or genetic blue print (vii) Free interbreeding.

Q.10 Give reasons for the appearance of new combination of characters in the F_2 progeny.

Ans. **Independent Assortment.** The two forms of a gene separate and pair independent of the two forms of other genes during gametogenesis and fertilisation. It causes new combination of characters, *e.g.*;

Parents Rr Yy Rr Yy

Gametes (RY)(Ry)(rY)(ry) (RY)(Ry)(rY)(ry)

	(RY)	(Ry)	(rY)	(ry)	
(RY)	RRYY Round Yellow	RRYy Round Yellow	Rr YY Round Yellow	RrYy Round Yellow	Round Yellow - 9
(Ry)	RRYy Round Yellow	RRyy Round Green	RrYy Round Yellow	Rr yy Round Green	Round Green - 3
(rY)	Rr YY Round Yellow	Rr Yy Round Yellow	rr YY Wrinkled Yellow	rr Yy Wrinkled Yellow	Wrinkled Yellow - 3 Wrinkled Green - 1
(ry)	Rr Yy Round Yellow	Rr yy Round Green	rr Yy Wrinkled Yellow	rryy Wrinkled Green	Recombinants - 6/16

Q.11 If a trait A exists in 10% of a population of an asexually reproducing species and a trait B exists in 60% of the same population, which trait is likely to have arisen earlier?

Ans. In asexual reproduction, the reproducing cells produce a copy of their DNA through some chemical reactions. However, this copying of DNA is not accurate and therefore, the newly formed DNA has some variations.

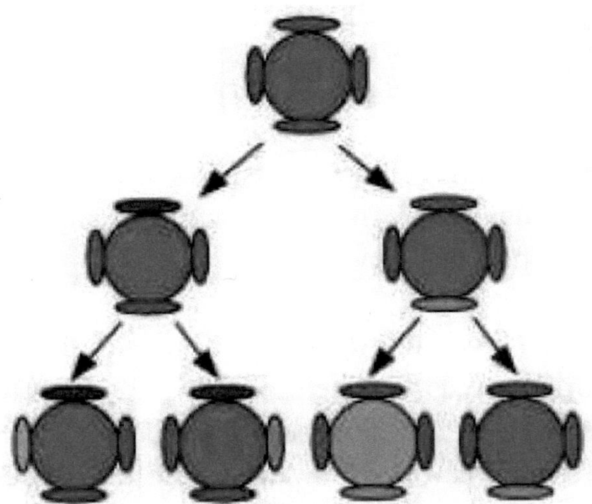

It can be easily observed in the above figure that in asexual reproduction, very few variations are allowed. Therefore, if a trait is present in only 10% of the population, it is more likely that the trait has arisen recently. Hence, it can be concluded that trait B that exists in 60% of the same population has arisen earlier than trait A.

Q.12 How does the creation of variations in a species promote survival?

Ans. Sometimes for a species, the environmental conditions change so drastically that their survival becomes difficult. For example, if the temperature of water increases suddenly, most of the bacteria living in that water would die. Only few variants resistant to heat would be able to survive. If these variants were not there, then the entire species of bacteria would have been destroyed. Thus, these variants help in the survival of the species.

However, not all variations are useful. Therefore, these are not necessarily beneficial for the individual organisms.

Q.13 How do Mendel's experiments show that traits may be dominant or recessive?

Ans. Mendel selected true breeding tall (TT) and dwarf (tt) pea plants. Then, he crossed these two plants. The seeds formed after fertilization were grown and these plants that were formed represent the first filial or F_1 generation. All the F_1 plants obtained were tall.

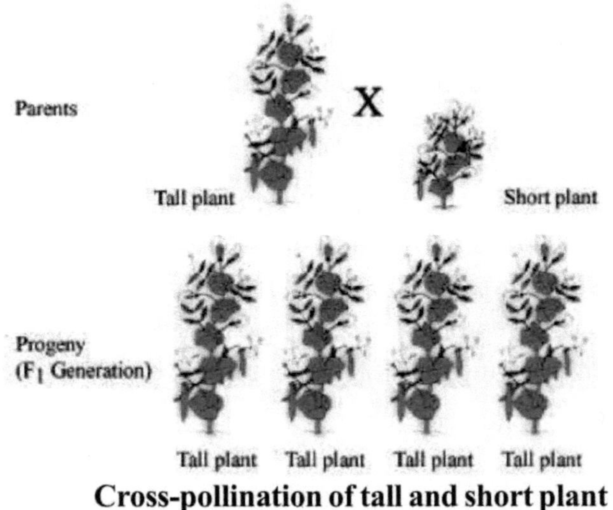

Cross-pollination of tall and short plant

Then, Mendel self-pollinated the F_1 plants and observed that all plants obtained in the F_2 generation were not tall. Instead, one-fourth of the F_2 plants were short.

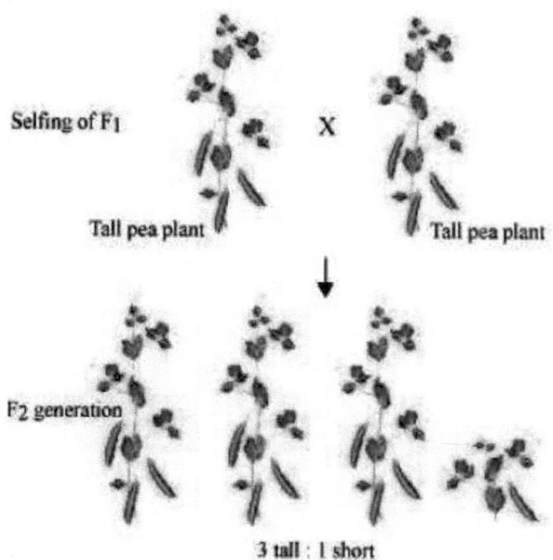

Self-pollination of F_1 plants

From this experiment, Mendel concluded that the F_1 tall plants were not true breeding. They were carrying traits of both short height and tall height. They appeared tall only because the tall trait is dominant over the dwarf trait.

Q.14 How do Mendel's experiments show that traits are inherited independently?

Ans. Mendel crossed pea plants having round green seeds (RRyy) with pea plants having wrinkled yellow seeds (rrYY).

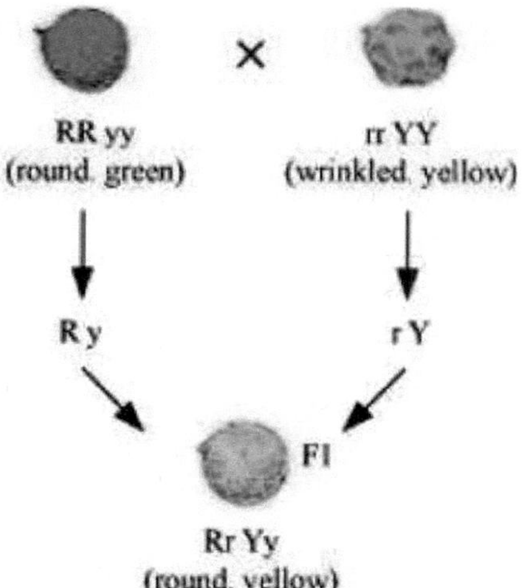

An example of dihybrid crosses

Since the F_1 plants are formed after crossing pea plants having green round seeds and pea plants having yellow wrinkled seeds, F_1 generation will have both these characters in them. However, as we know that yellow seed colour and round seeds are dominant characters, therefore, the F_1 plants will have yellow round seeds. Then this F_1 progeny was self-pollinated and the F_2 progeny was found to have yellow round seeds, green round seeds, yellow wrinkled seeds, and green wrinkled seeds in the ratio of 9:3:3:1.

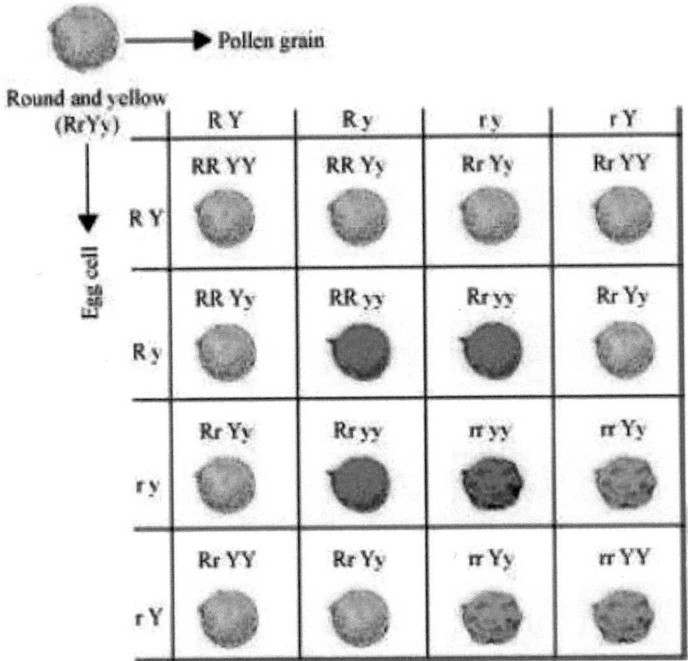

Independent inheritance of two different traits

In the above cross, more than two factors are involved, and these are independently inherited.

Q.15 A man with blood group A marries a woman with blood group O and their daughter has blood group O. Is this information enough to tell you which of the traits . blood group A or O is dominant? Why or why not?

Ans. No. This information is not sufficient to determine which of the traits . blood group A or O is dominant. This is because we do not know about the blood group of all the progeny. Blood group A can be genotypically AA or AO. Hence, the information is incomplete to draw any such conclusion.

Q.16 How is the sex of the child determined in human beings?

Ans. In human beings, the females have two X chromosomes and the males have one X and one Y chromosome. Therefore, the females are XX and the males are XY.

The gametes, as we know, receive half of the chromosomes. The male gametes have 22 autosomes and either X or Y sex chromosome.

Type of male gametes: 22 + X OR 22 + Y.

However, since the females have XX sex chromosomes, their gametes can only have X sex chromosome.

Type of female gamete: 22 + X

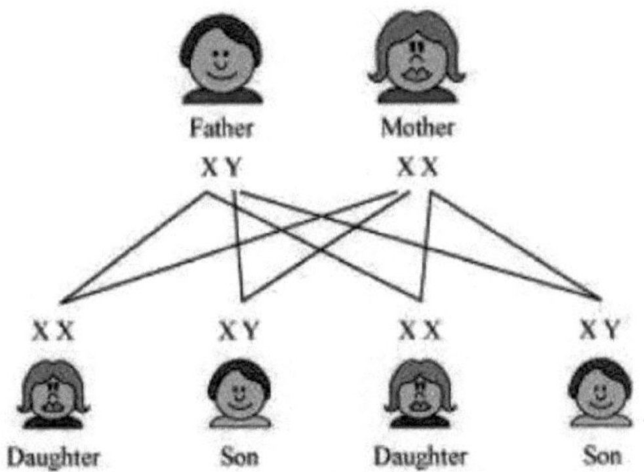

Sex determination in humans

Thus, the mother provides only X chromosomes. The sex of the baby is determined by the type of male gamete (X or Y) that fuses with the X chromosome of the female.

Q.17 What are the different ways in which individuals with a particular trait may increase in a population?

Ans. Individuals with a particular trait may increase in a population as a result of the following:

(i) Natural selection: When that trait offers some survival advantage.

(ii) Genetic drift: When some genes governing that trait become common in a population.

(iii) When that trait gets acquired during the individual in its lifetime.

Q.18 Why are traits acquired during the life-time of an individual not inherited?

Ans. This happens because an acquired trait involves change in non-reproductive tissues (somatic cells) which cannot be passed on to germ cells or the progeny. Therefore, these traits cannot be inherited.

Q.19 Why are the small numbers of surviving tigers a cause of worry from the point of view of genetics?

Ans. Small numbers of tigers means that fewer variations in terms of genes are available. This means that when these tigers reproduce, there are less chances of producing progeny with some useful variations. Hence, it is a cause of worry from the point of view of genetics.

Q.20 What factors could lead to the rise of a new species?

Ans. Natural selection, genetic drift and acquisition of traits during the life time of an individual can give rise to new species.

Q.21 Will geographical isolation be a major factor in the speciation of a self-pollinating plant species? Why or why not?

Ans. Geographical isolation can prevent the transfer of pollens among different plants. However, since the plants are self-pollinating, which means that the pollens are transferred from the anther of one flower to the stigma of the same flower or of another flower of the same plant, geographical isolation cannot prevent speciation in this case.

Q.22 Will geographical isolation be a major factor in the speciation of an organism that reproduces asexually? Why or why not?

Ans. Geographical isolation prevents gene flow between populations of a species whereas asexual reproduction generally involves only one individual. In an asexually reproducing organism, variations can occur only when the copying of DNA is not accurate. Therefore, geographical isolation cannot prevent the formation of new species in an asexually reproducing organism.

Q.23 Give an example of characteristics being used to determine how close two species are in evolutionary terms.

Ans. The presence of feathers in dinosaurs and birds indicates that they are evolutionarily related. Dinosaurs had feathers not for flying but instead these feathers provided insulation to these warm-blooded animals. However, the feathers in birds are used for flight. This proves that reptiles and birds are closely related and that the evolution of wings started in reptiles.

Q.24 What are fossils? What do they tell us about the process of evolution?

Ans. Fossils are the remains of organisms that once existed on earth. They represent the ancestors of plants and animals that are alive today. They provide evidences of evolution by revealing the characteristics of the past organism and the changes that have occured in these organisms to give rise to the present organisms.

Q.25 Why are human beings who look so different from each other in terms of size, colour and looks said to belong to the same species?

Ans. A species is a group of organisms that are capable of interbreeding to produce a fertile offspring. Skin colour, looks, and size are all variety of features present in human beings. These features are generally environmentally controlled. Various human races are formed based on these features. However, there is no biological basis to this concept of races. Therefore, all human beings are a single species as humans of different colour, size and looks are capable of reproduction and can produce a fertile offspring.

Q.26 In evolutionary terms, can we say which among bacteria, spiders, fish and chimpanzees have 'better'of body design? Why or why not?

Ans. Evolution cannot always be equated with progress or better body designs. Evolution simply creates more complex body designs. However, this does not mean that the simple body designs are inefficient. In fact, bacteria having a simple body design are still the most cosmopolitan organisms found on earth. They can survive hot springs, deep sea, and even freezing environment. Therefore, bacteria, spiders, fish, and chimpanzees are all different branches of evolution.

Q.27 A Mendelian experiment consisted of breeding tall pea plants bearing violet flowers with short pea plants bearing white flowers. The progeny all bore violet flowers, but almost half of them were short. This suggests that the genetic make-up of the tall parent can be depicted as

(A) TTWW (B) TTww (C) TtWW (D) TtWw

Ans. (C) The genetic make-up of the tall parent can be depicted as TtWW

Since all the progeny bore violet flowers, it means that the tall plant having violet flowers has WW genotype for violet flower colour.

Since the progeny is both tall and short, the parent plant was not a pure tall plant. Its genotype must be Tt.

Therefore, the cross involved in the given question is

TtWw × ttww

↓

TtWw – ttww

Therefore, half the progeny is tall, but all of them have violet flowers.

Q.28 An example of homologous organs is

(A) our arm and a dog's fore-leg.
(B) our teeth and an elephant's tusks.
(C) potato and runners of grass.
(D) all of the above.

Ans. (B)An example of homologous organs is our teeth and an elephant tusks.

Q.29 In evolutionary terms, we have more in common with

(A) a Chinese school-boy
(B) a chimpanzee.
(C) a spider.
(D) a bacterium.

Ans. (A) In evolutionary terms, we have more in common with a Chinese school boy.

Q.30 A study found that children with light-coloured eyes are likely to have parents with lightcoloured eyes. On this basis, can we say anything about whether the light eye colour trait is dominant or recessive? Why or why not?

Ans. Let us assume that children with light-coloured eyes can either have LL or LI or II genotype. If the children have LL genotype, then their parents will also be of LL genotype.

$$LL \times LL$$
$$\downarrow$$
$$LL$$

If the children with light-coloured eyes have ll genotype, then their parents will also have II genotype.

$$II \times II$$
$$\downarrow$$
$$II$$

Therefore, it cannot be concluded whether light eye colour is dominant or recessive.

CONCEPT APPLICATION LEVEL - II

SECTION - A

Q.1 Define genetics. What is the contribution of Mendal in the field of Genetics?

Ans. The branch of biology that deals with the study of Heredity & evolution is known as genetics. Gregor Johann Mendal was the first person to carry out experiments regarding the heredity of certain characters from one generation to another. The worked mainly on the garden pea plant. This observation regarding the occurence of contrasting characters in various generations of garden pea led him to interpret that these are controlled by units which he called factors (Genes). "He is also known as the father of Genetics."

Q.2 How do embryological studies provide evidence for evolution?

Ans. The embryology of different vertebrates provide very strong evidence favoring organic evolution. The early embryos of different vertebrates show shiking similarities. This indicates common origin & oncestory of different vertebrates.

Q.1 A study found that children with light-coloured eyes are likely to have parents with light-coloured eyes. On this basis, can we say anything about whether the light eye colour trait is dominant or recessive? Why or why not?

Ans. As per the findings of study, children and parents both have the light-coloured eyes as the common trait, we can say light eye colour trait is dominant because only dominant traits from parents are inherited by the children in the first generation

Q.2 Can the wing of a butterfly and the wing of a bat be considered homologous organs? Why or why not?

Ans. No, the wing of a butterfly and the wing of a bat can not be considered homologous organs because they both perform the same function of flying but their origin and structure is not similar. The bird's wing has well developed bone structure supported with flesh and feathers whereas insect's wing has evolved from hardening of membrane cover with a few associated muscles. Homologous organs have similar basic structure but perform different functions, where as analogous organs have different origin and structure but perform same functions.

Q.3 What is Heredity ?

Ans. The continuity of features from one generation to another is known as heredity.It can be also defined as transmission of traits from parents to offsprings.

Q.4 Define variations ?

Ans. Changes in the phenotype and genotype are known as variations.

Q.5 Define a gene ?

Ans. It is the functional unit of DNA. It is also responsible for the transmission of characters from one generation to another.

Q.6 What are the components of a chromosome?

Ans. A chromosome consists of two chromatids joined together at centromere. It consists of DNA material wound over histone proteins.

Q.7 What is sex chromosome?

Ans. Chromosome which are responsible for the determination of sex of an individual are known as sex chromosome. These are of two types: X chromosome and Y chromosome. Male have one X and one Y chromosome while Female have two X chromosome.

Q.8 Explain Darwin theory of evolution ?

Ans. Darwin theory also known as **Theory of natural selection**. He explained that despite have enormous potential of fertility, the population size of any kind of organism remains in limit. It is due to struggle between members of same species and different species for space,food and mate. This struggle eliminates the unfit individual. In other words, the fit individual possesses some variations which are favourable which can be passed to next generation (Survival of the fittest).

SECTION – B
(Previous Years Questions)

Q.1 If a particular animal has shelled egg, hair and teats on the body and has cloaca, then it may be a connecting link between - **[NTSE Stage-I_2005]**
(A) Reptile and aves (B) Aves and mammal
(C) Reptile and mammal (D) Mammal and aves

Q.2 If heterozygous tall plant is crossed with the homozygous dwarf plant, then the percentage of dwarf plants in progeny will be - **[NTSE Stage-I_2005]**
(A) 25% (B) 75% (C) 50% (D) 100%

Q.3 Contractile vacuole of amoeba is equivalent to which organ of human ? **[NTSE Stage-I_2006]**
(A) Spleen (B) Kidney (D) Lung (D) Liver

Q.4 Dissimilarity found in Aves and Mamalia is – **[NTSE Stage-I_2013]**
(A) Warm Blooded Animal (B) Lay eggs
(C) Breathe through Lungs (D) Four chambered Heart

Q.5 The author of the book 'Systema Naturae' is **[NTSE Stage-I_2014]**
(A) Lamarck (B) Darwin (C) Theophrastus (D) Carolus Linnaeus

Q.6 Knightia is a fossil of **[NTSE Stage-I_2015]**
(A) tree trunk (B) invertebrate (C) fish (D) dinosaur skull

Q.7 Raja saurus is a fossil of **[NTSE Stage-I_2017]**
(A) Tree trunk (B) Invertebrate (C) Fish (D) Dinosaur

Statement for Q.8-Q.9 : A group of red beetles lives on green leaves of a tree. Beetles multiply through sexual reproduction. One day, some green beetles are seen among the red beetles. Green beetles breed to produce green progeny. Crows on the tree eat beetles.

Q.8 Some green beetles appear among the red beetle because **[NTSE Stage-II_2013]**
(A) beetles become green by accumulating chlorophyll from the green leaves that they eat.
(B) natural variations occur during sexual reproduction.
(C) red beetles mimic green colour of leaves whenever they see crows.
(D) beetles change colour from red to green with change of season.

Q.9 The colour composition of beetle population is likely to change in the following manner **[NTSE Stage-II_2013]**

(A) Both red and green beetle survive equally. (B) Only the red beetle survives.
(C) More red beetles survive than the green. (D) More green beetles survive than the red

Q.10 Which one of the following statements is **NOT** true about evolution ? **[NTSE Stage-II_2014]**

(A) Evolution leads to generation of diverse forms of life.
(B) Time dating and fossil studies help in understanding of evolution.
(C) Evolution is not always progressive series of changes that occur in organism.
(D) Human beings have not evolved form chimpanzees.

Q.11 A pea plant with round green (RRyy) pea seed is crossed another pea plant with wrinkled yellow (rrYY) seeds What would be the nature of seed in the first generation (F_1 generation) ? **[NTSE Stage-II_2014]**

(A) Round green (B) Wrinkled green (C) Wrinkled yellow (D) Round yellow

Q.12 A group of laboratory mice having tails are bred together and their progeny studied. The progeny are again bred for four successive generations. What do you think would be the nature of the new progeny? **[NTSE Stage-II_2014]**

(A) All mice born will have tails.
(B) All mice born will have no tails.
(C) The ratio of tail less to tailed mice will be 1 : 3
(D) The ratio of tail less to tailed mice will be 1 : 4

Q.13 The gene for hemophilia is present on X chromosome. If a hemophilic male marries a normal female, the probability of their son being hemophilic is **[NTSE Stage-II_2015]**

(A) nil (B) 25% (C) 50% (D) 100%

Q.14 In the experiment conducted by Mendel, RRyy (round, green) and rrYY (wrinkled, yellow) seeds of pea plant were used. In the F_2 generation 240 progeny were produced, out of which 15 progeny had specific characteristics. What were the characteristics? **[NTSE Stage-II_2016]**

(A) Round and green (B) Round and yellow (C) Wrinkle and yellow (D) Wrinkle and green

Q.15 A tall plant (TT) is crossed with a dwarf plant (tt). All F_1 plants showed tall phenotype. Which of the following correctly defines a test cross? **[NTSE Stage-II_2017]**

(A) TT (F_1) × Tt (P) (B) Tt (F_1) × Tt (P) (C) tt (F_1) × Tt (P) (D) Tt (F_1) × tt (P)

Q.16 Varieties of vegetables such as cabbage, broccoli and cauliflower have been produced from a wild cabbage species. Such process of producing new varieties of living organisms is called **[NTSE Stage-II_2017]**

(A) Natural selection (B) Artificial selection (C) Speciation (D) Genetic drift

Q.17 Which of the following are pairs of analogous organs? **[NTSE Stage-II_2017]**

I. Forelimbs of horse – Wings of bat II. Wings of bat – Wings of butterfly
III. Forelimbs of horse – Wings of butterfly IV. Wings of bird – Wings of bat

(A) I and II (B) II and IV (C) III and IV (D) II and III

Q.18 Occurrence of tall and dwarf plants in the F_2 generation of pea plant indicates that **[NSEJS Stage-I_2008]**
(A) both the traits were present in the parent plant
(B) both the traits were present in the F_1
(C) tall is dominant over dwarf
(D) tall and dwarf traits have equal effect in expression

Q.19 The basic event in evolution is **[NSEJS Stage-I_2008]**
(I) change in DNA (II) change in habitat
(III) change in nature of food (IV) change in climate
(A) I and III both (B) II and IV Both (C) I, II and IV (D) All of these

Q.20 The one that **cannot** be used for DNA fingerprinting is **[NSEJS Stage-I_2009]**
(A) leucocytes (B) erythrocytes (C) hair bulbs (D) sperms

Q.21 The family pedigree of Queen Victoria shows a number of haemophilic descendents as **[NSEJS Stage-I_2011]**
(A) she herself was haemophilic
(B) haemophilia is autosomal recessive disorder.
(C) haemophilia is sex linked recessive disorder and Queen Victoria was a carrier.
(D) haemophilia is caused by contact and therefore it was seen it the royal family descendents.

Q.22 Heterosis is the **[NSEJS Stage-I_2011]**
(A) superiority of male percent over the hybrid. (B) superiority of female parent over the hybrid.
(C) superiority of hybrid over the parents. (D) superiority of both the parents over the hybrid.

Q.23 Genome of a sexually reproducing organism is **[NSEJS Stage-I_2011]**
(A) all the chromosomes present in the diploid cell.
(B) total number of chromosomes present inthe haploid cell.
(C) total number of genes present in a cell.
(D) totality of DNA present in the haploid cell.

Q.24 In usual course, the progeny varies from its parents due to **[NSEJS Stage-I_2011]**
(A) mutation (B) pleiotropic effect
(C) chromosomal recombination (D) independent assortment

Q.25 Down's syndrome is a result of **[NSEJS Stage-I_2011]**
(A) XO genotype (B) XXY genotype
(C) Trisomy (chromosome 12) (D) Trisomy (chromosome 21)

Q.26 Sting of a honeybee represents modification of **[NSEJS Stage-I_2011]**
(A) Ovipositor (B) abdominal bristles
(C) abdominal appendage (D) Motion of a satellite around the earth

Q.27 Like sickle cell anaemia, the other genetic disorder related to blood pigment is **[NSEJS Stage-I_2011]**
(A) leukemia (B) phenylketoneuria (C) thalassemia (D) xeroderma pigmentosis

Q.28 Y varies inversely as x. If x is increased by 25%, then the value of percentage change to y is [NSEJS Stage-I_2012]

(A) 80% (B) 75% (C) 60% (D) 62.5%

Q.29 A lady has 4 kids with blood group AB and 1 kid with blood group O. If the father of these kids have blood group B, what is the possible genotype of the lady? [NSEJS Stage-I_2012]

(A) I^AI^B (B) I^AI^O (C) I^AI^A (D) I^BI^B

Q.30 Given here is a phylogenetic tree (family tree) of greater apes. Which of the following statements cannot be true from the tree ? (mya-million years ago) [NSEJS Stage-I_2013]

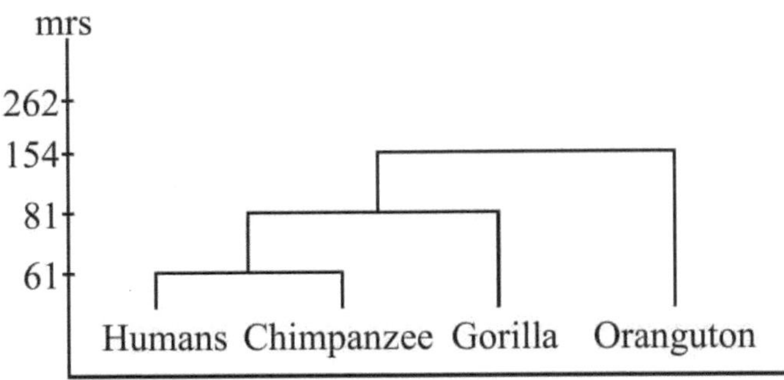

(A) Humans did not evolve from chimpanzees.
(B) Humans and chimpanzees are evolutionary cousins.
(C) Orangutans evolved much earlier then Humans.
(D) Humans are highly evolved among great apes.

Q.31 If the distance between genes - W, X, Y, and Z on a chromosome are as follows : from W-Y is 18 units, W-X is 26 units, W-Z is 40 units, X-Y is 8 units and X-Z is 14 units, the sequence of W, X, Y, Z genes on the chromosome would be : [NSEJS Stage-I_2014]

(A) W, Y, X, Z (B) X, Y, W, Z (C) Y, W, X, Z (D) W, X, Y, Z

Q.32 In biology, Polymerase Chain Reaction (PCR) refers to which of the following option? [NSEJS Stage-I_2015]

(A) In vitro multiplication of nucleic acids molecules.
(B) In vivo multiplication of nucleic acids molecules.
(C) Continuous protein synthesis from peptide.
(D) Synthesis of mRNA from DNA in vitro.

Q.33 Each chromosome contains [NSEJS Stage-I_2015]

(A) one long DNA molecule (B) one long RNA molecule
(C) one long sequence of amino acids (D) a single gene for a protein

CONCEPT APPLICATION LEVEL - III

SECTION-A

- **Fill in the blanks**

Q.1 The ratio phenotypic for the monohybrid cross is ________________.

Q.2 Characters that are expressed in any conditions are called ________________ and characters that are expressed only in homozygous conditions are called ____________.

Q.3 ________________ is physical and chemical expression of a character.

Q.4 Every organism have __________ sets of all genes, one inherited from ________________.

Q.5 The formation of new species is known as ________________ basis of heredity.

Q.6 Genes are ________________.

Q.7 ________________ are preserved traces of living organism.

Q.8 Classification of a species is infact a relation of their ________________.

SECTION-B

- **Multiple choice question with one correct answers**

Q.1 Genetics is the study of
(A) Inheritance (B) Cell structure (C) Only plants (D) Only animals

Q.2 If two parents have the genotypes AA × aa, the probability of having an aa genotype in the F_1, generation is
(A) 25 percent (B) 50 percent (C) 75 percent (D) None of these

Q.3 Sex-linked disorders such as colour blindness and hemophilia are
(A) caused by gene on the X-chromosome (B) caused by gene on the autosome
(C) caused by gene on the Y-chromosome (D) Expressed only in men

Q.4 Your arm is homologous with
(A) a seal flipper (B) an octopus tentacle (C) a bird wing (D) both (A) &(C)

Q.5 Which option represents test cross
(A) TT × TT (B) Tt × tt (C) Both (A) & (B) (D) None

Q.6 Mendel formulated some laws which are known as
(A) Law of germplasm (B) Law of origin of species
(C) Law of speciation (D) Law of inheritance

Q.7 Term 'GENE' was given by
(A) Mendel (B) Morgan (C) Bateson (D) Johnson

Q.8 Mendel choose pea plants because
(A) They were cheap (B) They were having seven pairs of contrasting characters
(C) They were attractive (D) Of great economic importance

Q.9 The resemblance of individual to their progenitors is due to
(A) Heredity (B) Genetics (C) Evolution (D) None of these

Q.10 Linkage is contradicton to_________law of Mendel
(A) Mutation (B) Independent assortment
(C) Dominance (D) Crossing over

Q.11 Law of purity of gametes is also known as
(A) Law of inheritance (B) Law of variation
(C) Law of independent assortment (D) Law of segregation

Q.12 Mendel formulated the law of purity of gametes on the basis of
(A) Dihybrid cross (B) Monohybrid cross (C) Back cross (D) Test cross

Q.13 A white flowered mirabilis plants rr was crossed with red coloured RR, if 120 plants are produced in F_2 generation. The result would be
(A) 90 uniformly red and 30 white (B) 90 Non-uniformly coloured and 30 white
(C) 60 Non-uniformly coloured and 60 white (D) All coloured and 40 white

Q.14 From the list given below, select the character which can be acquired but not inherited
(A) Colour of eye (B) Colour of skin (C) Size of body (D) Nature of hair

Q.15 The two versions of a trait (character) which are brought in by the male and female gametes are situated on
(A) Copies of the same chromosome (B) Two different chromosomes
(C) Sex chromosomes (D) Any chromosomes

Q.16 Select the statements that describe characteristics of genes
(i) Genes are specific sequence of bases in a DNA molecule
(ii) A gene does not code for proteins
(iii) In individuals of a given species, a specific gene is located on a particular chromosome
(iv) Each chromosome has only one gene.
(A) (i) and (ii) (B) (i) and (iii) (C) (i) and (iv) (D) (ii) and (iv).

Q.17 In peas, a pure tall plant (TT) is crossed with a short plant (tt). The ratio of pure tall plants to short plants in F_2 is
(A) 1 : 3 (B) 3 : 1 (C) 1 : 1 (D) 2 : 1

Q18 The number of pair(s) of sex chromosomes in the zygote of humans is
(A) One (B) Two (C) Three (D) Four

Q.19 The theory of evolution of species by natural selection was given by
(A) Mendel (B) Darwin (C) Morgan (D) Lamarck

Q.20 Some dinosaours had feathers although they could not fly but birds have feathers that help them to fly. In the context of evolution this means that
(A) Reptiles have evolved from birds
(B) There is no evolutionary connection between reptiles and birds
(C) Feathers are homologous structures in both the organisms
(D) Birds have evolved from reptiles.

Q.21 A gamete contains
(A) Two alleles of a gene (B) One allele of a gene
(C) All alleles of a gene (D) None of the above

Q.22 A breeding experiment dealing with a single trait is called
(A) Dihybrid (B) Monohybrid (C) Monozygous (D) Heterozygous

Q.23 Which one is not a vestigial organ in man?
(A) Vermiform appendix (B) Epiglottis
(C) Muscles of ear pinna (D) Nictitating membrane

Q.24 The wings of bat, locust and pigeon are the example of
(A) Homologous organs (B) Analogous organs
(C) Vestigial organs (D) Exoskeleton

Q.25 Homologous structures are
(A) Dissimilar in origin, similar in function (B) Dissimilar in origin and function both
(C) Similar in origin and similar in function (D) Similar in origin and dissimilar in function

Q.26 Palaentology is the study of
(A) Fossils (B) Bones (C) Birds (D) Embryo

Q.27 'Descent with modification' is the central theme of
(A) Recapitulation (B) Genetics (C) Evolution (D) Biogenesis

Q.28 The ultimate source of variation is
(A) Natural selection (B) Mutation
(C) Sexual reproduction (D) None of these

Q.29 Vestigial organs are
(A) Primitive organs (B) Primordial organs
(C) Organs reduced due to disuse (D) Organs marked only in embryonic stage

Q.30 Father of genetics is
(A) Morgan (B) Mendel (C) Darwin (D) Hutchinson

Q.31 Sudden inheritable change is called
(A) Recombination (B) Mutation (C) Natural selection (D) Segregation

Q.32 Exchange of genetic material takes place in
(A) Vegetative reproduction (B) Asexual reproduction
(C) Sexual reproduction (D) Budding

Q.33 Two pink coloured flowers on crossing resulted in 1 red, 2 pink and 1 white flower progeny. The nature of the cross will be
(A) Double fertilisation (B) Self pollination (C) Cross pollination (D) No fertilisation

Q.34 Which of the following statement is incorrect ?
(A) For every hormone there is a gene.
(B) For every protein there is a gene.
(C) For production of every enzyme there is a gene.
(D) For every molecule of fat there is a gene.

Q.35 The maleness of a child is determined by
(A) The X chromosome in the zygote
(B) The Y chromosome in zygote
(C) The cytoplasm of germ cell which determines the sex
(D) Sex is determined by chance

Q.36 A zygote which has an X-chromosome inherited from the father will develop into a
(A) Boy
(B) Girl
(C) X-chromosome does not determine the sex of a child
(D) Either boy or girl

Q.37 Select the incorrect statement
(A) Frequency of certain genes in a population change over several generations resulting in evolution.
(B) Reduction in weight of the organism due to starvation is genetically controlled
(C) Low weight parents can have heavy weight progeny
(D) Traits which are not inherited over generation do not cause evolution

Q.38 New species may be formed if
(i) DNA undergoes significant changes in germ cells.
(ii) Chromosome number changes in the gamete
(iii) There is no change in the genetic material
(iv) Mating does not take place
(A) (i) and (ii) (B) (i) and (iii) (C) (ii), (iii) and (iv) (D) (i), (ii) and (iii)

Q.39 A basket of vegetable contains carrot, potato, radish and tomato. Which of them represent the correct homologous structures?
(A) Carrot and potato (B) Carrot and tomato (C) Radish and carrot (D) Radish and potato

Q.40 Select the correct statement
(A) Tendril of a pea plant and phylloclade of *Opuntia* are homologous
(B) Tendril of a pea plan and phylloclade of *Opuntia* are analogous
(C) Wings of birds and limbs of lizards are analogous
(D) Wings of birds and wings of bat are homologous

Q.41 Which of the following statements is not true with respect to variation?
(A) All variation in a species have equal chance of survival
(B) Change in genetic composition results in variation
(C) Selection of variants by environmental factors forms the basis of evolutionary processes.
(D) Variation is minimum in asexual reproduction.

Q.42 According to the evolutionary theory, formation of a new species is generally due to
(A) Sudden creation by nature
(B) Accumulation of variations over several generations
(C) Clones formed during asexual reproduction
(D) Movement of individuals from one habitat to another

Q.43 From the list given below, select the character which can be acquired but not inherited
(A) Colour of eye (B) Colour of skin (C) Size of body (D) Nature of hair

Q.44 The two versions of a trait (character) which are brought in by the male and female gametes are situated on
(A) Copies of the same chromosome (B) Two different chromosomes
(C) Sex chromosomes (D) Any chromosome

Q.45 The number of pair(s) of sex chromosomes in the zygote of humans is
(A) One (B) Two (C) Three (D) Four

Q.46 Some dinosaurs had feathers although they could not fly but birds have feathers that help them to fly. In the context of evolution this means that
(A) Reptiles have evolved from birds
(B) There is no evolutionary connection between reptiles and birds
(C) Feathers are homologous structures in both the organisms
(D) Birds have evolved from reptiles

Q.47 From heredity point of view which marriage is not suitable
(A) Man Rh(–) and woman Rh(+) (B) Both Rh(+)
(C) Both Rh(–) (D) Man Rh(+) and woman Rh(–)

Q.48 If one parent has blood group A and other parent has blood group B. The offspring have which blood group
(A) AB (B) O (C) BO (D) A,B,AB,O

Q.49 Plants having similar genotypes produced by plant breeding are called
(A) Clone (B) Haploid (C) Autopolyploid (D) Genome

Q.50 Mendel formulated the law of purity of gametes on the basis of
(A) Dihybrid cross (B) Monohybrid cross (C) Back cross (D) Test cross

Q.51 In human sex of body is decided by is due to
(A) X-chromosome (B) Y-chromosome (C) A-chromosome (D) B-chromosome

Q.52 The famous book "Origin of species" was written by Charles Darwin in
(A) 1809 (B) 1859 (C) 1885 (D) 1871

Q.53 Which of the following are fossils?
(A) pollen grain buried in land
(B) the skeleton of archeapteryx
(C) the impression a clam shell made in mud preserved in mudstone
(D) All of the above

Q.54 Which of the following is Heterozygous?
(A) TT (B) RR (C) r r (D) Tt

Q.55 Vestigeal organs are
(A) Primitive organs (B) Primordial organs
(C) Organs reduced due to disuse (D) Organs marked only in embryonic stage

Q.56 Mendel worked on
(A) Pisum (B) Solanum (C) Lathyrus (D) Dolichos

Q.57 Father of genetics is
(A) Morgen (B) Mendel (D) Darwin (D) Hutchinson

Q.58 Mendel noted as many pairs of contrasting traits in pea plants
(A) 2 (B) 5 (C) 7 (D) 9

Q.59 The book "Origin of Species by Natural Selection" was written by
(A) Oparin (B) Wallace (C) Darwin (D) Darwin and Wallace

Q.60 Sudden inheritable change in called
(A) Recombination (B) Mutation (C) Natural selection (D) Segregation

Q.61 Inheritance of acquired characters was proposed by
(A) Drawin (B) Lamarck (C) Wallace (D) Oparin

Q.62 Exchange of genetic material takes place in
(A) Vegetative reproduction (B) Asexual reproduction
(C) Sexual reproduction (D) Budding

Q.63 Two pink coloured flowers on crossing resulted in 1 red, 2 pink and 1 white flower progeny. The nature of the cross will be
(A) Double fertilisation (B) Self pollination (C) Cross fertilisation (D) No fertilisation

Q.64 A cross between a tall plant (TT) and short pea plant (tt) resulted in progeny that were all tall plants because
(A) Tallness is the dominant trait (B) Shortness is the dominant trait
(C) Tallness is the recessive trait (D) Height of pea plant is not governed by gene 'T'or 't'

Q.65 Which of the following statement is incorrect ?
(A) For every harmone there is a gene.
(B) For every protein there is a gene
(C) For production of every enzyme there is a gene
(D) For every molecule of fat there is a gene

Q.66 If a round, green seeded pea plant (RR, yy) is crossed with wrinkled, yellow seeded pea plant. (rr YY) the seeds produced in F_1 generation are
(A) Round and yellow (B) Round and green
(C) Wrinkled and green (D) Wrinkled and yellow

SECTION-C

- **Assertion & Reason**

Instructions: In the following questions as Assertion (A) is given followed by a Reason (R). Mark your responses from the following options.
(A) Both Assertion and Reason are true and Reason is the correct explanation of 'Assertion'
(B) Both Assertion and Reason are true and Reason is not the correct explanation of 'Assertion'
(C) Assertion is true but Reason is false
(D) Assertion is false but Reason is true

Q.1 **Assertion:** Chemical basis of heridity is DNA.
Reason: Cellular DNA is the information source for making protein in the cell.

Q.2 **Assertion:** Genes are functional segment DNA.
Reason: Genes are responsible for the expression of an enzyme.

Q.3 **Assertion:** Variation are formed during reproduction.
Reason: Errors in DNA copying and sexual reproduction do not causes evolution.

Q.4 **Assertion:** Speciation is the phenomenon by which new sps. comes into existence.
Reason: Genetic drift does not lead to speciation.

Q.5 **Assertion:** The birds have pneumatic or hollow bones with air sacs
Reason: These adaptations help them during flight

SECTION-D

- **Match the following (one to one)**

Q.1

	Column I		Column II
(A)	Minor differences in progeny	(P)	Theory of evolution
(B)	Gregor Mendel	(Q)	Transmission of characters from parents to child
(C)	Heridity	(R)	Genetic drift
(D)	Change in frequency of gene	(S)	Due to inaccuracies in copying of DNA
(E)	Charles Darwin	(T)	Law of inheritance

Q.2

	Column I		Column II
(A)	Monohybrid cross	(P)	Wings of Bat and Bird
(B)	Sex-chromosomes	(Q)	Not neccesary better then old
(C)	Artificial selection	(R)	One pair (xx/XY)
(D)	Analogous organ	(S)	production of different varities of cabbage from wild cabbage
(E)	New species formed	(T)	3 : 1

ANSWERS

CONCEPT APPLICATION LEVEL - II

SECTION - B

Q.1	C	Q.2	C	Q.3	B	Q.4	B	Q.5	D	Q.6	C	Q.7	D
Q.8	B	Q.9	B	Q.10	D	Q.11	D	Q.12	A	Q.13	A	Q.14	D
Q.15	D	Q.16	B	Q.17	A	Q.18	A	Q.19	D	Q.20	B	Q.21	C
Q.22	C	Q.23	D	Q.24	C	Q.25	D	Q.26	A	Q.27	C	Q.28	A
Q.29	B	Q.30	A	Q.31	A	Q.32	A	Q.33	A				

CONCEPT APPLICATION LEVEL - III

SECTION-A

Q.1.	3 : 1	Q.2	dominant, recessive	Q.3	Phenotypes
Q.4	two, each parent	Q.5	Speciation	Q.6	Physical
Q.7	Fossils	Q.8	Evolutionary relationship		

SECTION-B

Q.1	A	Q.2	D	Q.3	A	Q.4	D	Q.5	B	Q.6	D	Q.7	D
Q.8	B	Q.9	A	Q.10	B	Q.11	D	Q.12	B	Q.13	A	Q.14	C
Q.15	A	Q.16	B	Q.17	C	Q.18	A	Q.19	B	Q.20	D	Q.21	B
Q.22	B	Q.23	B	Q.24	B	Q.25	D	Q.26	A	Q.27	C	Q.28	B
Q.29	C	Q.30	B	Q.31	B	Q.32	C	Q.33	B	Q.34	D	Q.35	B
Q.36	B	Q.37	B	Q.38	A	Q.39	C	Q.40	A	Q.41	A	Q.42	B
Q.43	C	Q.44	A	Q.45	A	Q.46	D	Q.47	D	Q.48	D	Q.49	A
Q.50	B	Q.51	B	Q.52	B	Q.53	D	Q.54	D	Q.55	C	Q.56	A
Q.57	B	Q.58	C	Q.59	C	Q.60	B	Q.61	B	Q.62	C	Q.63	B
Q.64	A	Q.65	D	Q.66	A								

SECTION-C

Q.1.	A	Q.2	B	Q.3	C	Q.4	C	Q.5	A

SECTION-D

Q.1 (A–S),(B–T),(C–Q),(D–R),(E–P)   Q.2 (A–T), (B–R), (C–S), (D–P), (E–Q)

5 OUR ENVIRONMENT

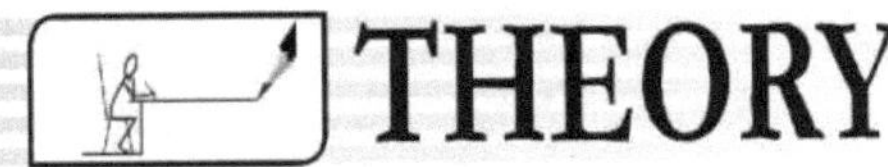

THEORY

ENVIRONMENT

- Environment is everything that surrounds an organism and influences its life i.e. physical and biological world in which one lives.
- It has the following three important parts.

(i) Living organisms constitute environment are plants, animals, human beings and microorganisms.
(ii) Physical surroundings, make up the environment are land, water bodies and air.
(iii) Meteorological factor or climatic factors, form a part of our environment, are sunlight temperature, rainfall, humidity.

ECOSYSTEM

- The term Ecosystem was coined by Tansley. According to him Ecosystem is a symbol of structure and function of nature.
- The term Ecology was coined by **Reiter.**
- The term Ecology was first of all described by **E.Haeckel.**
- Father of India Ecology - Prof. **Ramdeo Mishra**.
- The boundaries of ecosystem are indistinct and have an overlapping character with each other.
- "The total group of living things and environment of factors present in a particular place is called as **ecosystem.**
- It means any structural and functional unit of the environment that can be identified and studied is called as **ecosystem**.
- Ecosystem may be natural or artificial, permanent or temporary. Large ecosystem is called as **biome** such as desert, forest etc.
- **Homeostasis :** Self maintainable characteristic is found in ecosystem. It means an ecosystem maintains the balance between the different trophic levels. Each trophic level controls the other trophic level in an ecosystem.
- **Cybernetics :** A science of self control [homeostasis] in an ecosystem is called as "**cybernetics**"

TYPES OF ECOSYSTEMS

- **Ecosystems are of two types :**

1. Natural Ecosystems :

- The natural ecosystems are terrestrial (land) as well as aquatic. The common examples of land ecosystem are forests, grasslands, deserts, etc. The common examples of aquatic ecosystem are ponds, lakes, rivers, ocean, etc.

- It is further of two types :

(A) **Fresh water :** It may be lentic (standing water) or lotic (running wate) ecosystem.
(a) Lentic – Pond, pool and ditch ecosystem.
(b) Lotic – River, stream and spring ecosystem.

(B) **Marine** – Ocean and sea.

2. Human made or Artificial Ecosystems :

- The artificial ecosystems are made by human beings. The common examples of artificial ecosystems are crop fields, gardens, parks, aquarium, etc.
- An ecosystem may be as small as a drop of pond water. Such small ecosystem is called as **micro ecosystem**.
- Human activities may modify or convert natural ecosystem into man made ecosystem.
- Cutting tree or forests and the conversion of land for tree plantation or agriculture etc. are some of the examples of conversion of natural ecosystem to man made ecosystem.

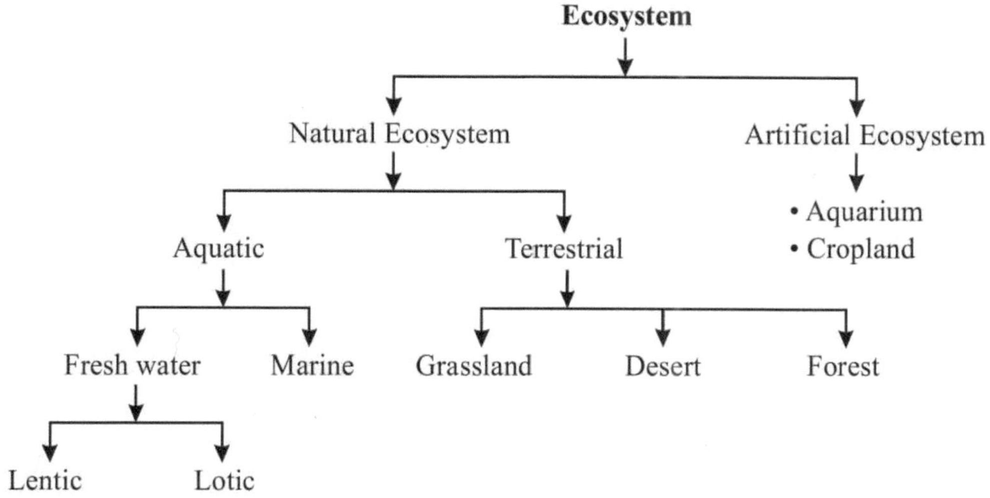

COMPONENTS OF ECOSYSTEM :

- Ecosystem consists of two components :
(i) Abiotic component (environment, soil etc.)
(ii) Biotic component

(i) **Abiotic components :** It means the non-living part of the environment - air, water, soil and minerals. The climatic or physical factors such as sunlight, temperature, rainfall, humidity, pressure and wind are a part of the abiotic environment.

- **Inorganic materials :** They are involved in the material cycles e.g. Carbon, Nitrogen, CO_2 and H_2O.
- **Organic compounds :** These are present in dead organic matter and include carbohydrates.
- **Climatic and edaphic factor :** Climatic factors include physical factors of environment e.g., light, temperature etc. The edaphic factor is soil.

(ii) **Biotic Components :** It means the living organisms of the environment - plants, animals, human being and microorganisms like bacteria and fungi, which are distinguished on the basis of their nutritional relationship.

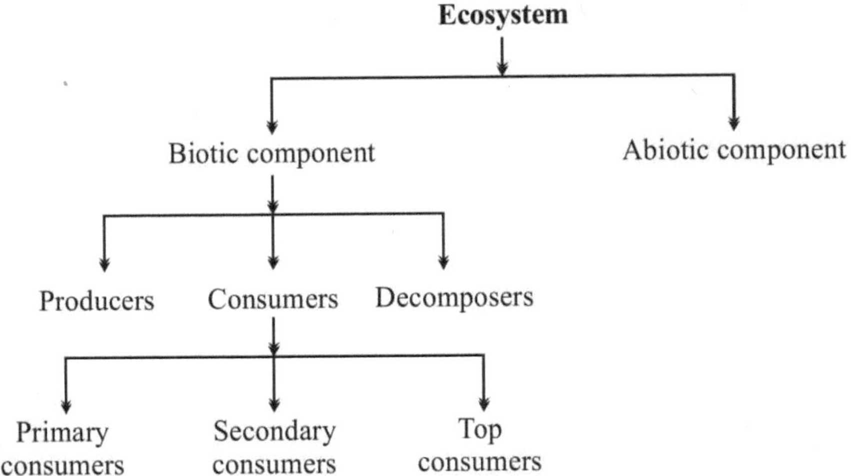

◆ Biotic components are of three types which are essential for ecosystem.

(A) Producers :

- All the autotrophs of ecosystem are called as **producers**.
- The green plants are the main producers.
- Green plants absorb solar energy and convert it into chemical energy.
- It means energy enters into the ecosystem through the producers.
- The solar energy is the only ultimate source of energy in ecosystem.
- This energy is available to the remaining living organisms through the medium of food.

(B) Consumers:

- All the heterotrophy of the ecosystem are known as **consumers**.
- Animals are the main consumers.
- They directly (herbivorous) or indirectly (carnivorous) depend upon the producers.
- **There are various types of consumer which are as follows :**

(i) **Primary consumers :** They are also known as secondary producers because they synthesize complex materials in the cells by the digestion of food which they obtain from the plants. Such living organisms which obtain food form the producers are known as primary consumers. Such as all the herbivores of ecosystem.

(ii) **Secondary consumers :** Animals which feed upon primary consumers and obtain their food. It means those carnivorous which kill and eat the herbivorous. So that they are called as predators e.g. Dog, Cat, Snake etc. In aquatic system whale fish is a secondary consumer.

(iii) **Top consumers :** Those animals which kill other animals and eat them but they are not eaten by other animals in the nature .e.g Lion, Vulture, Peacock and Man (human) in our ecosystem. Man and peacock may be omnivorous.

(C) Decomposers or Microconsumer :

- Those living organisms which decompose the dead bodies of producers and consumers and release mineral substances again into the soil which are present in the dead bodies.

- So that decomposers help in mineral into the soil which are present in the dead bodies.
- So that decomposers help in mineral cycle.
- Only because of this land is the main source of minerals.
- The main decomposers in ecosystem are - bacteria and fungi which decompose continuously dead animals and dead plants.

(D) Scavengers :

- Vulture never kills any animal so that vulture is a scavenger, not a decomposer.
- The process of decomposition takes place outside the body of bacteria.
- The break down of the food materials takes place in the body of vulture and minerals are released into the soil in the form faecal material.
- They are also called as **reducers** because they decomposes and remove the dead bodies of the organism.

STRUCTURE OF AN ECOSYSTEM

- The structure of an ecosystem is characterized by the physical organization of biotic & abiotic components.
- The major structural features of an ecosystem are species composition, stratification, trophic organization and nutrients.
  - **(i) Species composition :** Each ecosystem has its own type of species composition. Different ecosystems have different species composition. A great variety of species is found in forest ecosystem, whereas a few species occur in a desert ecosystem.
  - **(ii) Stratification :** The organisms in each ecosystem form one or more layers or strata, each comprising the population of particular kind of a species.
  - **(iii) Trophic organization :** Food relationship of producers and consumers is another way to predict ecosystem structure. In an ecosystem there can be only 4 - 5 successive trophic levels because

(A) All the food available in one tropic level is not being eaten by another animal in the next trophic level.

(B) All the food eaten by an animal is not useful, thus a part of energy containing food is passed out as waste products.

(C) A large amount of energy is lost in respiration to drive organisms metabolism and thus, there is not much energy left to support higher trophic levels.

- The amount of nutrients such as nitrogen, phosphorus and calcium present in the oil at any given time is termed as standing state.

FUNCTIONS OF AN ECOSYSTEM

(i) Productivity : Ecosystem helps to maintain the productivity, of the system. The rate of organic matter or biomass production is called as productivity. The study of biomass production in the ecosystem is called as production ecology.

(ii) Energy flow : Energy flow in an ecosystem is a key function of an ecosystem. It determines the following two laws of Thermodynamics :

(A) First law : It states, that energy can neither be created nor destroyed, but can be transferred from one from to other.

(B) **Second law :** It states, that every energy change involves the degradation or dissipation of energy, from concentrated to the dispersed form due to metabolic functions, so that only a small part of energy is stored in the biomass.

(iii) **Nutrient cycles :** All living organisms get matter from the biosphere component i.e. lithosphere, hydrosphere and atmosphere. Essential elements or inorganic substances are provided by earth and are required by organisms for their body building and metabolism, they are known as biogeochemical or biogenetic nutrients.

(iv) **Development and stabilization :** This function is necessary for the development and giving stability to various life forms by undergoing certain modifications.

FOOD CHAIN

- The chain of organisms which involves transfer of energy from one trophic level to next trophic level is called as food chain.
- The flow of food or energy in an ecosystem is called **Food chain**. Those organisms which join with the food chain are termed as Trophic levels.
- Usually, there are four trophic levels present in the ecosystem because level of energy decreases during the flow of energy from one trophic level to the another trophic level.

First trophic level [T1]	:	Producers
Second trophic level [T2]	:	Primary consumers
Third trophic level [T3]	:	Secondary consumers
Fourth trophic level [T4]	:	Top consumers

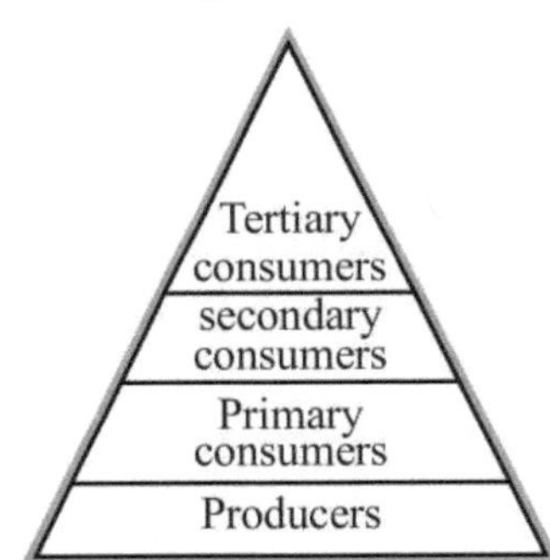

- The flow of energy occurs in an ecosystem from the first trophic level to the fourth trophic level in the food chain.
- There are five trophic levels also found in a highly complex ecosystem in which tertiary consumers are present in between the secondary consumer and top consumers, then fifth trophic level (T5) formed by the top consumers.

TYPES OF FOOD CHAIN :

- There are three types of food chains which are found in nature.
  1. Predator food chain
  2. Parasitic food chain
  3. Saprophytic food chain
- Predator food chain extends from producers through herbivores to carnivores, parasitic food chain start from producers but ends with parasites and saprophytic food chain starts with decomposers.

- Producers are autotrophic organisms which synthesize organic food from simple inorganic raw material through photosynthesis by utilizing solar energy.
- A part of food synthesized by the producers is used in their body building, while the rest is utilized in providing energy for various life activities.

Food chain in nature (a) in forest , (b) in grassland & (c) in a pond

- **Some common predator food chains are given below :**
  - Vegetation → Grasshopper → Shrew → Hawk
  - Vegetation → Rabbit → Wolf → Tiger
  - Vegetation → Frog → Snake → Peacock
  - Plant → Rat → Snake → Hawk.
- **Aquatic food chains :**
  - Phytoplanktons → Zooplanktons → Small crustacians
    Predator insect → Small fish → Large fish → Crocodile
  - Phytoplanktons → Zooplanktons → Small fish → Large fish (Shark)
  - Phytoplanktons → Zooplanktons → Fish → Crane → Hawk.

SIGNIFICANCE OF FOOD CHAIN

- The study of food chain helps in understanding of food relationship and interactions among various organisms in an ecosystem.
- With such studies one can follow the basic mechanism of transfer of food energy and nutrients through various components of nature.
- One can also understand the movement of toxic substances in an ecosystem and the problem of their biological magnification.

FOOD WEB

- In nature, the food chains are not isolated sequences but are rather interconnected with one another.
- "A network of food chains which are interconnected at various trophic levels, so as to form a number of feeding connection amongst different organisms of a biotic community is called as **food web**.
- The food web opens several alternate pathways for the flow of energy.
- Generally, food web operates according to taste and food performances of the organisms at each trophic level, yet availability of food source and other compulsions are equally important.
- The concept of food web appears to be more real than that of simple food chain.
- The food web increases the stability of an ecosystem by providing alternate source of the food and allowing endangered population to grow in size.
- Many food chains are interlinked together to form food web in a big ecosystem in which flow of food takes place through many directions such as forest.
- A food web which is present in forest ecosystem is a highly complex and permanent (stable) type of food web.

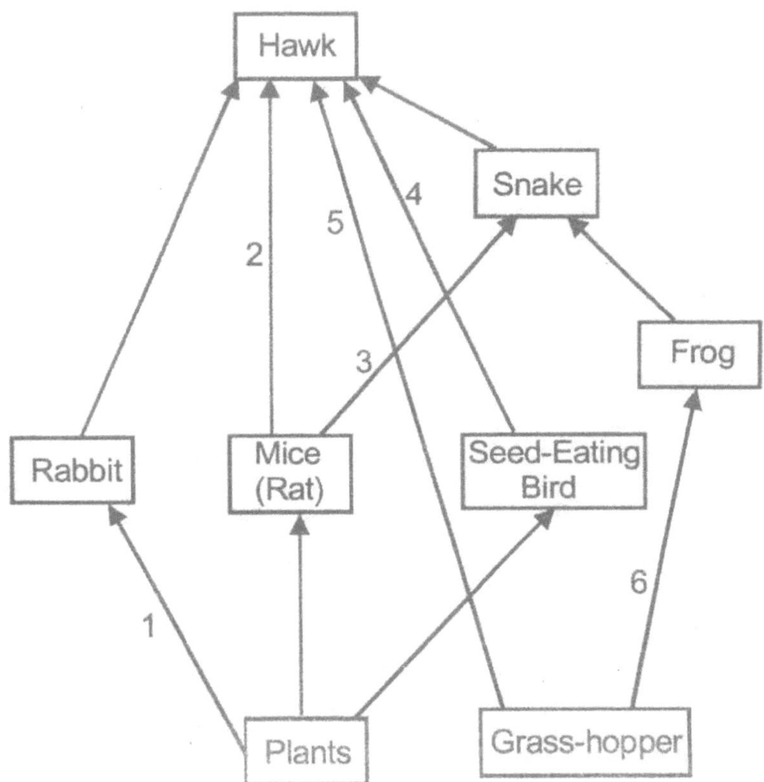

- As much as food web complexes are there as much ecosystem is permanent or stable, such type of ecosystem does not degenerate naturally and continues for longer timeperiod.
- The ecosystems which have simple food webs are not more stable. It means that this type of food web can be finished at any time. Any attack or cutting of plants can causes the destruction of ecosystem e.g. Gondwana forest is converted into the desert by the activity of men. this is the example of desertification by men.

Difference Between Food Chain and Food Web

Food chain	Food web
1. It consists of a single unit of food relations.	It is a complex formed by several units of food relations.
2. It is a straight line sequence of organisms.	It is a network of many linkages among the connected food chains.
3. It has a maximum of 4-6 populations of different species.	A food web consists of numerous populations of different species.
4. Only one type of organism is used as food by a particular type of organism.	An organism can use two to several types of organisms as food.

ECOLOGICAL PYRAMIDS

- An ecological pyramid is a graphical representation of an ecological parameter like number of individuals or amount of biomass or amount of energy present in various trophic levels of a food chain with producers forming the base and top carnivores from the tip.
- Ecological pyramids could be upright, inverted or spindle shaped.
- There are three important parameters of each trophic level in a food chain i.e. number of individual, amount of biomass and amount of energy.

Pyramid of Number :

- In this type of pyramid the number of individual organisms in various trophic levels is shown.
- These pyramids may be upright or inverted.
- The number of organisms of any trophic level depends upon the availability of organisms which are used as food on lower level so that availability of food is the main factor.
- These producers are of two types :
  - **(i)** **Phytoplanktons :** They are the inactive floating plant, because they do not have locomotors organs e.g. Diatoms.
  - **(ii)** **Phytonektons :** These plants swim actively in water, because in them locomotary organs are present. Usually flagella are preset in these plants. e.g. Chlamydomonas and dinoflagellates. The number of phytoplanktons and phytonketons are higher per unit area of water because they are unicellular.

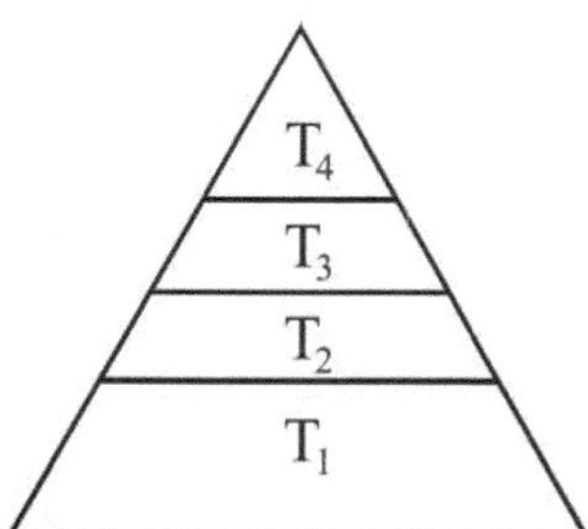

- In a tree ecosystem the pyramid of number is inverted. This is called as **parasitic ecosystem** because bird depend upon tree and parasites depend upon birds. Therefore with the increase in the number of trophic levels, the number of the organisms increases sequentially.

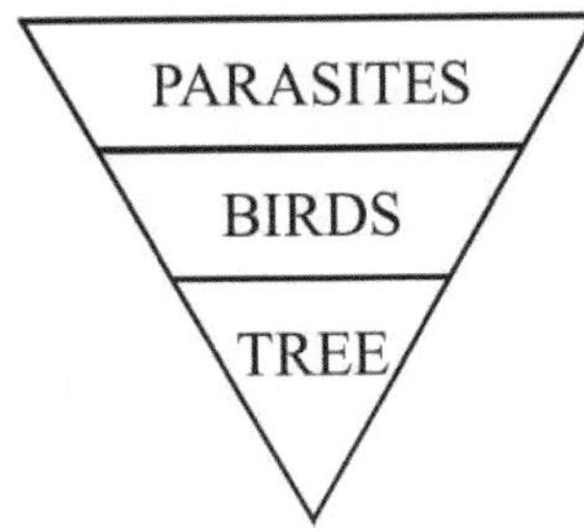

- Pyramid of number shows biotic potential of an ecosystem.
- The number of members of any particular species in a favorable condition is called as their **biotic potential**.
- When the number of the members of any species increases then it is called as **population explosion**.

Pyramid of Biomass :

- The biomass of each trophic level is shown by this pyramid. Mostly these pyramids are also upright (erect). e.g. Tree ecosystem :
  - Pyramid of biomass in aquatic ecosystem is inverted, because in this producers are micro organisms and their biomass is lesser than other trophic levels.
  - Pyramids of biomass show the standing crop of ecosystem. It means total amount of living matter at a particular time in an ecosystem is called as standing crop.
  - Total amount of nonliving matter in an ecosystem is called as standing state.

Pyramid of Energy :

- It always remains erect, because flow of energy is not cyclic. i.e. during the flow of energy at each trophic level goes on decreasing.
- According to the 10% law of Linderman the 90% part of obtained energy of each organism is utilized in their various metabolic activities and only 10% energy transferred to the next trophic level. So that 90% energy is lost at each trophic level therefore, top consumers like lion etc., are weakest ecologically.
- Pyramids of energy show the productivity of any ecosystem.

PLANT COMMUNITY

- All types of plants present at a particular place form a community, is called as **plant community**.
- The distribution of any species at a place depends upon social nature of the species which indicates cooperation between them.
- **Synecology :** The ecological study of any plant community is called as "**synecology**"
- **Phytogeography :** The study of distribution of the plants on the earth is called as "**phytogeography**". Some characteristics of plant community are as follows :
  - **(i)** **Species diversity :** There are many varieties of organisms found in a community. The total number of species of plants called as **population**. The ecological study of population is called as Autecology. The maximum species diversity is found in tropical forest. The plants are called as **flora** and animals are termed as **fauna**. The lowest species diversity is found in **Tundra biome** or **Arctic desert**.
  - **(ii)** **Dominant species :** The highest number of plants of a species present in a community is called as **dominant species** and whole plant community is knows as the name of the **species**. Such as Prosop is community on Aravali hills and Pinus community on Himalaya.

FLOW (TRANSFER) OF ENERGY IN AN ECOSYSTEM :

- Energy transfers in the biosphere in food chains obey the laws of thermodynamics
- The food chain in a community actually represents a stepwise transfer of food and the energy contained in food.
- About 1% of the sun's energy falling on the leaves is used by the plants in the process of photosynthesis and stored as chemical energy of food.

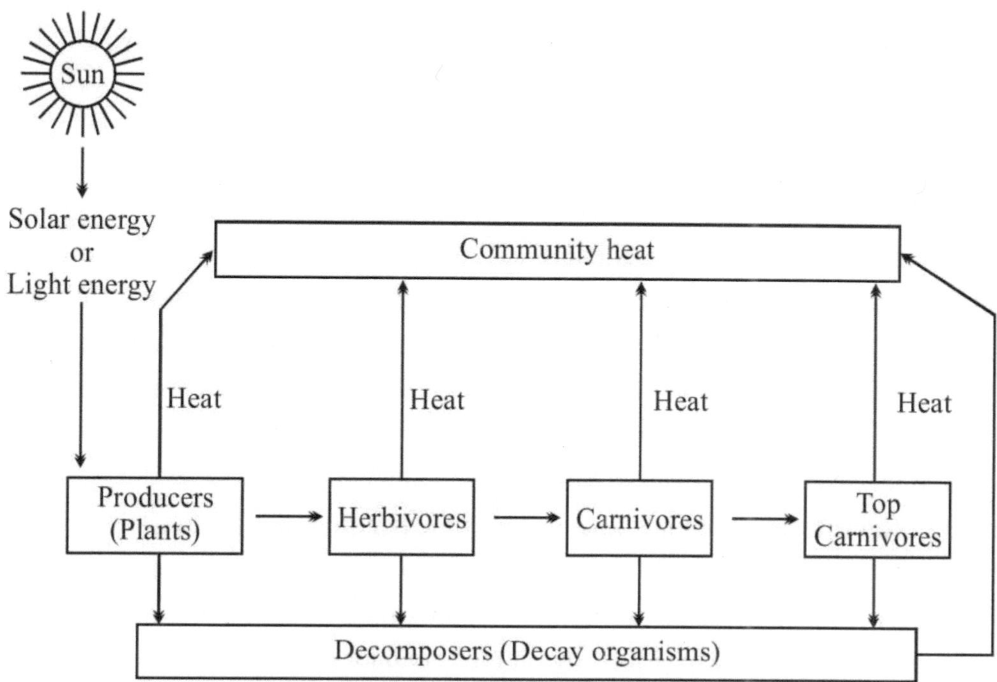

Transfer of energy in the ecosystem :

- Energy is not created in the ecosystem. Energy is only converted from one form to another.
- There is a continuous transfer of energy from one trophic level of organisms to the next in a food chain.

  Example: **Food Chain : Plants → Dear → Lion**

  This transfer of energy takes place in the form of chemical energy of food.
- At each trophic level of organisms, some of the energy is utilized by the organisms for their metabolic activities like respiration and for growth.
- A part of the energy at each tropic level (like produces, herbivores and carnivoures) is utilized for the functioning of decomposers.
- There is a loss of energy at each energy transfer in various trophic levels of organisms which goes into the environment and remains unutilized is called **community heat**.

Flow of Material in Ecosystem is Cyclic but Flow of Energy in Unidirectional

The flow of energy in the ecosystem is said to be unidirectional because the energy lost as heat from the living organisms of a food chain cannot be reused by plants in photosynthesis.

The 10% Law

- Given by Lindeman in 1942
- According to the ten percent law, only 10% of the total energy entering a particular trophic level is available for transfer to the next trophic level.

- For example, suppose 1000 J of solar energy is received by green plants, then only 1% of solar energy available on earth is utilized by plants. So only 10 J (1% of 1000 J) is trapped by plants and the rest 990 J of energy is lost to the environment. So, plant utilizes only 10 J of energy.
- Next, only 10% of the 10 J energy of plants, that is, 1 J, is available to the herbivore animal while 9 J is lost to the environment.
- Again, just 10% of the 1 J of energy of herbivore animals is utilized by carnivore animals. Thus carnivore animals have only 0.1 J of energy while 0.9 J is lost to the environment.

BIOLOGICAL MAGNIFICATION

- As human beings usually occupy the highest trophic level of the food chain, they get the maximum quantity of harmful chemicals accumulate in their bodies.
- Increase in the concentration of harmful chemical substances in the body of living organisms at each trophic level of a food chain is called **biological magnification** or **biomagnification.**
- Some harmful non-biodegradable chemicals (pesticides, e.g., D.D.T. and heavy metals such as mercury, arsenic, cadmium etc.) enter the bodies of organisms through the food chains and go on concentrating at each trophic level through process of **biomagnification.**
- Accumulation of mercury lead to disease Minimata.
- Accumulation of fluorine lead the knee-knock syndrome bending of legs fluorisis.
- Water bodies usually contains a small amount - 0.02 ppm (parts per million) of harmful chemicals. When this water is consumed by phytoplanktons and zooplanktons, the concentration of these chemicals increases to 5 ppm. Fishes feeding on these planktons were found to contain 240 ppm of harmful chemicals. Birds feeding on these fishes were found to contain 1600 ppm of these chemicals. Thus, there is an increase on the concentration of the chemicals at each trophic level.

EFFECTS OF HUMAN ACTIVITIES ON ENVIRONMENT

- Changes in the environment affect us and our activities change the environment. It is polluted beyond the capacity of cleaning agents of nature, ecological balance is lost and the environment becomes polluted.
- Our activities pollute the environment in various ways and some of the environment problems are depletion of ozone layer and disposal of waste.

OZONE LAYER DEPLETION :

Between 20 km to 26 km above the sea level ozone layer is present and the part of atmosphere containing it is called ozonosphere (Stratosphere). This layer is established due to an equilibrium between photo dissociation of ozone by UV - radiations and regeneration of ozone. The thickness of this ozonosphere averages 5 mm. The ozone layer acts as an ozone shield and absorbs the harmful UV - radiations of the sunlight so protect the earth's biota form the harmful effects of strong UV - radiations. So this layer is very important for the survival and existence of life on earth.

(a) Causes of Thinning of Ozone Layer :

- The decline in spring - layer (general thickness) is called ozone hole.
- Ozone hole is largest over Antarctica and was just short of 27 million sq. km. during September 2003.
- Main chemicals to be responsible for destruction of ozone - layer are : chlorofluorocarbons (CFCs), halogens (used in fire extinguishers), methane and nitrous oxide.
- Out of these, most damaging is the effect of CFCs which are a group of synthetic chemicals and are used as coollants in refrigerations and air conditioners; as cleaning solvents, propellants and sterilant etc.
- These CFCs produce "active chlorine" in the presence of UV - radiations.
- These active chlorine radicals catalytically destroy ozone and convert it into oxygen.
- Ozone at the higher levels of the atmosphere is a product of UV radiation acting on oxygen (O_2) molecule.
- The higher energy UV radiations split apart some molecular oxygen (O_2) into free oxygen (O) atoms.
- These atoms then combine with the molecular oxygen to form ozone as shown -

$$O_2 \xrightarrow{UV} O + O$$

$$O + O_2 \longrightarrow \underset{\text{(Ozone)}}{O_3}$$

- In 1987, the United National Environment Programme (UNEP) succeeded in forgoing an agreement to freeze CFC production at 1986 levels.
- **Nitrous oxide:** is produced in industrial processes, forest fires, solid waste disposal, spraying of insecticides and pesticides, etc. Methane and nitrous oxide also cause ozone destruction.
- **Dobson spectometer** is used to measure amount of ozone and is expressed as **Dobson unit (DU)**.

(b) Effects of Ozone Layer Depletion :

- The thinning of ozone layer results in increase in the UV radiation (in the rage of 290 - 320 nm) reaching the earth's surface.
- It is estimated that 5 percent loss of ozone results in 10 per cent increase in UV - radiations.
- These UV - radiations can :

(i) Increases in incidences of cataract and skin cancer.
(ii) Decrease in the functioning of immune system.
(iii) Inhibit photosynthesis in most of phytoplankton so adversely affecting the food chains of aquatic ecosystems.
(iv) Damage nucleic acids of the living organisms.

Garbage Management :

- More quantity of waste material is generated due to the improvement of our day to day lifestyle.
- Nowadays, more and more disposable items are used to change in our life style.
- Changes in packaging have resulted much of our non-biodegradable waste.
- Proper method of garbage disposal by segregating biodegradable, non-biodegradable and recycling material to the used.

Replacement of Non-biodegradable Waste to Biodegradable Waste : An example

- Few years back, tea was served in trains in reusable glasses.
- For hygienic reasons glasses were replaced by disposable plastic cups.
- But disposal of these cups were a major environment challenge.
- Plastic cups were then replaced by disposable clay cups but making of these cups in large scale had resulted loss of fertile top soil.
- Now, disposable paper-cups are used which are biodegradable.

WATER POLLUTION

- The presence of some inorganic, organic, biological, radiological or physical foreign substances or particles, in the water that tends to degrade its quality.
- Most of our water bodies as ponds, lakes, steams, rivers, sea, oceans have become polluted due to industrial growth, urbanisation and other man made problems.
- The chief sources of water pollution are :

(i) Sewage and other wastes.
(ii) Industrial effluents.
(iii) Agricultural discharges.
(iv) Industrial wastes from chemical industries, fossil fuels, plants and nuclear power plants.

SEWAGE

- It consists of excreta of animals.
- A major source of water pollution is raw or partially discharged sewage thrown into natural resources of water (e.g. rivers, lakes, streams etc.).

INDUSTRIAL WASTES

- The industries that cause pollution are printing, electroplating, soap manufacture, rubber, plastics etc.
- Caustic soda and chlorine factories release heavy metals, such as mercury, cadmium, chromium, copper, lead etc.
- **Mercury poisoning** occurred in **Minamata city, Japan** in 1953, where more than 100 persons died or suffered serious nervous damage from eating fish taken from Minamata Bay.
- **Cadmium poisoning** causes itai-itai (ouch-ouch) disease.
- Adding large amount of inorganic fertilizers to crop fields results in fertilizer pollution.
- Nitrite poisoning or methaemoglobinemia occurs in infants and farm animals by poisoning or nitrite.

Eutrophication :

- It means enrichment of nutrients by human activity.
- **Eutrophic :** Refers to lakes that are highly productive in terms of organic matter formed and well supplied with nutrients.

BIOLOGICAL OXYGEN DEMAND (BOD)

- It is the amount of oxygen required for biological oxidation by microbes in any unit volume of water.
- The greater the amount of organic matter in water, higher the **BOD**.
- **BOD** is higher in polluted sewage water and is connected with both microbes and organic matter.
- The excessive use of pesticides causes water pollution by penetrating through soil and getting dissolved in soil water.
- Pesticide means any substance that is used for control pests.
- Spraying of **DDT** on crops produces pollution of air, soil and water.

Biological Amplification (Magnification)

- Increase in the concentration of a persistent chemical by the organisms at successive trophical levels in a food chain.

BIOLOGICAL MONITORING

- Direct measurement of changes in the biological component of a habitat based on evaluation of the number and / or distribution of organisms or species.

Effect of Heavy Metal of Water Pollution on Man		
S.No.	**Metal**	**Toxic Effect**
1.	Cadmium	Diarrohea, bone deformation, kidney damage, retarded growth, CNS injury etc.
2.	Copper	Hypertension, uremia, coma etc.
3.	Mercury	Abdominal pain, headache, haemolysis, diarrhoea etc.
4.	Lead	Anaemia, vomitting, brain damage etc.
5.	Chromium	Cancer, nephritis, gastrointestinal ulcer etc.
6.	Zinc	Vomitting, renal damage, cramps etc.
7.	Cobalt	Paralysis, low blood pressure, bone defects, lung irritation etc.

SOIL POLLUTION

- Soil is the most important component of earth. All the plants grow over earth's crust (soil).
- These plants serve as food for herbivore animals, thus supports the animal life on earth.
- Like air and water, soil is subjected to pollution.
- Any foreign substance (organic pollutants) that enters the soil will adversely affect the soil productivity.
- **Three types of soil pollution may be found in nature :**
  - (i) Pollutants that are washed out of atmosphere when came in contact with it, may pollute the soil.
  - (ii) Pesticides, insecticides and weedicides, sprayed over the crops may find their way along with water to the soil.
  - (iii) Nitrogenous fertilizers, mixed with soil to increase its productivity may sometimes have negative effects on the soil.
- One of the major soil pollution problem in large cities is the disposal of **plastics**.
- Plastics articles are non-biodegradable.
- Exposure of man to radiation may cause cancer, genetic damage and infant mortality.

- The most outstanding danger at present for survival of living beings on earth is radiation hazard.
- **Chernobyl disaster** occurred in Ukraine, USSR on 26th April 1986. It was an explosion at the **nuclear power station** releasing huge amount of radioactive substance into the atmosphere.
- Strontium-90, a radioactive pollutant causes bone cancer and degeneration of tissues in human beings.
- Iodine-131, a radioactive isotopes is used in the detection of **thyroid cancer**.
- Mothers who received abnormal doses of **X-rays** for diagnostic purposes during their pregnancy tend to produce an above average number of **mongoloid children**.
- Due to radioactive pollution, **radiation stress** leads to **reduction** in **species diversity** at the ecosystem level.
- Disposal of waste heat produced in nuclear energy production causes **thermal pollution**.
- Thermal pollution raises the temperature of water, thereby increasing the metabolic rate and oxygen consumption of micro-organisms.

NOICSE POLLUTION

- Means the unwanted sound dumped into the atmosphere.
- The main sources of noise pollution are factories and industries, transportation (air, rail and road), community and religious activities.
- **There are two basic properties of sound :**
  - **(i) Loudness :** It is the strength of sensation of sound perceived by the individual. It is measured in **decibel**.
    - Sounds beyound **80 dB** can be safely regarded as pollutant as it harms hearing system.
    - The **WHO** has fixed **45 dB** as the safe noise level for a city.
    - Loudness is also expressed in **sones**.
    - 1 sone = loudness of 40 dB sound pressure at **1000 Hz**.
  - **(ii) Frequency :** Number of vibrations per second. Its unit is **hertz (Hz)**.
    - The noise has adverse effect on man reducing hearing capacity, flushing the skin and constricting stomach muscles.
    - **Deafness** can be caused due to continuous noise exposure.
    - Noise also produces ulcers, headache, heart diseases, high blood pressure, nervousness etc.

POINTS TO REMEMBER

1. Our environment is composed of various biotic and abiotic factors which interact with each other.
2. Human activities have a great impact on the functioning of the environment.
3. The wastes generated by the various human activities may be biodegradable or non- biodegradable.
4. The enzymes present in the body of decomposers are capable of breaking down the biodegradable substances, but not the non- biodegradable materials.
5. The non-biodegradable materials like plastic and synthetic pesticides persist in the environment for a long duration and may harm its biotic factors.
6. In an ecosystem, the abiotic and biotic factors interact to form a stable unit.
7. The size of an ecosystem ranges in size from as small as a pond or a backyard garden to as large as an entire rain forest.
8. An ecosystem may be natural (like lakes and forests) or artificial (like crop fields and aquarium).
9. The biotic factors may be classified as producers, consumers and decomposers depending on their mode of nutrition.
10. The food manufactured by the producers from simple inorganic substances is utilized directly or indirectly by the consumers.
11. Herbivores, carnivores, omnivores and parasites are the various types of consumers.
12. The decomposers break down the dead bodies and wastes of organisms and help in nutrient recycling.
13. Food chains are present in every ecosystem. Each food chain is composed of three to five trophic levels.

Trophic level	Organisms comprising the trophic level
First	Autotrophs / Producers
Second	Herbivores / Primary consumers
Third	Small carnivores / Secondary consumers
Fourth	Large carnivores / Tertiary consumers

14. There is flow of energy between the various trophic levels.
15. Producers convert solar energy into chemical energy, which is then utilized by the consumers and decomposers.
16. About 1% of solar energy falling on leaves is utilized by plants in photosynthesis to produce food.
17. A large amount of energy loss occurs when the organisms of the higher trophic level feeds on the lower trophic level organisms.
18. There is only 10% flow of energy from one trophic level to the next higher level. Due to this energy loss, only 4 or 5 trophic levels are present in each food chain.
19. The number of individuals in a trophic level decreases as we go up the food chain.
20. Food webs, consisting of several interconnected food chains, are more common in mature.

21. Flow of energy is unidirectional and cannot be utilized by the previous trophic levels.
22. The non-biodegradable chemicals like pesticides and insecticides enter the food chains in land and aquatic ecosystems and then accumulate progressively at each trophic level. This is known as biological magnification.
23. Human activities can cause several environmental problems like ozone layer depletion and waste disposal.
24. Ozone, composed of three oxygen atoms, is a toxic chemical. It is formed by the combination of free oxygen atom with molecular oxygen.
25. The atmospheric ozone layer prevents the entry of solar ultraviolet rays and thus protects all organisms on Earth.
26. Use of chemicals like chlorofluorocarbons has greatly depleted the atmospheric ozone layer, which could endanger the environment.
27. The disposal of large amounts of garbage produced in any human settlement, especially in cities and towns is causing major environmental problems.
28. Changes in our lifestyle and attitude have created many disposable items, many of which are non-biodegradable.
29. Effective methods of waste disposal should be found in order to reduce the harmful effects on our environment.

CONCEPT APPLICATION LEVEL - I [NCERT Questions]

Q.1 Why is improper disposal of wastes a curse to environment ?

Ans. An improper disposal of wastes means addition of pollutants into environment air, water, soil. They will harm living beings, human assets and human beings. For example, passage of sewage into water body will cause entrophication, stink development of sludge, killing of animals and source of water borne pathogens.

Q.2 Write the common food chain of a pond ecosystem.

Ans. Phytoplankton (and other aquatic plants) ⟶ Zooplankton (and other small aquatic animals and larvae) ⟶ Fish ⟶ Bird (King Fisher).

Q.3 What are the advantages of cloth bags over plastic bags during shopping ?

Ans. Advantages of Cloth Bags

(i) Cloth bags are stronger and more durable as compared to plastic bags.
(ii) They are washable.
(iii) They are reused again and again.
(iv) Cloth bags do not pollute environment.
(v) They are made of biodegradable material which can also be recycled.

Q.4 Why are crop fields known as artificial ecosystems ?

Ans. Crop fields are known as artificial ecosystems because they are raised, maintained, nourished and reaped by human beings.

Q.5 Explain the role of decomposers in the environment.

Ans. Decomposers are saprophytes which feed on organic remains by a process of external digestion and absorption of soluble materials. *e.g.*, many bacteria, fungi. In the process they perform the following functions :

(i) Cleansing the earth of organic remains and continuously creating space for newer generations of organisms.

(ii) Release of minerals from organic remains. The phenomenon is called **mineralisation**. The released minerals become available to plants for utilization in synthesis of new organic matter. Decomposers, therefore, take part in biogeochemical recycling.

Q.6 Select the mismatched pair in the following and correct it.

(a) *Biomagnification*. Accumulation of chemicals at the successive trophic levels of a food chain.

(b) *Ecosystem*. Biotic component of environment.

(c) *Aquarium*. A man-made ecosystem.

(d) *Parasites*. Organisms which obtain food from other living organisms.

Ans. **(b) Ecosystem.** It is an ecological system, consisting of a distinct biotic community and the **physical environment** (consisting of a number of abiotic factors) both interacting and exchanging materials between them.

Q.7 We do not clean ponds or lakes but an aquarium needs to be cleaned. Why?

Ans. An aquarium is an **artificial system** which is also incomplete due to absence of producers, food chains and decomposers. There is no recycling and self cleaning. However, a pond or a lake is a self sustained, natural and complete ecosystem where there is perfect recycling of nutrients.

Q.8 Suggest any four activities in daily life which are ecofriendly.

Ans. (i) Use of cloth bags instead of polythene or plastic bags.
(ii) Separation of biodegradable and non-biodegradable in green and blue coloured bins.
(iii) Use of compact fluorescent lamps instead of incandescent lamps.
(iv) Harvesting of rain water and preventing wastage of resources.

Q.9 Name the wastes which are generated in your house daily. What measures would you take for their disposal ?

Ans. **Wastes :**

(i) Vegetable and fruit peels and rind, stale food, food leftovers, used tea leaves.
(ii) Milk pouches, polythene bags, empty cartons.
(iii) Waste paper (newspaper, bags, envelopes), packing paper, empty bottles, torn cloth pieces, etc.
(iv) Dust and other sweepings.

Disposal :

(i) Separation into biodegradable and non-biodegradable, recyclable and non-recyclable wastes.
(ii) Recyclable wastes (waste paper, cloth, polythene or plastic bags, cartons, bottles, cans etc.) can be given to rag pickers for recycling.
(iii) Preparation of compost or vermicompost from kitchen wastes for home garden (kitchen garden).
(iv) In the absence of kitchen garden, the household garbage and other wastes can be given to waste collectors for disposal.

Q.10 What are the by products of fertilizer industries ? How do they affect the environment.

Ans. The most common by product of fertilizer industries are oxides of nitrogen and sulphur. They pass into atmosphere and spread to all nearby places. The gases have a corrosive effect on several items besides being harmful to living beings. They also give rise to **acid rain**. Acid rain is highly destructive to forests, crops and aquatic biota.

Q.11 Explain some harmful effects of agricultural practices on the environment.

Ans. **(i)** **Soil.** Fertilizer added to soil not only changes the chemistry of the soil but also kills many useful microbes.

(ii) **Ground Water.** A part of fertilizer always leaches down into soil and reaches ground water. It raises the salt content of ground water.

(iii) **Eutrophication.** Run-off from fields sprayed with fertilizer reaches water bodies. It results in their eutrophication.

(iv) **Pesticides.** Pesticides sprayed over crops reach water bodies killing the biota. Persistent pesticides undergo biomagnification and prove highly harmful to higher organisms.

(v) **Ground Water.** Continued use of ground water in agriculture has resulted in lowering of water table at most of the places.

(vi) **Irrigation.** It causes water-logging and salivation of soils.

(vii) **Genetic Erosion.** Use of only selected high yielding varieties has resulted in genetic erosion of the crop plants.

(viii) **Damage to Nature.** Natural ecosystems and habitats haw been damaged during clearing band for agriculture.

Q.12 Why are some substances biodegradable and some non-biodegradable?

Ans. All substances are divided in to two broad categories i.e. bio-degradable and Non-biodegradable. Substances which are broken down by biological process are called biodegradable and those substances which cannot be broken down in this manner are called non-bio-degradable.

Q.13 Give any two ways in which biodegradable substances would affect the environment.

Ans. (i) They accumulation of these in more amounts or in water bodies may produce foul smell during decomposition process and causes degradation of water and hence killing of aquatic animals and diseases to human being.

(ii) The accumulation and decomposition of these may produce harmful gases such as ammonia, methane, carbon dioxide.

Q.14 Give any two ways in which non-biodegradable substances would affect the environment.

Ans. (i) Non-biodegradable substances may chock sewer systems or drains resulting in water logging and hence water borne diseases;

(ii) They are inert and may persist in environment for a long time causing pollution and harms to our eco-system.

(iii) They also kill micro-organisms;

(iv) Pesticides substances like DDT, BHC enter in the food chain and cause biomagnifications.

Q.15 What are trophic levels? Give an example of food chain and state the different trophic levels in it.

Ans. Trophic levels are each step or level of the food chain. Trophic levels are different steps/levels of a food chain. A trophic level is the level of species in an ecosystem on the basis of the source of nutrition such as producers, primary consumers, secondary consumers, etc. The producers form the first trophic level as they manufacture food. The primary consumers form the second trophic level, the secondary consumers form the third, and the tertiary consumers form the fourth trophic level.

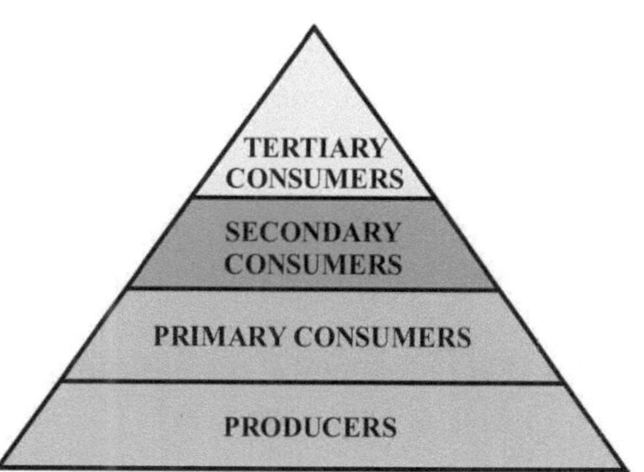

An example of food chain and the different trophic levels.

1st – Trophic level	Green Plants	(Autotrophs/Producer)
2nd – Trophic level	Grasshopper	(herbivores/Primary consumers)
3rd – Trophic level	Frog	(Small Carnivores/Secondary Consumers)
4th – Trophic level	Snake/Eagle	(larger Carnivores/Tertiary Consumers)

Q.16 What is the role of decomposers in the ecosystem?

Ans. They play the following role:

(i) They are micro-consumers and they decomposes & break down the complex organic degradable compounds of dead plants and animals in to useful inorganic compounds;

(ii) It releases the inorganic useful compounds in to environment/soil which are used by the producers.

(iii) They clean the environment.

Q.17 What is ozone and how does it affect any ecosystem?

Ans. **OZONE:** Ozone (O_3) is a molecule formed by three atoms of oxygen.

It's affect on any Eco-system:

At the higher levels of the atmosphere, ozone performs an essential function. It shields the surface of the earth from ultraviolet (UV) radiation from the Sun. This radiation is highly damaging to organisms, for example, it is known to cause skin cancer in human beings.

Q.18 How can you help in reducing the problem of waste disposal? Give any two methods.

Ans. The following two methods could be adopted to reduce the problem of waste disposal:

(i) First and foremost method is to segregate or separate the biodegradable and non-biodegradable waste

(ii) By adopting the different suitable methods to properly dispose them off like composting for biodegradable and recycling the non-biodegradable waste;

Q.19 What will happen if we kill all the organisms in one trophic level?

Ans. If we kill all the organisms of one trophic level it will create an imbalance in food chain and food web. It may also decrease the food and energy availability to the next higher trophic levels. It will result the instability and disturbance of the ecosystem.

Q.20 Will the impact of removing all the organisms in a trophic level be different for different trophic levels? Can the organisms of any trophic level be removed without causing any damage to the ecosystem?

Ans. Yes, the impact of removing all the organisms in a trophic level will be different for different trophic levels. Take for example; if we remove all producers from primary level then it will adversely affect all the above trophic levels, primary consumers, secondary consumers and so on.

Whereas if we remove all herbivores/primary consumers, then it would not affect the primary producers but it would affect the carnivores only.

NO, the removal of all organisms of any trophic level will adversely affect or damage the eco-system. Removing any trophic level from a food chain will cause imbalance in an ecosystem.

Q.21 What is biological magnification? Will the levels of this magnification be different at different levels of the ecosystem?

Ans. Biological magnification is defined as the phenomena of progressive accumulation or increase in the concentration of pesticides and harmful chemicals substances at each trophic level.

Yes, the level of this magnification will be different at different levels of the ecosystem. The chemical substances are progressively accumulated from the different sources at each trophic level. The animals at the higher trophic levels get more poison along with their food than animals at lower trophic level. As human being occupies the the top level in any food chain, the maximum concentration is found in our bodies.

Q.22 What are the problems caused by the non-biodegradable wastes that we generate?

Ans. Following are some problems caused by non-biodegradable wastes:

(A) The cause biomagnification.

(B) They increase pollution.

(C) They make environment unclean.

(D)They kill useful microorganisms.

Q.23 If all the waste we generate is biodegradable, will this have no impact on the environment?

Ans. If all the waste generated would be biodegradable this will also create problem for the environment and ecosystem. The rate of decomposition of biodegradable is a slow process. If rate of increase of biodegradable waste accumulation is more than its decomposition, it will lead to environmental pollutions. It may lead to loss of natural environment and un-hygienic conditions along with various diseases due to foul smell and toxic gases. It may lead to choking of sewer and drainage and may also lead to the water pollution and thereby affecting the aquatic life also.

Q.24 Why is damage to the ozone layer a cause for concern? What steps are being taken to limit this damage?

Ans. Ozone shields the surface of the earth from ultraviolet (UV) radiation from the Sun. The damage to ozone layer is a cause of concern because UV radiation will pass through the ozone layer due its depletion. It is highly damaging to organisms, for example, it is known to cause skin cancer/eye diseases/immune system/etc in human beings.

Steps to reduce the damage:

(1) International agreement to reduce the use CFC production;

(2) Reducing and banning of the use of other chemicals like aerosols, solvents, etc

CONCEPT APPLICATION LEVEL - II

SECTION–A

Q.1 Why is the ozone layer lost more in cold region?

Ans. Ozone layer is most severe in the worlds coldest region, because of clouds in the stretosphere, known s polar stretospheric clouds. They provide surface on which chemical reactions that result in the destruction of ozone takes place.

Q.2 Explain the human activity on environment.

Ans. Any type of change that people make in our enviroment affects animals plants & land. Some changes are helpful, while some are harmful to the environment. Clearing land for farming, construction of homes, roads and shopping centres are helpful to the people but animal habitats & plants destroyed clearing of land may result in soil erosion & the eventual lost of top soil.

Q.3 List four components in food chain.

Ans. Various component of food chain includes plants, herbivours, coarnivorus & decomposers.

Q.4 Define environemt.

Ans. The biotic & abiotic factors which surrounds any living organisms is considered as its environment. It can be generally degined as a community of organism living in a particular environment and the physical elements in that environment with which they interact.

SECTION – B
(Previous Years Questions)

Q.1 The chemical which destroys ozone layer is **[NTSE Stage-I_2006]**
(A) CH_4 (B) CFC (C) SO_2 (D) NO_2

Q.2 The source of energy in any star is **[NTSE Stage-I_2014]**
(A) Nuclear fission reaction (B) Nuclear fusion reaction
(C) Solar energy (D) Fossil fuel

Q.3 The human made synthetic chemical used in refrigerator is **[NTSE Stage-I_2015]**
(A) LPG (B) CFC (C) CH_4 (D) PVC

Q.4 Which of the following groups constitutes a correct food chain? **[NTSE Stage-I_2016]**
(A) Grass → Rabbit → Snake → Eagle (B) Grass → Goat → Fox → Lion
(C) Goat → Grass → Elephant → Snake (D) Grass → Wheat → Frog → Goat

Q.5 Which radiation harms ozone layer in the atmosphere? **[NTSE Stage-I_2017]**
(A) Ultraviolet radiation (B) Infrared radiation
(C) Radio radiation (D) Red radiation

Q.6 In the following food chain who gets less energy than the tertiary consumer and more than the primary consumer? **[NTSE Stage-II_2013]**
Grass → Grasshopper → Frog → Snake → Eagle
(A) Grasshopper (B) Frog (C) Snake (D) Eagle

Q.7 If a non-degradable and fat soluble pollutant, such as DDT enters the food chain, the pollutant **[NTSE Stage-II_2013]**
(A) magnifies in concentration at each trophic level.
(B) degrades at first trophic level.
(C) accumulates in the body fat of organism at first trophic level and does not pass to second trophic level.
(D) decreases in concentration at each trophic level.

Q.8 Some organisms are sensitive to different levels of air pollution and are used as pollution-indicators. Suggest which among the following fits into the category **[NTSE Stage-II_2014]**
(A) Fungi (B) Fresh water algae (C) Bacteria (D) Lichens

Q.9 Which of the following is a result of biological magnification **[NTSE Stage-II_2016]**
(A) Top level predators may be most harmed by toxic chemicals in environment.
(B) Increase in carbon dioxide.
(C) The green-house effect will be most significant at the poles.
(D) Energy is lost at each tropic level of a food chain.

Q.10 What is the main reason for increase in temperature in a glass house? **[NTSE Stage-II_2016]**
(A) Sunlight in completely absorbed by plants in the glass house.
(B) Radiation fails to escape from the glass house completely.
(C) Plants do not utilize sunlight in a glass house.
(D) Plants produce heat inside the glass house

Q.11 What is the main reason for increase in temperature in a glass house? **[NTSE Stage-II_2017]**
(A) Sunlight in completely absorbed by plants in the glass house.
(B) Radiation fails to escape from the glass house completely.
(C) Plants do not utilize sunlight in a glass house.
(D) Plants produce heat inside the glass house.

Study the following diagram and answer the questions 12 to 16 :

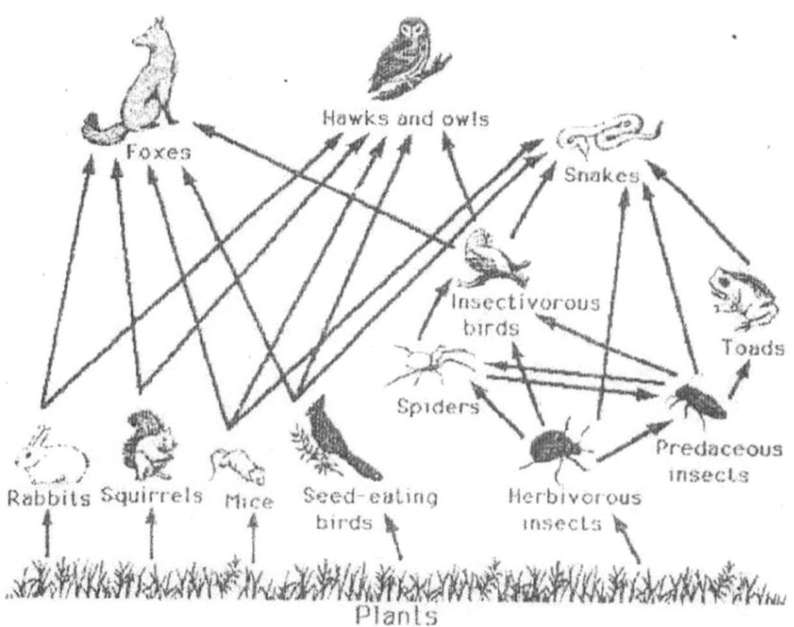

Q.12 Which of the following are tertiary consumers? **[NSEJS Stage-I_2012]**
(A) Snake, toads and spiders
(B) Foxes, Hawks and Snakes
(C) Rabbit, Squirrels and MIce
(D) Spiders, Predacious insects and herbivorous insects.

Q.13 The shortest and the longest food chains have____ and _____ number of organisms respectively. **[NSEJS Stage-I_2012]**
(A) 2 and 6 (B) 2 and 5 (C) 3 and 5 (D) 3 and 6

Q.14 An insecticide is sprayed to protect the plants. Which of the following statements is true? **[NSEJS Stage-I_2012]**
(A) Toads and insectivorous birds will prosper as they will get ample supply of dead insects.
(B) Herbivores will be greatly affected, plants will be safe and carnivores will move to other areas and will not be affected greatly.
(C)Some insects will die, some will become resistant and prolifer more and top carnivore will be affected most.
(D) Some insects will die, but there will be no long term effects as the pesticides will get washed away.

Q.15 What should be the preferred food of snakes to ensure minimum loss of solar energy. **[NSEJS Stage-I_2012]**
(A) Mice (B) Toads (C) Insectivorous birds (D) Faxes

Q.16 Organisms having low chances of survival produce larger number of offsprings to ensure their survival. Which of the following can be a characteristic feature of such organisms. **[NSEJS Stage-I_2012]**
(A) Short lifecycle (B) Better defense strategies
(C) Large body size (D) Good parental care

Q.17 Mud flats with mangrove plants export a lot of organic matter to waters in contact. This is primarily because: **[NSEJS Stage-I_2012]**
(A) there are fewer consumers in mangrove community
(B) excreta of animals in mangrove community is richer in fibers
(C) detritivores are lacking in mangrove community
(D) aerobic decomposers cannot survive in waterlogged mud

Q.18 Green house effect is related to **[NSEJS Stage-I_2012]**
(A) Ozone layer depletion (B) Carbon dioxide emission and absorption
(C) Nitrogen radiation (D) Oxygen radiation

Passage for (Q.19–Q.21) : In a field one summer's day a Grasshopper was hopping about, chirping and singing to its hearts's content. An Ant passed by, bearing along with great toil an ear of pea he was taking to the nest. "Why not come and chat with me," said the Grasshopper, "instead of to toiling and moling in that way?" "I am helping to lay up food for the winter," said the Ant, "and recommend you to do the same." "Why bother about winter?" said the Grasshopper ; "We have got plenty of food at present." But the Ant went on its way and continued its toil. When the winter came the Grasshopper had no food an found itself dying of hunger - while it saw the ants distributing every day corn and grain from the stores they had collected in the summer. Then the Grasshopper knew : It is best to prepare for days of need

Q.19 In the passage given above there seems to be a factural error with respect to the ant carrying the food to the nest.The most probable reason for this mistake would be **[NSEJS Stage-I_2013]**
(A) Pea pod is too heavy for an ant to carry to its nest.
(B) Pea cannot be carried by an ant in the summber because it is a Rabi crop.
(C) Ant couldn't have passed by easily since it is the favourite food of grasshoppers.
(D) Grasshoppers avoid coming out in summber and thus there cannot be grasshopper in the story.

Q.20 What could be the most plausible reason that all the ants that toiled and moiled in the summer were happy and content in the winter ? **[NSEJS Stage-I_2013]**
(A) Ants were probably happy since their food was not shared with Grasshopper.
(B) Ants need not worry to work anymore since they had food stocked.
(C) Ants were happy since they enjoyed working together in summer.
(D) Food that was procured was efficiently distributed and managed so that all the ants were fed equality.

Q.21 Grasshopper was at fault in this story mostly because **[NSEJS Stage-I_2013]**
(A) Of its attitude towards ants who were working tirelessly.
(B) Of not having a forethought to store food for the upcoming winter season.
(C) Of chirping and singing to its heart's content in the summer.
(D) It should have asked ants for the food and managed to surpass the winter somehow.

Q.22 The term Biodiversity refers to **[NSEJS Stage-I_2013]**
(A) Species Diversity (B) Genetic diversity
(C) Ecosystem diversity (D) All of the above

Q.23 After hearing to an influential lecture on "how to conserve environment by avoiding usage of plastic"? Ghan Shyam resolved that he should also contribute towards protecting the environment from plastic menace. Can you suggest him the first step how should he go about doing this effectively **[NSEJS Stage-I_2013]**
(A) He should urge his parents to stop using plastic materials at home.
(B) He should write a letter to the local civic body against selling plastic materials around his locality.
(C) He should practice minimising plastic usage himself.
(D) He should ask his teacher to advice people on his behalf to stop usage of plastics.

Q.24 Which of the following conditions will give the most benefits to the farmers? **[NSO–2010]**
(A) Use of high quality seeds, fertilizers and no irrigation.
(B) Use of quality seeds, irrigation, fertilizers and crop protection measures.
(C) Use of ordinary seeds, irrigation and fertilizers.
(D) Use of quality seeds, irrigation and protection measures.

Q.25 In a grassland ecosystem which of the following groups of animals are likely to occupy the same trophic level ? **[NSO–2010]**

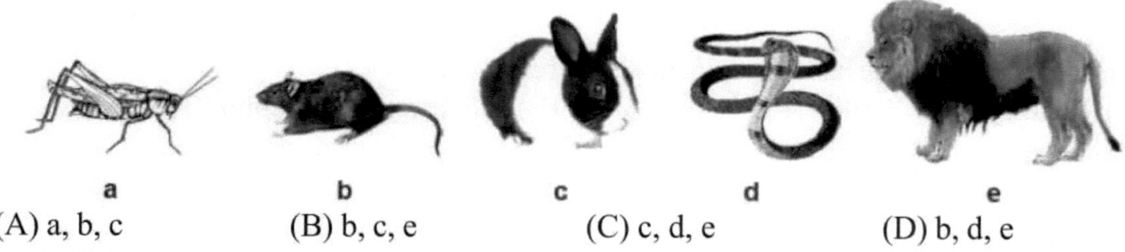

(A) a, b, c (B) b, c, e (C) c, d, e (D) b, d, e

Q.26 Cutting down forests and using the land for other purposes is known as deforestation. It has adverse effects on the environment. Which of the following are correct regarding these effects? **[NSO–2011]**

(i) Decrease in soil erosion
(ii) Increase in temperature
(iii) Ground water level gets lowered
(iv) Droughts and floods
(v) Increase in water holding capacity of the soil

(A) (i), (ii), (iii) & (iv) (B) (ii), (iv) & (v) (C) (ii), (iii) & (iv) (D) (i), (ii), (iv) & (v)

Q.27 Which of the following options is correct about India alligator and Indian giant squirrel? **[NSO–2012]**

(A) Both are examples of extinct species.
(B) Both are found in Satpura National Park.
(C) Both are examples of endemic species.
(D) Both are examples of exotic species.

Q.28 Which of the following is incorrect for the given figure? **[NSO–2012]**

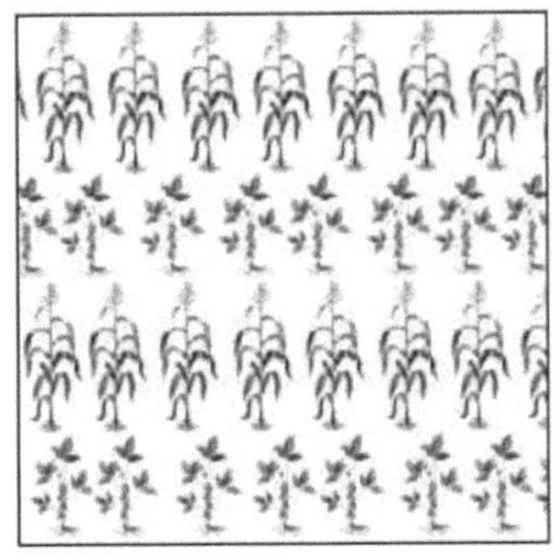

(A) It is a type of cropping pattern called intercropping.
(B) The given cropping pattern increases the productivity of crops per unit area.
(C) The given cropping pattern helps in maintaining soil fertility and makes better use of resources.
(D) None of these.

Q.29 Study the following table regarding different species and their status Select the correct option for a-e. **[NSO–2013]**

(A) a - Extinct; b - Hog badger; c - Thick billed parrot; d - Endangered; e - Vulnerable
(B) a - Vulnerable; b - Thick billed parrot; c - Hog badger; d - Extinct; e - Endangered
(C) a - Endangered; b - Hog badger; c - Thick billed parrot; d - Vulnerable; e - Extinct
(D) a - Extinct; b - Thick billed parrot; c - Hog badger; d - Extinct; e - Endangered

Q.30 Read the given statements and select the correct option. **[NSO–2013]**

Statement-I: Shivam, an environmental researcher, is working in the buffer zone of a biosphere reserve where limited human activity is allowed.

Statement-2 : Buffer zone provides space for settlements, farming, fisheries, research and recreation.

(A) Both statements 1 and 2 are correct and statement 2 is the correct explanation of statement 1.
(B) Both statements 1 and 2 are correct but statement 2 is not the correct explanation of statement 1.
(C) Statement 1 is correct and statement 2 is incorrect.
(D) Both statements 1 and 2 are incorrect.

Q.31 Select the option which has the complete set of fresh-water fishes. **[NSO–2013]**

(A) Rohu, Calbasu, Sardine, Eel
(B) Sanghara, Hilsa, Salmon, Pomphrets
(C) Mrigal, Catla, Malhi, Rohu
(D) Mackerels, Tuna, Bombay duck, Flatfish

Q.32 Match Column-I with Colunm-II and select the correct option from the codes given below : [NSO–2014]

	Column-I (National Park)		Column-II (State)
a.	Bandipur National Park	I.	Karnataka
b.	Dachigam National Park	II.	Madhya Pradesh
c.	Corbett National Park	III.	Uttarakhand
d.	Dudhwa National Park	IV.	Jammu & Kashmir
e.	Gir National Park	V.	Uttar Pradesh
f.	Kanha National Park	VI.	Assam
g.	Kaziranga National Park	VII.	Gujarat

(A) a-I, b-IV, c-III, d-V, e-VII, f-II, g-VI (B) a-V, b-I, c-IV, d-III, e-II, f-VII, g-VI
(C) a-I, b-IV, c-III, d-V, e-VII, f-VI, g-II (D) a-III, b-II, c-I, d-VII, e-V, f-IV, g-VI

Q.33 The diagram given below shows a river and its surrounding area.

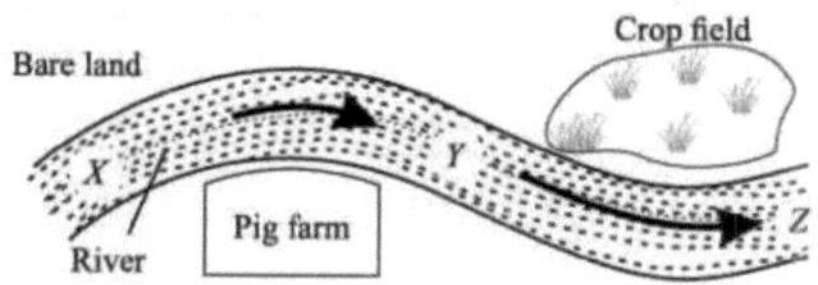

Which of these statements holds true regarding the given diagram? [NSO–2014]
(A) Site X has the highest content of dissolved oxygen while site Y has the lowest content of dissolved oxygen.
(B) There is a high concentration of nitrogen compounds at site Z.
(C) There are very few fishes found at site Z.
(D) All of these

Q.34 Match column-I with column-II and select the correct option from the codes given below. [NSO–2014]

	Column-I		Column-II
a.	Bottom feeder	(i)	Surti
b.	Cow breed	(ii)	Tharparkar
c.	Buffalo breed	(iii)	Common carp
d.	Surface feeder	(iv)	Murrah
		(v)	Mrigal
		(vi)	Red sindhi
		(vii)	Catla

(A) a-(iii), (vi); b-(ii); c-(i), (iv); d-(v), (vii) (B) a-(i), (ii), (v); b-(iii), (vi); c-(iv); d-(vii)
(C) a-(v); b-(i), (ii), (vi); c-(iv); d-(iii), (vii) (D) a-(iii), (v); b-(ii), (vi); c-(i), (iv); d-(vii)

Q.35 In an ecosystem, four major interdependent components were in the given proportions. If male cats are removed from the given ecosystem, then which of these figures would show the new composition of the same ecosystem after a gap of 3 years? [NSO–2014]

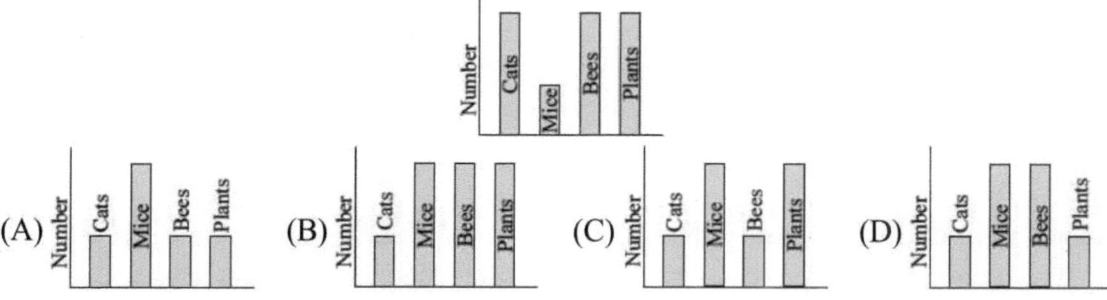

CONCEPT APPLICATION LEVEL - III

SECTION-A

- **Fill in the blanks**

Q.1 The biodegradable substances were broken down by the activity of __________ secreated by __________.

Q.2 Increase in temperature of earth due to green house gases is called __________

Q.3 The series of organism feeding on one another is called __________.

Q.4 UNEP stands for __________.

Q.5 The process by which producers prepare their own food in presence of sunlight is called __________.

Q.6 All interacting organism in an area together with abiotic components of an environment forms an __________.

Q.7 Ozone is getting depleted due to __________ used in refrigerants and in fire extinguishers.

Q.8 The process by which the harmful chemicals entered in food chain are not degradable and get accumulated progressively at each level is called __________.

Q.9 Herbivores, carnivores, omnivores and parasites are examples of __________.

Q.10 __________ can be taken as average value for the amount of organic matter that is present at each step and reaches the next level of consumers.

SECTION-B

- **Multiple choice question with one correct answers**

Q.1 The best source of energy is

(A) Water (B) Soil (C) Plants (D) Ponds

Q.2 Ozone hole means

(A) Hole in the straptosphere (B) Same concentration of ozone

(C) Decrease in concentration of ozone (D) Increase in concentration of ozone

Q.3 As a biologist, if you become very intrested in the study of the interaction of organism with each other and the environment your subspeciality will be

(A) Zoology (B) Ecology (C) Protany (D) Herpetology

Q.4 As energy is passed from one trophic level to another, the amount of usable energy

(A) Increases

(B) Decreases

(C) Remains same

(D) Energy is not passed from one trophic level to another

Q.5 In the biosphere which of the following is the ultimate source of energy

(A) Carbon (B) Water (C) Sunlight (D) Nitrogen

Q.6 Individual of any species at a place form

(A) Biotic community (B) Ecosystem (C) Population (D) Biome

Q.7 Pyramid of energy are
(A) always upright (B) always inverted (C) mostly upright (D) mostly inverted

Q.8 The maximum energy is stored at the following trophic level in an ecosystem
(A) Producers (B) Herbivores (C) Carnivores (D) Top carnivores

Q.9 Sun gives radiations in form of
(A) Infra-red radiation (B) Visible light (C) Ultra-voilet (D) All of the above

Q.10 Minimum energy is transfered in step:
(A) Grass → deer (B) Deer → lion (C) Grass → Lion (D) Sun → Plant

Q.11 Excessive exposure of humans to U V-rays results in
(i) damage to immune system (ii) damage to lungs
(iii) skin cancer (iv) peptic ulcers
(A) (i) and (ii) (B) (ii) and (iv) (C) (i) and (iii) (D) (iii) and (iv)

Q.12 In the following groups of materials, which group(s) contains only non-biodegradable items?
(i) Wood, paper, leather (ii) Polythene, detergent, PVC
(iii) Plastic, detergent, grass (iv) Plastic, bakelite, DDT
(A) (iii) (B) (iv) (C) (i) and (iii) (D) (ii) and (iv)

Q.13 Which of the following limits the number of trophic levels in a food chain?
(A) Decrease in energy at higher trophic levels (B) Dufficient food supply
(C) Polluted air (D) Water

Q.14 Which of the statement is incorrect ?
(A) All green plants and blue green algae are producers
(B) Green plants get their food from organic compounds
(C) Producers prepare their own food from inorganic compounds
(D) Plants convert solar energy into chemical energy.

Q.15 Which group of organisms are not constituents of a food chain ?
(i) Grass, lion, rabbit, wolf (ii) Plankton, man, fish, grasshopper
(iii) Wolf, grass, snake, tiger (iv) Frog, snake, eagle, grass, grasshopper
(A) (i) and (iii) (B) (iii) and (iv) (C) (ii) and (iii) (D) (i) and (iv)

Q.16 The percentage of solar radiation absorbed by all the green plants for the process of photosynthesis is about
(A) 1 % (B) 5 % (C) 8 % (D) 10 %

Q.17 In the given figure the various trophic levels are shown in a pyramid. At which trophic level is maximum energy available?
(A) T_4 (B) T_2 (C) T_1 (D) T_3

Q.18 What will happen if deer is missing in the food chain given below ?

Grass $\rightarrow$ Deer $\rightarrow$ Tiger

(A) The population of tiger increases
(B) The population of grass decreases
(C) Tiger will start eating grass
(D) The population of tiger decreases and the population of grass increases

Q.19 The decomposers in an ecosystem
(A) convert inorganic material, to simpler forms
(B) convert organic material to inorganic forms
(C) convert inorganic materials into organic compounds
(D) do not breakdown organic compounds.

Q.20 If a grass hopper is eaten by a frog, then the energy transfer will be from
(A) producer to decomposer (B) producer to decomposer
(C) primary consumer to secondary consumer (D) secondary consumer to primary consumer

Q.21 The reason for excessive generation of waste is
(A) Use and throw policy (B) Increased availability of food
(C) Non-utilisation of all components of food (D) Increased construction wastes

Q.22 Combustible material can be hygienically disposed off through
(A) Dumping (B) Incineration (C) Composing (D) Recycling

Q.23 The first conference on ozone layer was held in
(A) 1987 (B) 1989 (C) 1992 (D) 2000

Q.24 Rag pickers remove
(A) Plastic, polythene, paper and metal wastes (B) Rags, cardboard, glass articles
(C) Both (A) and (B) (D) Food articles

Q.25 Carcinogenic chemicals produced during recycling of plastics and polythene are
(A) Formaldehyde (B) Polycyclic aromatic compounds
(C) Vinyl chloride (D) Dioxins and furans

Q.26 Who coined the term ecosystem?
(A) Tansley (B) Odum (C) Warming (D) Darwin

Q.27 In every food chain green plants are
(A) Decomposers (B) Producers (C) Consumers (D) None of the above

Q.28 An artificial ecosystem is
(A) Lake (B) Ocean (C) Aquarium (D) Forest

Q.29 Organisation involved in formulating programs for protecting environment is
(A) WHO (B) UNDP (C) UNEP (D) UNICEF

Q.30 Which chemical has been replaced recently?
(A) Malathion (B) Chlorofluorocarbons
(C) Chloroform (D) Ethylene dibromide

Q.31 In the given food chain, suppose the amount of energy at fourth trophic level is 5kJ, what will be the energy available at the producer level?
Grass ⟶ Grasshopper ⟶ Frog ⟶ Snake ⟶ Hawk
(A) 5 kJ (B) 50 kJ (C) 500 kJ (D) 5000 kJ

Q.32 Organisms which synthesise carbohydrates from inorganic compounds using radiant energy are called
(A) decomposers (B) producers (C) herbivores (D) carnivores

Q.33 In an ecosystem, the 10% of energy available for transfer from on trophic level to the next is in the form of
(A) heat energy (B) light energy (C) chemical energy (D) mechanical energy

Q.34 Flow of energy in an ecosystem is always
(A) unidirectional (B) bidirectional (C) multi directional (D) no specific direction

Q.35 In the following groups of materials, which group(s) contains only non-biodegradable items?
(i) Wood, paper, leather (ii) Polythene, detergent, PVC
(iii) Plastic, detergent, grass (iv) Plastic, bakelite, DDT
(A) (iii) (B) (iv) (C) (i) and (iii) (D) (ii) and (iv)

Q.36 Which of the following limits the number of trophic levels in a food chain?
(A) Decrease in energy at higher trophic levels (B) Dufficient food supply
(C) Polluted air (D) Water

Q.37 Which of the statement is incorrect?
(A) All green plants and blue green algae are producers
(B) Green plants get their food from organic compounds
(C) Producers prepare their own food from inorganic compounds
(D) Plants convert solar energy into chemical energy.

Q.38 Which group of organisms are not constituents of a food chain?
(i) Grass, lion, rabbit, wolf (ii) Plankton, man, fish, grasshopper
(iii) Wolf, grass, snake, tiger (iv) Frog, snake, eagle, grass, grasshopper
(A) (i) and (iii) (B) (iii) and (iv) (C) (ii) and (iii) (D) (i) and (iv)

Q.39 What will happen if deer is missing in the food chain given below?

Grass $\longrightarrow$ Deer $\longrightarrow$ Tiger

(A) The population of tiger increases
(B) The population of grass decreases
(C) Tiger will start eating grass
(D) The population of tiger decreases and the population of grass increases

Q.40 Which one is recyclable waste ?
(A) paper (B) Torn clothes
(C) Metallic and plastic discards (D) All the above

Q.41 Rag pickers remove
(A) Plastic, polythene, paper and metal wastes (B) Rags, cardboard, glass articles
(C) Both (A) and (B) (D) Food articles

Q.42 Carcinogenic chemicals produced during recycling of plastics and polythene are
(A) Formaldehyde (B) Polycyclic aromatic
(C) Vinyl chloride (D) Dioxins and furans.

Q.43 Which is abiotic component of ecosystem?
(A) Humus (B) Bacteria (C) Plants (D) Fungi

Q.44 Who coined the term ecosystem ?
(A) Tansley (B) Odum (C) Warming (D) Darwin

Q.45 In every food chain green plants are
(A) Decomposers (B) Producers (C) Consumers (D) None of the above

Q.46 Which one is present in maximum number an ecosystem?
(A) Herbivores (B) Carnivores (C) Producers (D) Omnivores

Q.47 An artificial ecosystem is
(A) Lake (B) Ocean (C) Aquarium (D) Forest

Q.48 Organisation involved in formulating programmes for protecting environment is
(A) WHO (B) UNDP (C) UNEP (D) UNICEF

Q.49 Which chemical has been replaced recently
(A) Malathion (B) Chlorofluorocarbons
(C) Chloroform (D) Ethylene dibromide

Q.50 Which one of the following is an artificial ecosystem ?
(A) Pond (B) Crop field (C) Lake (D) Forest

Q.51 In a food Chain, the third trophic level is always occupied by
(A) Carnivores (B) Herbivores (C) Decomposers (D) Producers

Q.52 An ecosystem includes
(A) all living organisms
(B) non-living objects
(C) both living organisms and non-living objects
(D) sometimes living organisms and sometimes non-living objects

Q.53 In the given food chain, suppose the amount of energy at fourth tropic level is 5 kJ, what will be the energy available at the producer level ?
Grass $\rightarrow$ Grasshopper $\rightarrow$ Frog $\rightarrow$ Snake $\rightarrow$ Hawk
(A) 5 kJ (B) 50 kJ (C) 500 kJ (D) 5000 kJ

Q.54 Accumulation of non-biodegradable pesticides in the food chain in increasing amount at each higher trophic level is known as
(A) eutrophication (B) Pollution (C) biomagnification (D) accumulation

Q.55 Depletion of ozone is mainly due to
(A) Chloroflurocarbon compounds (B) carbon monoxide
(C) methane (D) pesticides

Q.56 Organisms which synthesis carbohydrates from inorganic compounds using radiant energy are called
(A) decomposers (B) produces (C) herbivores (D) carnivores

Q.57 In an ecosystem, the 10% of energy available for transfer from one trophic level to the next is in the form of
(A) heat energy (B) light energy (C) chemical energy (D) mechanical energy

Q.58 Organisms of a higher trophic level which feed on several types of organisms belonging to a lower trophic level constitute the
(A) food web (B) ecological pyramid (C) ecosystem (D) food chain

Q.59 Flow of energy in an ecosystem is always
(A) unidirectional (B) bidirectional (C) multi directional (D) no specific direction

Q.60 Which of the following constitute a food-chain?
(A) Grass, wheat and mango (B) Grass, goat and human
(C) Goat, cow and elephant (D) Grass, fish and goat

Q.61 Which of the following are environment-friendly practices?
(A) Carrying cloth-bags to put purchases in while shopping
(B) Switching off unnecessary lights and fans
(C) Walking to school instead of getting your mother to drop you on her scooter
(D) All of the above

SECTION-C

- **Assertion & Reason**

Instructions: In the following questions as Assertion (A) is given followed by a Reason (R). Mark your responses from the following options.

(A) Both Assertion and Reason are true and Reason is the correct explanation of 'Assertion'
(B) Both Assertion and Reason are true and Reason is not the correct explanation of 'Assertion'
(C) Assertion is true but Reason is false
(D) Assertion is false but Reason is true

Q.1 **Assertion:** Each step or level of the food chain forms a trophic level. Generally there are four trophic level in a food chain.
Reason: Very less energy remains after fourth trophic level.

Q.2 **Assertion:** The length and complexity of food chain vary greatly
Reason: It food web is more stable.

Q.3 **Assertion:** Increase in temperature of earth is due to green house gases.
Reason: Ozone increase due to chlorofluoro carbon used in refrigerants and in fire extinguishers.

Q.4 **Assertion:** Supersonic jet cause pollution as they thin out ozone.
Reason: Depletion of ozone cause cataract.

Q.5 **Assertion:** Each ecosystem contain only biotic components
Reason: The autotrophs synthesize food material while heterotrophs utilise and resynthesize it.

SECTION-D

- Match the following (one to one)

Q.1

Column I	Column II
(A) Autotroph	(P) Chlorofluoro carbon
(B) Ozone	(Q) United Nations environment programme
(C) UNEP	(R) Ist Tropic level
(D) CFC	(S) Three atoms of oxygen (O_3)

Q.2

Column I	Column II
(A) Abiotic factor	(P) Food chain
(B) Natural ecosystem	(Q) Forest, Ponds and Lakes
(C) Ozone protects us from	(R) Physical factors
(D) Trophic level	(S) Ultraviolet radiation

ANSWERS

CONCEPT APPLICATION LEVEL - II

SECTION-B

Q.1	B	Q.2	B	Q.3	C	Q.4	B	Q.5	A	Q.6	B	Q.7	A
Q.8	D	Q.9	A	Q.10	B	Q.11	B	Q.12	B	Q.13	D	Q.14	C
Q.15	A	Q.16	A	Q.17	D	Q.18	B	Q.19	B	Q.20	D	Q.21	B
Q.22	D	Q.23	C	Q.24	B	Q.25	C	Q.26	C	Q.27	C	Q.28	D
Q.29	A	Q.30	C	Q.31	C	Q.32	A	Q.33	D	Q.34	D	Q.35	A

CONCEPT APPLICATION LEVEL - III

SECTION-A

1. Enzyme, Microorganism
2. Green house effect
3. Food chain
4. United Nations environment programme
5. Photosynthesis
6. Ecosystem
7. Chlorofluoro carbon (CFC)
8. Biomagnification
9. Consumers
10. 10%

SECTION-B

Q.1	C	Q.2	C	Q.3	B	Q.4	B	Q.5	C	Q.6	D	Q.7	A
Q.8	A	Q.9	D	Q.10	D	Q.11	C	Q.12	D	Q.13	A	Q.14	B
Q.15	C	Q.16	A	Q.17	C	Q.18	D	Q.19	B	Q.20	C	Q.21	A
Q.22	B	Q.23	A	Q.24	C	Q.25	D	Q.26	A	Q.27	B	Q.28	C
Q.29	C	Q.30	B	Q.31	D	Q.32	B	Q.33	C	Q.34	A	Q.35	D
Q.36	A	Q.37	B	Q.38	C	Q.39	D	Q.40	D	Q.41	C	Q.42	D
Q.43	A	Q.44	A	Q.45	B	Q.46	C	Q.47	C	Q.48	C	Q.49	B
Q.50	B	Q.51	A	Q.52	C	Q.53	D	Q.54	C	Q.55	A	Q.56	B
Q.57	C	Q.58	A	Q.59	A	Q.60	B	Q.61	D				

SECTION-C

1.	A	2.	B	3.	C	4.	B	5.	D

SECTION-D

1. (A)-(R), (B)-(S), (C)-(Q), (D)-(P)
2. (A)-(R), (B)-(Q), (C)-(S), (D)-(P)

6 MANAGEMENT OF NATURAL RESOURCES

RESOURCE

- **Resource is** a source of supply kept in reserve.

NATURAL RESOURCE

- *"Natural Resources are those components of our environment which are used to support life."* They can be drawn upon from air, water or soil, means any part of our environment.
- Natural Resource are non living and living components of nature which are being used or have the potential of being used by human beings for meeting their requirements of food, fodder, shelter, clothing, articles of use and recreation.
  Example : Forests, wildlife, water, coal and petroleum.
- Depending upon their availability, natural resources are either inexhaustible or exhaustible.

(i) **Inexhaustible resources** are those resources which occur in such abundance that they are unlikely to get exhausted with time, e.g., water, and solar energy.

(ii) **Exhaustible resources** are resources which are likely to diminish and get exhausted with continuous exploitation. They are of two types, renewable and non-renewable.

(a) **Renewable resources** are exhaustible resources that are being replenished naturally and are, therefore, likely to remain available if they are not used beyond their renewability, e.g., forests, wildlife, soil.

(b) **Non-renewable resources** are those resources which are likely to get exhausted with continued use because of lacks of regeneration, e.g., fossil fuels.

MANAGEMENT OF NATURAL RESOURCES :

Introduction :

- We often hear or read about environmental problems.
- These are often global-level problems and we feel helpless to make any changes.
- There are international laws and regulations, and then there are our own national laws and acts for environmental protection.
- There are national and international organisations also working towards protecting our environment.
- The multi core project of Ganga Action Plan came about in 1985 because the quality of water in the ganga was so poor.

Sustainable Development :

- Sustainable development is related to judicious use of resources and due care of the environment.
- It means use of resources for development in a more meaningful manner.
- A very good definition of sustainable development is "**Sustainable development is the development that meet the needs of present without compromising the ability of future generations to meet their own needs.**"
- Economic development must be linked to environmental conservation.
- Government alone or some non-government organisations cannot make it possible.
- It requires involvement of all people.
- For a healthy environment 33% of land should be under forest cover.

Why is Management of Resources Required ?

Management of resources is required for following reasons :

(i) Many of the important resources are not everlasting, they are present in limited amount. Therefore, there is a need to use them judiciously.

(ii) To use them in an ecofriendly manner. It means to extract and use the resources in such a way that it does not affect the environment adversely. (No pollution, no harm to wild life).

(iii) To ensure their availability for future generation.

(iv) To ensure their equal and round the year, distribution to all.

(v) Moreover, it is our normal responsibility also to hand over a same or better environment to our future generations.

(vi) There is minimum wastage, disposal of waste is safe in sustainable management.

Pollution of the Ganga:

- The Ganga runs its course of over 2500 km from Gangotri in the Himalayas to Ganga Sagar in the Bay of Bengal.
- It is being turned into a drain by more than a hundred towns and cities in Uttar Pradesh, Bihar and West Bengal that pour their garbage and excreta into it.
- Largely untreated sewage is dumped into the Ganga every day.
- In addition pollution is caused by other human activities like bathing, washing of clothes and immersion of ashes or unburnt matter also. And then, industries contribute chemical effluents to the Ganga's pollution load and the toxicity kills fishes in large section of the river.

THREE R'S TO SAVE THE ENVIRONMENT :

- **Reduce :** This means 'to use less'. We can save electricity by switching off unnecessary lights and fans. We can save water by repairing leaky taps.
- **Recycle :** This means that we can collect plastic, paper, glass and metal items and recycle these materials to make required things instead of synthesizing or extracting fresh plastic, paper, glass or metal. In order to recycle, we first need to segregate our waste so that the material that can be recycled is not dumped along with other waste.
- **Reuse :** This is actually even better than recycling because the process of recycling uses some energy. In the 'reuse' strategy, we can simply use things again and again.

Knowledge Enhancer

- **Environmental Laws**
- One of the fundamental rights, according to the Indian constitution is the 'Right to life' which means right to healthy environment.
- Various laws have been enacted by the Government of India at different time.
- Some of the important ones are given below :
  - Forest Act, 1972, 1980.
  - Wildlife Protection Act, 1972 (amended in 1991)
  - The Water (Prevention and control of Pollution) Cess Act, 1977 (amended in 1991)
  - The Air (Prevention and control of Pollution) Cess Act, 1981 (amended in 1987)
  - The Environment Protection Act, 1986
  - Prevention of Cruelty of Animal Act, 1960
  - The Motor Vehicle Act, 1938 (amended in 1988)
  - **UNEP (United Nations Environment Programme)**
  - **IPCC (Intergovernmental Panel on Climatic Change)**

Need of Manage Our Resources :

Our natural resources are limited with the rapid increase in human population. Due to improvement in health care, the demand for all resources is also increasing. Management of natural resources requires long term perspective to meet the needs and aspirations of future generations. Natural resources should be managed in such a way that every one of the society is benefited from its development. The waste generated from exploration of natural resources should be disposed off safely. For instance, mining causes pollution due to discard of large amount of slag during metal extraction.

Do you known

- There are two main categories of conservation :

(i) **In-situ** conservation where conservation is done in their natural habitats.
For example, National parks, wild life sanctuaries etc.

(ii) **Ex-situ** conservation where conservation is done outside their habitats.
For example, Botanical gardens, Zoos, seed banks, tissue culture etc.

BIODIVERSITY :

- It is the existence of a wide variety of species of plants, animals and microorganism in a natural habitat within a particular environment.
- Biodiversity of an area is the number of species or range of different life forms found there. Forests are 'biodiversity hotspots'.

Use of forests (Significance of Forests)

- They serve many economic, protective and regulatory functions.

(i) Forests are great centres of biodiversity. They provide habitat to large number of animals.

(ii) Forests give us many substances of economic importance, like timber, fuels, wood, medicine, food item, spices, gum, resin, bamboo and many other useful material, Tendu leaves for making bidi.

(iii) They help in maintaining fix amount of oxygen and carbon dioxide in atmosphere.
(iv) They help in bringing rain, reduce temperature of the area.
(v) They absorb pollutants and control flood.
(vi) They serve as source of aesthetics, inspiration.
(vii) There are many forest based industries, like timber, paper, lac, sports equipments etc.
(viii) They check soil erosion.

PRACTICES FOR CONSERVATION AND PROTECTION OF ENVIRONMENT:

- Conservation means 'to keep safe' whereas preservation means 'to maintain the environment as it is'.
- Various practices which can help in conserving and protecting our environment are as follows
  - The practice of crop rotation helps in conserving soil.
  - Judicious use of fertilizers, intensive cropping, proper irrigating and drainage help in the conservation of soil.
  - The treatment of sewage prevents pollution of water bodies and helps in conserving fishes and other aquatic life forms.
  - National parks and wildlife sanctuaries should be established throughout the country in order to protect and conserve wild animals, birds and plant species.
  - New trees should be planted in place of those cut for various purposes, which will protect the earth from excessive heating.
  - Harvesting of rain helps in the conservation of groundwater.
  - Composting of solid organic waste for biogas and manure.

WILDLIFE :

- It means all those naturally occurring animals, plants and their species which are not cultivated, domesticated and tamed.

Wildlife Conservation :

- It is the sensible use of the earth's natural resources in order to avoid excessive degradation and betterment of the environment.
- It includes – the search for alternative food and fuel supplies when these are endangered, an awareness of the dangers of pollution and the maintenance and preservation of habitats and its biodiversity.

Steps for conservation of wildlife :

(A) Laws should be imposed to ban poaching or capturing of any animal or bird belonging to an endangered species.
(B) The natural habitats of wild animals and birds should be preserved by establishing National Parks, Sanctuaries and Biosphere reserves throughout the country.
(C) The Government Department should conduct periodic surveys of National Parks, Sanctuaries and Biosphere Reserves to have a knowledge of all the species of wild animals and birds.
(D) More attention should be given to conserve the endangered species of wild animals and birds to prevent their extinction.
(E) Unauthorized cutting of forest trees should be stopped.

STAKEHOLDERS OF FORESTS :

- The conservation of forests depend on its forest resources or its various stakeholder, who are as follows :

People Who Live in or Around Forests :

(i) They depend on forest produce, for various aspects of their life.
(ii) The local people need large quantities of firewood, small timber.
(iii) Bamboo is used to make slates for huts and baskets for collecting and storing food.
(iv) Implements for agriculture, fishing and hunting are largely made of wood.
(v) People collect fruits, nuts and medicines from forests, their cattle also graze in forest.

Forest Department of the Government :

(i) Which owns the land and controls the forest resources.
(ii) People develop practices to ensure that forest resources are used in a sustainable manner.
(iii) The forest resources were overexploited after the British took control of the forest.
(iv) Forest department of independent India then owned the land and control the resources of the forest but local needs such as herbs, fruits and fodder were ignored.
(v) Monoculture of pine, teak or eucalyptus have been started which can destroy the bio-diversity of the area.

Industrialist :

(i) Industries consider the forest as a source of raw material for its factories.
(ii) These industries are not interested for the sustainability of the forest in one area as they go to a different area after cutting down all tree in one area.

Wildlife and Nature Enthusiasts :

(i) They are not dependent of the forest but conserve nature and take part in its management.
(ii) Conservationists started with conserving large animals but are now preserving biodiversity as a whole.
(iii) The local people, for instance the Bishnoi community in Rajasthan worked for conservation of forest and wildlife as a religious act. Thus management of forest resources has to take the interests of various stakeholder into account.
(iv) Environment Conservationists and Nature Enthusiasts who are not in any way dependent on the forests. NGOs like the World Wide Fund for Nature (WWF), Centre for Science and Environment (CSE), International Union for Conservation of Nature and Natural Resources (IUCN) often exercise a considerable say in policy and management of forests. Historically. conservationists took up causes of protecting large animals like tigers (Project Tiger), lions, elephants and rhinoceros.

BISHNOI COMMUNITY OF RAJASTHAN

- For Bishnoi community of Rajasthan conservation of forest and wildlife is religious belief. For these people conservation of nature is the work of utmost importance.
- **Khejri** is known as **State Tree of Rajasthan**.
- A brave lady of Bishnoi community Amrita Devi sacrificed her life in 1731 alongwith 363 others for the protection of Khejri trees in Khejarali village near Jodhpur in Rajasthan.
- The Government of India has instituted an **Amrita Devi Bishnoi National Award for wildlife conservation** in the memory of Amrita Devi Bishnoi.

CHIPKO MOVEMENT

- The **Chipko Andolan** (Chipko movement) also shows love and care of people to the nature and natural resources.
- The word 'Chipko andolan' means, Hug the tree movement.
- The movement originated from an incident in a remote village named Reni in Garhwal, Uttarakhand during the early 1970s.
- A logging contractor was allowed to fell trees in a forest close to this village.
- The local people opposed this decision.
- They were of the opinion that cutting of this forest would disturb the ecological balance.
- On day, when all the men of that village were out for work, the contractor's worker came in the forest to cut the trees.
- The woman of the village fought with this situation with tremendous courage.
- They reached the forest quickly and clapsed the tree trunks (hug the tree trunk with both hands open) preventing the workers from felling the trees.
- In this way, forest trees were saved. The contractor, then ran away from the forest.
- Magsaysay Award recipient Sunderlal Bahuguna gave momentum to the 'Chipko Andolan' in Tehri Gharwal district in Uttrakhand.

Do you Know

Botanical name of Khejri is *Prosopis cineraria*.

- Local people live in harmony with the forests.
- Local people living traditionally with forest do not do any harm to the forest, rather they help the forest replenishment.
- The relationship is mutually beneficial. Here is an example; The **alpine meadow of Himalayan** area were regularly grazed by the sheeps of the nomadic shephered.
- Meadows are grasslands of the great Himalayan National Park. During summer season only these shephered used to take their sheeps up to these meadow.
- When the area was declared as a National Park, this practice was stopped.
- Now it has been seen that without the regular grazing by sheeps the area has lost its special features.
- The grass, now grows very tall and then falls over, therefore, there is no fresh growth.
- It is clear that limited interactions between human and their domesticated animals with their habitat like forest is mutually beneficial to both.

- It also shows that keeping the local people out, by using force from the management of protected area cannot be successful in long run.
- Local people only cannot be blamed for the depletion of forest resources.
- The main cause of deforestation is ever increasing needs of industries or development projects, like buildings, roads and dams.
- The so called **Eco-tourism** has also caused great damage to these reserves.
- Making roads in forest area which lead to hotels/lodge and other arrangements made for the convenience of tourists damage the ecosystem.

BEST STRATEGY FOR FOREST MANAGEMENT

- Now it has been realized that limited human activities have been very much a part of the forest.
- Limited activities of locals do not damage the forests.
- Yes, we have to ensure the limit of human interference.
- The management of the forest resources should be environmentally and developmentally sound.
- It means that on one hand, it should support local people; while on the other hand, it should not degrade quality of the forest.
- **The benefits of the controlled exploitation must go to local people.**
- It is an example of decentralised economic growth and ecological conservation going hand in hand. Environment has enough to fulfil our needs not greed.

METHOD OF USE OF RESOURCES MAKES A DIFFERENCE

- The local people of the forest area and contractor both use forest. But the difference is in their method of use.
- The contractor would have felled the trees, destroying them forever.
- The local communities cut the dried branches and pluck the leaves.
- This practice allows the forest to replenish over time.
- The message of Chipko movement quickly spread across communities and media and forced the government to decide their priorities in use of forest produce.
- Forest resources were often made available for industrial use at rate far below the market value.
- Not only this, these are denied to local people.
- Now it has been realised even by forest department that participation of local people can indeed lead to efficient management of forests.

JOINT FOREST MANAGEMENT (JFM)

- This is an example of people's participation in management of forests.
- The condition of the forests of south western districts of West Bengal was very poor till 1972.
- Despite many sincere attempts the degraded Sal forests of the area could not be revived.
- To stop the interference of local people in forests the locals were sent far away from the forest area.
- There were frequent clashes between forest officials and villagers.
- An intelligent, far seeing forest officer Mr. A. K. Banerjee posted at **Arbari forest range** of Midnapore district used different strategy.
- He involved villagers in the protection of 1272 hectares of badly degraded Sal forests.
- In return of their services in protection of the forest villagers were given employment.

- They were employed in silviculture and harvesting of the forest products.
- In addition to this they were also given 25% of final harvest.
- They were also allowed to collect fuelwood and fodder on payment of a nominal fee.
- With the active and willing participation of the local inhabitants of the area the Sal forests recovered soon.
- The recovery was really remarkable, as a highly degraded and worthless forest was converted into a multicrore asset.

CONSERVATION OF FORESTS

- On the basis of above discussed facts forest can be conserved effectively by

(i) Checking deforestation and enforcing Forest Protection Act, strictly.

(ii) Better management of forests and involvement of local communities in forest protection (Joint Forest Management).

(iii) Bringing more land under forest cultivation, **Afforestation**.

(iv) Replenishing the cut forest, **Reforestation**.

(v) Making more biosphere reserves and national parks.

(vi) Public awareness.

- **Silviculture :** The scientific method of growing of forest trees is called silviculture.
- **Afforestation :** Planting trees in an area where there were no trees earlier is known as afforestation.
- **Reforestation :** Planting trees is an area which was under forest cover earlier is known as reforestation. It is done after felling of trees or after a forest fire etc.
- **Deforestation :** Felling of forest trees is known as deforestation. Deforestation leads to soil erosion, frequent floods, loss of habitats, loss of biodiversity and climatic change etc.

RED DATA BOOK

The IUCN (International Union for the Conservation of Nature and Natural Resources) maintains an international list, published as the Red Data Book. The aim of the list is to impart information to the public and policy makers about the urgency of conservation problems to the public and policy makers. The list recognises 8 Red list categories of species.

(i) Extinct
(ii) Extinct in the world
(iii) Critically endangered
(iv) Endangered
(v) Vulnerable
(vi) Low risk
(vii) Data deficient
(viii) Not evaluated

WILD LIFE

- Wildlife is conserved in **Wildlife Sanctuaries, National Parks, Biosphere Reserves, Community Reserves, Sacred groves** etc.
- A Wildlife Protection Act was enacted in 1972 which provides legal protection to wild life.
- Threatened species are being given special attention for conservation.
- We should say 'No' to animal products, like ivory etc.
- Their conservation can be ensured by conserving ecosystem as a whole.
- Public awareness plays a vital role in conservation of wild life.

WATER AS A BASIC NATURAL RESOURCE :

(i) It is a valuable national asset.
(ii) It is the main requirement of human being.
(iii) Water is of two types - salt water and fresh water.
(iv) Fresh water is an unlimited natural resource, it can be obtained from three natural resources - rain water, surface water and ground water.
(v) Human intervention pollutes water and also changes the availability of water in various regions.

Water Sources :

(i) Rain in India is due to monsoon.
(ii) Failure to sustain underground water due to loss of vegetative cover, development of water demanding crop and pollution from industrial effluents.
(iii) Small dams, canals and tank were used for irrigation purpose and to fulfill the basic minimum needs.
(iv) Large dams and canals were made by British as well as our own government.
(v) Due to the mega project, local irrigation methods got neglected and the local people lost control over management of local water sources.
(vi) Large dams and canals were made by British as well as our own government.

Management of Water Resources :

◆ It includes :
(i) Interacted water-shed plan for drinking, irrigation and industrial uses.
(ii) Flood control
(iii) Transfer of surplus water to water deficiet basins by inter-linking of rivers.
(iv) Hydro geological survey to identify over-exploited areas.
(v) Artificial recharging of the ground water.
(vi) Mass awareness programmes through public or private agencies.
(vii) **Dams :** They are massive barriers built across rivers and streams to confined and utilize the flow of water for human purposes such as irrigation and generation of electricity.
- Large dams can also ensure the storage of adequate water.
- Canal system leading from dams transfer large quantity of water upto great distances, e.g. Indira Gandhi Canal or Rajasthan brought greenery to considerable areas.
- Purposes for building a dam :
- Generation of electricity
- Irrigation
- Control of flood which either stops or slows the amount of water in the river.
- **Bhakra Dam** built across the river Sutlej in Punjab.
- **Sardar Sarovar Dam** built on river Narmada in 1940 in Gujarat.
- **Tehri Dam** on river Ganga in Tehri, Uttranchal.
- **Tawar Dam** on the Tawa river in Hoshangabad (MP).
- **Mettur Dam** in Cauveri river in Tamil Nadu is the oldest dam.
- **Criticism about large dams :**
- Social problems : They displace large number of farmers and tribals.
- Economic problems : They consume huge amount of public money without proportionate benefit.
- Environmental problems. As they cause deforestation and loss of biological diversity.

Mismanagement of Water Distribution :

- Due to mismanagement in distribution of water, the benefit of constructing a dam goes to few people only. For example, people close to the water source grow water intensive crop like sugarcane and rice while people further downstream do not get any water. This resulted in discontentment among the people who has been displaced by building of dam.

Groundwater Dams.

Run off and rain water is stored in underground dams connected to crop field and surface water tanks. The technique was perfected by Magassay Award winner **Water Man** of Rajasthan, Rajinder Singh.

Management of resources should ensure

(i) Equitable distribution of resources so that benefit of the resources reaches all the sections of society instead of a few rich ones.

(ii) Exploitation of resources should be just enough to meet the requirement.

(iii) There should be minimum wastage during processing of the resource.

(iv) Safe disposal of the waste should be ensured.
For example, several tonnes of slag is discarded for every tonne of metal extracted. A proper disposal of **slag** must be planned to prevent degradation of environment.

Management of Water Pollution:

Some common methods of measuring quality of water are

(i) **Coliform Count.** It measures the most probable number or MPN of coliform bacteria in 100 ml of water.

(ii) **BOD (Biochemical Oxygen Demand)**. It is amount of oxygen required in milligrams for five days for micro-organisms to metabolize organic matter in one litre of water at 20°C. Pollution is low if BOD is below 1500 mg/l, medium between 1500–4000 mg/l and high above 4000 mg/l.

(iii) **T.D.S. (Total Dissolved Substances).** It indicates hardness or softness in 200 CC of water. Hard water with TDS above 120 ppm is not suitable for drinking, cooking, washing, bathing and industrial purposes.

(iv) **pH.** It is the easiest method as universal pH indicator papers are available. Dipping a paper in water and comparing the change in colour with the standard chart gives information about pH of the water. **Acidic pH indicates pollution while alkaline pH indicates hardness.**

Watershed management :

It means scientific conservation of soil and water to increase the biomass production.

- Watershed is a high raised area which is source of run off to low lying areas. Growing more trees in watershed areas increases retention of more rain water and protection of soil from erosion. Therefore, watershed management develops the primary resources of land and water. It enhances the development of secondary resources of plants, animals and other biota. The enhanced productivity increases the income of watershed community. There are fewer droughts and floods downstream. Silting of downstream dams and reservoirs is also reduced.
- Watershed management not only increases the production and income of the watershed community but also overcomes drought and flood.
- It increases the life of downstream dam and reservoirs.
- The area from which rainfall flows into a reservoir river system is called catchment area.

Water harvesting :

It means capturing rainwater where it falls or capturing the runoff water in a local area and talking measures to keep the water clean by not allowing polluting activities to take place.

(A) Techniques of water harvesting : Water harvesting techniques are mainly location specific. It is an age - old concept in India.

- Khadins, tanks and nadis in Rajasthan.
- Bandharas and tals in Maharashtra
- Ahars and Pynes in Bihar
- Kulhs in Himanchal Pradesh
- Ponds in kandi belt of Jammu.
- Eris (tanks) in Tamilnadu.
- Suragams in kerala.
- Kattas in Karnataka.
- Due to own control of the local population over exploitation of the local water resources is reduced.

(B) Some of the water harvesting techniques are :

- Capturing of runoff water from roof tops.
- Capturing of runoff water from local catchments.
- Capturing seasonal flood water from local streams.

(C) Benefits of water harvesting :

- Provide drinking water.
- Provide irrigation water.
- Increase in ground water resources.
- Reduces storm water discharge, urban flood and overloading of sewage treatment plants.

(D) Advantages of ground water :

- It does not evaporate.
- It spreads out to recharge wells.
- It provides moisture for vegetation.
- It does not provide breeding grounds for mosquitoes.
- It is relatively protected from contamination by human and animal waste.

(E) Traditional water harvesting system :

- The water harvesting structures are mainly crescent shaped.
- Monsoon rains fill ponds behind the structures.
- The large structure hold water throughout the year while most dry up after monsoon.
- The main purpose of this system is to recharge the ground water and not to hold surface water.

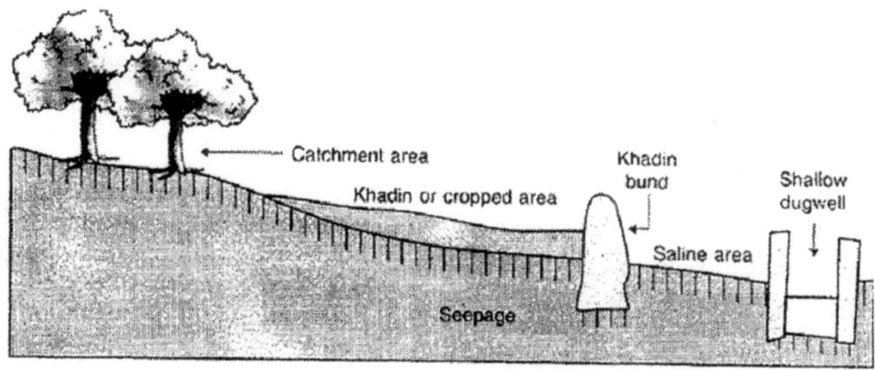

Traditional water harvesting system

FOSSIL FUELS :

- These fuels are obtained from the remain of plants and animals, which got buried beneath the earth millions of years ago, changed into coal, petroleum and natural gas due to excessive heat and high pressure inside the earth.

Non-Renewable Energy Sources :

- These are energy sources which cannot be replaced easily when they get exhausted and are also called conventional sources of energy. They are used traditionally for many years and take millions of years to form e.g. Fossil fuels.

(i) **Coal :** It contains carbon and its compound mainly with nitrogen, oxygen, sulphur and hydrogen. It also consists of inorganic matter.

Formation of coal. Coal is formed of organic matter which got buried under the earth 300 million years ago. Due to high pressure and temperature inside the earth, this organic matter changed into coal, that is why, coal is called fossil fuel.

(ii) **Petroleum :** 'Petro' means rocks and 'oleum' means oil, petroleum is therefore the oil found in rocks. It is a complex mixture of solid, liquid and gaseous hydrocarbons. It also contains small amounts of other compounds of carbon, hydrogen, oxygen, nitrogen and sulphur. Large reservoirs of petroleum have been preserved by nature for millions of years between porous rocks beneath the earth.

Formation of petroleum. It is formed by the decay of very small (tiny) marine animals and plant buried under the earth about 400 million years ago. Due to excess of heat and pressure it changed into oil called petroleum. It is a fossil fuel.

Conservation of Coal and Petroleum :

- It means more efficient use with regard to economic, social and environmental cost and benefits which result in attainment of higher efficiency, minimisation of wastage and protection of the environment.
- We can conserve coal and petroleum by their judicious use and substituting them by other resources wherever feasible.
- Conservation of coal and petroleum is a joint responsibility of the industries, citizens and government where each one has significant role in Management of Natural Resources.

Necessity of Judicious Use of Coal and Petroleum :

- The fossil fuels, coal and petroleum get exhausted and their combustion pollutes our environment, so a judicious use of these resources is necessary.
- When combustion take place, oxides of carbon, hydrogen, nitrogen and sulphur are formed.
- Carbon monoxide is formed instead of carbon dioxide if there is insufficient air.
- The oxides of sulphur, nitrogen and carbon monoxide are poisonous at high concentrations.
- Carbon dioxide is a green-house gas which leads to global warming.

Uses of Fossil Fuels :

(i) In thermal power plants and steam engines.

(ii) Petroleum products like petrol and diesel are used as fuel in motor vehicles and ships. Other products like kerosene and LPG are used for cooking purpose.

Management of Fossil Fuels :

- The natural gas is a good alternative to fossil fuels like coal and petroleum.
- The use of alternative source of non-conventional energy such as solar energy, wind energy, biomass energy, etc., should be promoted to save the reserves of fossil fuels.
- Biogas can also be used for various purposes.

Euro I and Euro II Norms

Emission norms for petrol driven cars are designated as euro-I (June 1999) and euro-II (April 2000). They are related to three parameters-hydrocarbons and nitrogen oxides, carbon monoxide and particulate matter

	Old	Euro–I	Euro–II
Hydrocarbons and Nitrogen oxides	3–4·6 ppm	0·97 ppm	0·5 ppm
Carbon monoxide	6·68–12·00 ppm	2·72 ppm	2·2 ppm
Particulate Matter	Not enforced	0·14 ppm	Nil

The less emission of pollutants has resulted from use of catalytic converters, tune ups and multiple-point fuel injection systems.

POINTS TO REMEMBER

Emission of Carbon Dioxide

- Find out the international norms to regulate the emission of carbon dioxide and discuss in class about how we can contribute meeting these norms.
- **Kyoto Protocol (Dec. 1997)** was signed by India in August 2002.
- Under the protocol India is to reduce CO_2 emission by 5.2% of 1990 level during 2008-2012.
- A national clean development mechanism (CDM) authority was set up in December 2003 to formulate projects for reducing emission of CO_2 and other gree house gases.
- The authority has approved 252 projects by March 2006. The major thrust areas are increasing vegetation cover, reducing CO_2 emission by improving technology and non-burning of organic wastes.

Organisation for Conservation of Environment and Natural Resources

- A number of non-governmental organisations (NGOs) are active in focussing attention of the public, industry and government over protecting the environment and natural resources.
- Green Peace Movement is an international non-governmental organisation of environmentalists.
- Chipko Movement and Environment Society are Indian organisations engaged in hightlighting environment issues.
- All schools are also required to establish eco clubs.
  - An eco-club is a club involved in creating environmental awarness amgonst its members, spreading the same in society and preventing environment degradation of surroundings.

1. The natural resources like water, soil, forests, wild-life, coal, petroleum etc. should be utilized in a sustainable manner in order to conserve our environment.
2. Over-exploitation of natural resources causes several environmental problems.
3. There are a number of laws at national and international level to safeguard our environment.
4. Ganga Action Plan was introduced in 1985 to improve the poor water quality of Ganga River.
5. The quality of water has to be assessed scientifically before utilizing it for various purposes.
6. We can adopt the 3 R's – Reduce, Recycle and Reuse, to conserve our environment.
7. Using our resources judiciously will prevent wastage and conserve our resources.
8. Recycling materials of paper, plastic, glass etc prevents their fresh extraction thereby reducing the pressure on environment.
9. Reusing items over and over again is another environment friendly method.
10. Sustainable development is the need of the hour to preserve our environment. Here at present human needs are met by keeping in mind the future generation needs.
11. The participation of every individual is essential to bring about sustainable development.
12. Solar energy is converted into usable form by autotrophs and several processes on Earth.
13. Our natural resources should be available equally to everyone and should be used without damaging the environment.
14. We should try to preserve the number and range of biodiversity present in a region.

15. The stakeholders of forests are the local and tribal people of the area, the Forest Department of the Government, the industrialists and the wild life and nature enthusiasts.
16. The local and tribal people depend on the forest products for fulfilling all their needs of shelter, food, transport, fuel, medicines and cattle grazing.
17. The Forest Department of India destroyed the huge biodiversity of forests by converting them into monocultures of commercially important plants. Such forests are useful for industrial purposes and not for local needs.
18. Industrialists are not dependent on the forests of a particular area and hence do not ensure sustainability of forests.
19. The nature and wild life conservationists play an active role in conserving the forest biodiversity.
20. The local people should be actively involved in forest management since they ensure its sustainability.
21. 'Amrita Devi Bishnoi National Award for Wildlife Conservation' is awarded by Government of India in the memory of late Amrita Devi Bishnoi, who laid down her life for protection of trees.
22. Deforestation is mainly caused by industrialism, tourism and development projects.
23. Economic and social development should be achieved with due consideration for ecological conservation.
24. There are many instances of strong protests by the local people against misuse and over-exploitation of forest resources.
25. In Chipko Andolan(which originated in the Reni village of Garhwal), the villagers used to hug the forest trees and prevent their mass felling by the contactors.
26. The local people use the forest resources without destroying the trees.
27. Destruction of forests affects the soil quality and water sources, in addition to reduced availability of forest resources.
28. Combined working of the Forest Department with the local people can ensure the protection and sustainability of forests.
29. By actively involving the villagers in the management of the Arabari forest range, the West Bengal Forest Department was able to revive the degraded Sal forests of the region.
30. Water is an important resource as we need water for fulfilling all our needs.
31. Failure to maintain the ground water level in spite of the plentiful monsoon rains is largely due to human activities like agriculture, pollution and deforestation.
32. In pre-British India, water management was carried out locally and optimally, according to the agricultural and daily needs of the local people.
33. Mega-projects like large dams and canals were initiated by the British and led to the neglect of the local water sources and irrigation methods.
34. Dual purpose of irrigation and electricity generation is achieved by large dams.
35. Mismanagement of large dams and canal systems leads to unequal distribution of water and benefits.
36. Building large dams brings about social, economic and environmental problems.
37. The construction of several dams like Tehri dam and Tawa Dam displaced several poor tribals and peasants without satisfactory rehabilitation or compensation.
38. In watershed management, land and water resources are developed scientifically to increase the biomass production with an aim to conserve the ecosystem.

39. Updating the ancient water harvesting systems has recharged ground water levels and is a viable option to the large scale water storage projects.
40. Water harvesting techniques reduces mismanagement of water resources and ensures benefits for the local people. State Water harvesting structures

State	Water harvesting structures
Rajasthan	Khadins, tanks, nadis
Maharashtra	Bandharas, tals
Uttar Pradesh	Bundhis
Madhya Pradesh	Bundhis
Bihar	Ahars, pynes
Himachal Pradesh	Kulhs
Jammu	Ponds
Tamil Nadu	Eris
Kerals	Surangams
Karnataka	Kattas

41. Water harvesting structures replenishes the ground water levels.
42. Ground water is polluted from pollution, breeding of mosquitoes and evaporation and constitutes an important source of water.
43. Fossil fuels like coal and petroleum have to be used very carefully due to the following reasons:
(i) They are present in extremely limited quantity.
(ii) Their combustion produces harmful gases such as oxides of nitrogen and sulphur and a green house gas i.e. carbon dioxide.
(iii) The huge reservoirs of carbon present in fossil fuels will be converted into carbon dioxide leading to increased global warming.
44. Each person can help in conservation of natural resources by making environment-friendly choices in life as much as possible.
45. Sustainable management of natural resources is the only option available to conserve our natural resources and ensure its equitable distribution to everyone.

CONCEPT APPLICATION LEVEL - I [NCERT Questions]

Q.1 List the advantages associated with water harvesting at the community level.

Ans. Water harvesting at the community level is capturing, collection and storage of rain water and surface run off for filling either small water bodies or recharging ground water. This is carried out through water shed management, check dams, earthen dams, roof top harvesting and filter wells in flood drains.

Benefits :

(i) It ensures water availability in non-rainy season.

(ii) It reduces the chances of flooding during rainy season.

(iii) Ground water level does not fall as it is regularly recharged.

(iv) Ground water recharge is the best form of water harvesting as the water is filtered and free-from contaminations. It also does not evaporate.

(v) Water becomes available for drinking as well as irrigation.

Q.2 In a village in Karnataka people started cultivating crops all around a lake which was always filled with water. They added fertilizers to their field in order to enhance the yield. Soon they discovered that the water body was completely covered with green floating plants and fishes started dying in large numbers.
Analyse the situation and give reasons for excessive growth of plants and death of the fish in the lake.

Ans. Fertilizer rich run off from fields must have passed into the lake. It caused nutrient enrichment of lake water. The result is excessive growth of algae and other aquatic plants which float on the water surface and produce **water bloom**. Old dead plants produce a lot of organic matter. The submerged plants are also killed due to shading. BOD of water increases. As more and more oxygen is consumed by decomposers little is left for respiration of aquatic animals. Therefore, fish begin to die. The phenomenon of nutrient enrichment of water body that causes formation of water bloom and subsequent killing of aquatic life is called **eutrophication**.

Q.3 Suggest a few measures for controlling carbon dioxide levels in the atmosphere.

Ans. **(i)** **Increasing Vegetation cover.** It will increase utilisation of atmospheric CO_2 in photosynthesis.

(ii) **Seeding of Oceans with phytoplankton.** Increased photosynthetic activity of oceans will result in decreasing CO_2 concentration.

(iii) **Carbonation.** CO_2 released during combustion should not be allowed to pass into atmosphere. Instead, it can be changed into carbonates.

(iv) **Alternate Sources of Energy.** Instead of fossil fuels, hydrogen fuel and solar energy should be used.

(v) **Burning of Litter.** Litter and crop residue should not be burnt but instead converted into manure.

Q.4 Is water conservation necessary ? Give reasons.

Ans. (i) Distribution of fresh water is highly uneven. Large tracts are deficient in rain as well as ground water.

(ii) At most places more water is withdrawn from reservoir and underground source than their recharging.

(iii) Requirement in urban and industrial areas is nearly always higher than the availability.

(iv) Further demand for water is rising by 4 - 8% annually in all fields, whether agriculture, industry or domestic use.

Therefore, water conservation is necessary. Wastage of the resource should be prevented. Waste water should be recycled. Water harvesting involving recharging of ground water should be practised.

Q.5 What changes can you make in your habits to become more environment-friendly?

Ans. We should switch off the electrical appliances when not in use. Water and food should not be wasted. Close the tap when not in use. Dump the objects made of plastic and glass in designated recycling boxes. Plastic, paper, or glass must be recycled or reused and not dumped with other wastes. This is because objects made of plastic do not get decomposed easily. Besides soil fertility, they badly affect our environment. We should dispose the wastes safely and not disperse in public places. These are a few things that can be done to become more environment- friendly.

Q.6 What would be the advantages of exploiting resources with short-term aims?

Ans. There should be a judicious use of natural resources as they are limited in nature. We should not exploit resources for our short term gains as this would only lead to depletion of natural resources for the present generation as well as generations to come. Hence, we can say that there are hardly any advantages of exploiting natural resources for short term gains.

Q.7 How would these advantages differ from the advantages of using a long-term perspective in managing our resources?

Ans. In the case of a long-time perspective in managing our resources, these resources will last for the generations to come. This management ensures uniform distribution among the people. It conserves the natural resources for many years and not just for a few years, as in the case of a short-term perspective in conserving natural resources.

Q.8 Why do you think there should be equitable distribution of resources? What forces would be working against an equitable distribution of our resources?

Ans. Natural resources of the Earth must be distributed among the people uniformly so that each and every one gets his share of the resource.

Human greed, corruption, and the lobby of the rich and powerful are the forces working against an equitable distribution of resources.

Q.9 Why should we conserve forests and wildlife?

Ans. We should conserve forests and wildlife to preserve the biodiversity (range of different life-forms) so as to avoid the loss of ecological stability. A large number of tribes are the habitants in and around the forests. If the forests are not conserved, then it may affect these habitants. Without proper management of forest and wildlife, the quality of soil, the water sources, and even the amount of rainfall may be affected. Without forest and wildlife, life would become impossible for human beings.

Q.10 Suggest some approaches towards the conservation of forests.

Ans. Some approaches towards the conservation of forests are as follows :

(a) People should show their participation in saving the forest by protesting against the cutting of trees. For example, **Chipko Andolan**.

(b) Planting of trees should be increased. Rate of afforestation must be more than that of deforestation.

(c) Some people cut precious trees such as Chandan to earn money. Government should take legal steps to catch these wood smugglers.

(d) Habitants of forests must not be bothered by the forest officials. Otherwise, this would result in the clash between tribal people and the government officials, thereby enhancing the naxal activities in forests.

Q.11 Find out about the traditional systems of water harvesting/management in your region.

Ans. One of the traditional systems of water harvesting used in our region is tanks.

Q.12 Compare the above system with the probable systems in hilly/mountainous areas or plains or plateau regions.

Ans. In plains, the water harvesting structures are crescent-shaped earthen embankments. These are low, straight, and concrete.
In hilly regions, the system of canal irrigation called Kulhs is used for water harvesting.
This involves a collection of rain water in a stream, which is then diverted into manmade channels down the hill sides.

Q.13 Find out the source of water in your region/locality. Is water from this source available to all people living in that area?

Ans. The source of water in our region is ground water. Water from the source is available to all the people living in that area.

Q.14 What changes would you suggest in your home in order to be environment-friendly?

Ans. Changes that can be undertaken in our homes to be environment-friendly are listed below:
(i) Switch off the electrical appliances when not in use.
(ii) Turn the taps off while brushing or bathing and repair the leaking taps.
(iii) Throw biodegradable and non-biodegradable waste into separate bins.
(iv) Construct composting pits.
(v) Food items such as jam, pickles, etc., come packed in plastic bottles. These bottles can later be used for storing things in the kitchen.

Q.15 Can you suggest some changes in your school which would make it environmentfriendly?

Ans. Changes that can be undertaken in our schools to make it environment friendly are listed below:
(i) Electricity can be saved by switching off lights and fans when not required.
(ii) Turn the taps off when not in use.
(iii) Biodegradable and non-biodegradable wastes should be thrown into separate bins.

Q.16 We saw in this chapter that there are four main stakeholders when it comes to forests and wildlife. Which among these should have the authority to decide the management of forest produce? Why do you think so?

Ans. The forest department of the government should have the authority to decide the management of forest produces. This is because the forest department is the care taker of the forest land and is responsible for any damage to the forest.

Q.17 How can you as an individual contribute or make a difference to the management of (a) forests and wildlife, (b) water resources and (c) coal and petroleum?

Ans. (a) **Forest and wildlife:**
(i) We should protest against the cutting of trees (deforestation).
(ii) We should protest against the poaching of wild animals.
(iii) We should stop the annexation of forest land for our use.

(b) **Water resources:**
(i) Turn the taps off while brushing or bathing and repair leaking taps.
(ii) We should practice rainwater harvesting.
(iii) We should avoid the discharge of sewage and other wastes into rivers and other water resources.

(c) Coal and petroleum:

(i) We should take a bus or practice car pooling to avoid excessive use of petroleum.

(ii) We should stop using coal as a fuel (angithis).

(iii) We should use alternative sources of energy such as hydro-energy and solar energy instead of depending largely on coal and petroleum.

Q.18 What can you as an individual do to reduce your consumption of the various natural resources?

Ans. Natural resources such as water, forests, coal and petroleum, etc. are important for the survival of human beings. The ways in which we can reduce the consumption of various natural resources are as follows :

(i) We should stop the cutting of trees (deforestation).

(ii) We should use recycled paper to reduce the cutting down of trees.

(iii) We should not waste water.

(iv) We should practice rainwater harvesting.

(v) We should practice car pooling to avoid the excessive use of petroleum.

(vi) We should use alternative sources of energy such as hydro-energy and solar energy.

Q.19 List five things you have done over the last one week to -

(a) conserve our natural resources

(b) increase the pressure on our natural resources

Ans. (a) To conserve our natural resources:

(i) Travel by a CNG bus for long distances and walk for short distances.

(ii) Use recycled paper

(iii) Throw biodegradable and non-biodegradable waste into separate bins

(iv) Plant trees

(v) Harvest rainwater

(b) To increase the pressure on our natural resources:

(i) Use non-renewable resources of energy

(ii) Waste water

(iii) Waste electricity

(iv) Use plastics and polythene bags for carrying goods

(v) Use escalators

Q.20 On the basis of the issues raised in this chapter, what changes would you incorporate in your life-style in a move towards a sustainable use of our resources?

Ans. One should incorporate the following changes in life-style in a move towards a sustainable use of our resources:

(i) Stop cutting trees and practice plantation of trees.

(ii) Stop using plastic and polythene bags for carrying goods.

(iii) Use recycled paper.

(iv) Throw biodegradable and non-biodegradable waste into separate bins.

(v) Waste minimum amount of water while using and repair leaking taps.

(vi) Practice rainwater harvesting.

(vi) Avoid using vehicles for short distances. Instead, one can walk or cycle to cover short distances. To cover long distances, one should take a bus instead of using personal vehicles.

(vii) Switch off electrical appliances when not in use.

(viii) Use fluorescent tubes in place of bulbs to save electricity.

(ix) Take stairs and avoid using lifts.

(x) During winters, wear an extra sweater to avoid using heaters.

CONCEPT APPLICATION LEVEL - II

SECTION - A

Q.1 List any four advantages of water harvesting.

Ans. Advantages of water harvesting :

– It provide drinking water.
– It provide irrigation water.
– It responsible for increase in ground level water.
– It reduces storm water discharge, urban flood and overloading of sewage treatment plant.

Q.2 Suggest any four changes that you would like to incorporate in the lifestyles of students of your age move towards the sustainable use of available sources.

Ans. Follow the principle of 3'RS
Plant more trees
Use public transport, buses & carpool
Switch of unnecessary lights, fans there by save electricities.

Q.3 Name any four catagories of people who depend on the forest resources. Mentioning major need of each catagory.

Ans. (1) Local people who live around forest, they use forest for grazing cattles, collecting foods, firewood and bamboo.
(2) Industrialist – They collect raw material for industries.
(3) Tourist – They visit forest for recretion.
(4) Forest department of you – They control resources of forest.

Q.4 "Burning fuel is a cause of global warming", Justify this statement.

Ans. Fossil fuels like coals, petroleum are formed from biomass. In addition to carbon they contain, hydrogen, nitrogen & sulphur. When fossil fuel are burnt, the product are CO_2, water vapour, oxides of nitrogen & sulphur. CO_2 is green house gas. Increase in the percentage of CO_2, increases to temperature of earth which leads to global warming.

Q.5 Define the term natural resources.

Ans. Natural resources are the stock of nature such as air, water, soil, coal, minerals, animals and plants that are useful to mankind in many ways.

Q.6 What are abiotic and biotic components of environment?

Ans. The physical components of the environment soil, water, air, light and temperature are termed as abiotic components. The biotic components are all living things such as plants, animals, microorganisms, parasites, predators and human beings which influence the organism's life directly or indirectly because of their presence.

Q.7 What is meant by management and conservation of resources?

Ans. Management and conservation of resources means scientific utilization of resources while maintaining their sustained yield and quality.

Q.8 What is meant by global warming?

Ans. Due to an unhealthy increase in the amount of green house gasses like CO_2 in the atmosphere, there in increase in the temperature of earth. This increase in temperature of earth is known as global warming. It is due to human activity like transportation sector emissions and industrial factory exhaust.

Q.9 Explain the three R's in the conservation of environment?

Ans. The three R's refer to Reduce, Recycle and Reuse. Reduce: Use less electricity by switching off unnecessary lights and fans, save water by repairing leaky taps, do not waste food. Recycle: Materials made of plastic, paper, glass and metal should be recycled to make new items. Reuse: To use the things again and again. This is even better than recycling as the process of recycling uses some energy.

Q.10 What is the cause of over exploitation of natural resources?

Ans. To meet the demands of increasing population, the land is continuously be cleared and converted to grow more food up and to make dwelling places. The industrial and technological revolution and consequent new demands for materials and lifestyle needs is another cause. Both these reasons are causing a large pressure for tapping the natural resources quickly and extensively.

Q.11 Why do we need to manage our resources?

Ans. With the enormous increase in human population and advancement in technology, the natural resources are being over exploited, without caring for the resultant consequences. If the natural resources are not managed then the future generation have to suffer with its consequences of not having them at all.

Q.12 Why are some forests known as biodiversity hot spots?

Ans. Forests where a large number of flora and fauna species are found are termed as 'biodiversity hot spots'. The range of different life forms like bacteria, fungi, ferns, flowering plants, nematodes, insects, birds, reptiles and so on are present in forests. Certain areas in the western ghats of Maharashtra and Kerela are examples of biodiversity hot spots.

Q.13 What direct value does a forest have for man?

Ans. Forests contribute to the economic development of our country by providing goods and services to people and industry. They are intimately linked with our culture and civilization. Forests are useful to humans for the following reasons:

(1) Forests provide timber for the building and furniture.

(2) Forests provide raw materials for the paper industry, board industry, plywood industry etc.

(3) Forests yield bamboos, which is called poor man's timber. Industrially bamboos are used as a raw material in paper and rayon industry.

(4) Forests provide fuel energy needs to villagers staying in their vicinity. They also provide fodder and grazing grounds for their animals.

(5) Forests provide various minor forest products such as fruits, nuts, gums, resins, tannins, rubber, lac, dyes, fibres, medicines, katha, insecticides, camphor, essential oils, soap substances, cooking oils and spices.

(6) Forests also provide various animal products such as musk, honey, wax, tusser or mooga silk etc.

SECTION – B
(Previous Years Questions)

Q.1 In opium source of substance of medicinal value is : **[NTSE Stage-I_2006]**
(A) Seed (B) Latex of young fruit (C) Latex of ripe fruit (D) Latex of leaves

Q.2 The state brid of Rajasthan is : **[NTSE Stage-I_2006]**
(A) Peacock (B) Pigeon (C) Godawan (D) Vulture

Q.3 The state tree of Rajasthan is : **[NTSE Stage-I_2006]**
(A) Neem (B) Peeple (C) Banyan (D) Khejri

Q.4 The use of disposable paper-cups is more beneficial over disposable plastic-cups, because **[NTSE Stage-I_2014]**
(A) it is cheaper
(B) it is easily available
(C) it can be reused
(D) its recycling process has no harmful impact on environment

Q.5 Amrita Devi Visnoi of Rajasthan is related with **[NTSE Stage-I_2017]**
(A) Plant conservation (B) Education
(C) Sports (D) Politics

Q.6 Which one of the following signifies *ex situ* conservation? **[NTSE Stage-II_2016]**
(A) National parks and Biosphere reserves
(B) Wild animals in their natural habitats
(C) Inhabitants of natural ecosystems
(D) Conservation methods practiced in Zoo and Botanical garden.

Q.7 Which of the following organisms is used as a biopesticide? **[NTSE Stage-II_2017]**
(A) Azolla (B) Anabaena (C) Rhizobium (D) Trichoderma

Q.8 Bio fuels are the fuels which are obtained from plants. Which of the following statements is incorrect regarding this? **[NSO 2013]**
(A) Seeds of the plant *Jatropha* yield oil and are used to make bio-diesel.
(B) *Jatropha* is a cultivated plant which requires only certain specific soil to grow and also requires much irrigation.
(C) Bio-fuels are an environment-friendly altemative to fossil fuels.
(D) Animals usually do not eat the plant *Jatropha*.

Q.9 Choose the incorrect statement among the following. **[NSO 2013]**
(A) Natural gas is used as a starting material for the manufacture of a number of chemicals and fertilisers.
(B) Over millions of years, presence of air, high temperature and low pressure transformed the dead organisms into petroleum.
(C) Naphthalene balls used to repel moths and other insects are obtained from coal tar.
(D) Minerals, coal, petroleum, natural gas, etc. are exhaustible natural resources.

CONCEPT APPLICATION LEVEL - III

SECTION - A

- **Fill in the blanks**

Q.1 ____________ means development which meets the needs of the present generation as well as of the furture generation.

Q.2 Recycling and reuse is an example of____________.

Q.3 ____________ important source of resource for the forest development.

Q.4 Amrita Devi Bishnoi National award is for ____________.

Q.5 Another name for Chipko movement is ____________.

Q.6 CITES is ____________.

Q.7. The main purpose of water harvesting structure is not the hold the surface water but to____________.

Q.8 Combustion of fossil fuel in presence of less oxygen leads to formation of____________.

Q.9 Conservation of fossil fuel depends upon ____________.

Q.10 Oxides of____________ & ____________ are poisonous at high concentration.

SECTION - B

- **Multiple choice question with one correct answers**

Q.1 Mild grazing in grasslands by herbivores
(A) Retards growth of grasses (B) Stimulates growth of grasses
(C) Destroys vegetation (D) Arrests growth of grasses

Q.2 Measurement of water pollution is made by
(A) Coliform count (B) BOD (C) pH (D) All the above

Q.3 Waste produced during extraction of metal is called
(A) Scrap (B) Slag (C) Ore (D) Waste

Q.4 Which of the following is not the function of forest?
(A) It is used to make paper. (B) Resin, gum and drugs are obtained
(C) Controls flood (D) Causes soil erosion

Q.5 An effect of deforestation is
(A) Desertification (B) Soil erosion and floods
(C) Depletion of wildlife (D) All the above

Q.6 Euronorms for vehicles are related to
(A) Hydrocarbon emission (B) Nitrogen oxide emission
(C) Carbon monoxide emission (D) All the above

Q.7 Bishnoi community people lost their lives while protecting
(A) Khejri tree (B) Sal tree (C) Pinus tree (D) Teak tree

Q.8 Which of the following is not the cause of water scarcity?
(A) Increasing urbanisation (B) Rising living standard
(C) Rising demand for cash crops (D) Precipitation

Q.9 Animals get extinct mainly due to
(A) Predation (B) Habitat destruction
(C) Afforestation (D) Pollution

Q.10 Find the incorrect match
(A) Himachal Pradesh – Khatri (B) Maharashtra – Bandharas
(C) Bihar – Bundhis (D) Kerala – Surangams

Q.11 Which of the following bacteria is found in Ganga water?
(A) Coliform bacteria (B) *Streptococcus* bacteria
(C) *Staphylococcus* bacteria (D) *Diplococcus* bacteria

Q.12 Biodiversity hotspots are
(A) Oceans (B) Glaciers (C) Rivers (D) Forests

Q.13 Kyoto Protocol was signed in
(A) 1992 (B) 1995 (C) 1997 (D) 1999

Q.14 Opposition to the construction of large dams is due to
(A) Social reasons (B) Economic reasons
(C) Environmental reasons (D) All the above

Q.15 Khadins, Bundhis, Ahars and Kattas are ancient structures that are examples for
(A) Grain storage (B) Wood storage (C) Water harvesting (D) Soil conservation

Q.16 Pick the right combination of terms which has no fossil fuel.
(A) Wind, ocean and coal (B) Kerosene, wind and tide
(C) Wind, wood, sun (D) Petroleum, wood, sun

Q.17 Ever increasing human population, urbanization & industrialization have led to
(A) over exploitation (B) under exploitation (C) monetary exploitation (D) All

Q.18 Petroleum is a complex mixture of compounds of
(A) Hydrogen & carbon (B) Lead & Zinc
(C) Chloride & Flouride (D) Sodium & Chloride

Q.19 The word forest has been derived from a Latin word –
(A) Foris (B) Floris (C) Forestry (D) Flora & Fauna

Q.20 Rains in India are largely due to
(A) Monsoon (B) Day & night change
(C) Humidity differences (D) All

Q.21 Which among them is not a water harvesting method.
(A) Kulhs (B) Ahars (C) Khadins (D) Sigri

Q.22 Which amoung them is a local system of canal irrigation in Himachal pradesh.
(A) Kulhs (B) Ahars (C) Khadins (D) Sigri

Q.23 Rain water harvesting not only increases water availability but also checks the declining –
(A) Soil erosion (B) Water table (C) Deforestation (D) Extinct species

Q.24 Tribal women of which village started 'Chipko movement'?
(A) Reni in Garhwal (B) Dehradoon (C) Rajasthan (D) West Bengal

Q.25 Which among them is the National Award for wildlife conservation –
(A) Savitri devi (B) Amrita devi (C) Amrita Rao (D) A.K. Banerjee

Q.26 What was grass root cause of 'Chipko Andolan'
(A) Industrialization
(B) effort to end the alienation of people from their forests
(C) Deforestation (D) All

Q.27 Soil erosion can be prevented by
(A) Afforestation (B) Deforestation (C) Overgrazing (D) Removal of vegetation

Q.28 Mild grazing in grasslands by herbivores
(A) Retards growth of grasses (B) Stimulates growth of grasses
(C) Destroyer vegetation (D) Arrests growth of grasses

Q.29 Measurement of water pollution is made by
(A) Coliform count (B) BOD (C) pH (D) All the above

Q.30 Waste produced during extraction of metal is called
(A) Scrap (B) Slag (C) Ore (D) Waste

Q.31 Which of the following is not the function of forest ?
(A) It is used to make paper (B) Resin, gum and drugs are obtained
(C) Controls flood (D) Controls flood

Q.32 An effect of deforestation is
(A) Desertification (B) Soil erosion and floods
(C) Depletion of wildlife (D) All the above.

Q.33 Euronorms for vehicles are related to
(A) Hydrocarbon emission (B) Nitrogen oxide emission
(C) Carbon monoxide emission (D) All the above

Q.34 Bishnoi community people lost their lives while protecting
(A) Khejri tree (B) Sal tree (C) Pinus tree (D) Teak tree

Q.35 Which of the following is not the cause of water scarcity ?
(A) Increasing urbanisation (B) Rising living standard
(C) Rising demand for cash crops (D) Precipitation

Q.36 Animals get extinct mainly due to
(A) Predation (B) Habitat destruction (C) Afforestation (D) Pollution

Q.37 Raisins are dried
(A) Grapes (B) Pomegranates seeus
(C) Apricot (D) Emblic

Q.38 Raisins kept in water swell up because water is
(A) Hypotonic (B) Isotonic (C) Hypertonic (D) None of the above

Q.39 Raisins absorb water and swell up due to
(A) Plasmolysis (B) Deplasmolysis (C) Endossmosis (D) Exosmosis

Q.40 Raisins were kept in water for (i) 15 minutes (ii) 30 minutes (iii) 45 minutes and (iv) 60 minutes. Which lot absorbed more water
(A) i (B) ii (C) iii (D) iv

Q.41 Two lots of raisins were placed in water, one kept at 15°C (i) and second at 35°C. (ii) After about one hour raisins were taken out, wiped and weighed.
(A) Weight is same in two lots
(B) Weight is more in first lot
(C) Weight is more in second lot
(D) Second lot has gained double the weight increase in first lot.

Q.42 10 g of raisins were placed in pure water for 1 hr. On weighing again it was found that raisins now weigh 12g. What is the percentage of water absorbed by raisins ?
(A) 2% (B) 20% (C) 10% (D) 30%

Q.43 Before weighing, the wet raisins are wiped off by
(A) Cloth (B) Tissue paper (C) Cotton wool (D) Blotting paper.

Q.44 5 g of raisins were placed each in pure water, 5% sugar solution and 25% sugar solution.
(A) Raisins swelled up in pure water but did not do so in others
(B) Raisins swelled up in all the three
(C) Raisins swelled up in the first two but not in the third
(D) Swelling occurred in raisins kept in 5% sugar solution and not in others.

Q.45 Raisins kept in water gained weight 10%, 20%, 25% and 30%. Which lot was kept in water for longest period.
(A) First (B) Second (C) Third (D) Fourth

Q.46 Endosmosis is
(A) Entry of water into a substance
(B) Exit of water from substance
(C) Expulsion of water through a semipermeable membrane
(D) Entrance of water into a system through a semipermeable membrane.

Q.47 A semipermeable membrane is the one which allows
(A) Passage of both solutes and water
(B) Passage of water but not solutes
(C) Passage of solutes but not water
(D) Passage of water and some solutes but holds back other solutes.

Q.48 Raisins absorb water due to
(A) Osmosis (B) Imbibition (C) Diffusion (D) All the above

Q.49 Which part of the raisins functions as semipermeable membrane
(A) Skin (B) Walls of individual cells
(C) Plasma membrane of individual cells (D) Vacuoles of individual cells.

Q.50 For determining the percentage of water absorbed by raisins in a given time, apart from water, raisins and a watch, we shall require.
(A) A breaker, a graduated cylinder, a thermometer, a filter paper
(B) A watch glass, a graduated cylinder, a thermometer, a weighing balance
(C) A breaker, a thermometer, a weighing balance
(D) A graduated cylidner, a thermometer, a weighing balance. **[CBSE Delhi 2007]**

Q.51 A student soaked 5 gms of raisins in 25 ml of distilled water in each of two beakers X and Y. Beaker X was maintained at 25°C and beaker Y at 50°C. After one hour, the student observed that the water absorbed by raisins was **[CBSE AI 2007]**
(A) Same in case of X and Y (B) Less in case of X then in Y
(C) Exactly double in X of that in Y (D) Exactly four times in X, of that in Y.

Q.52 While performing an experiment to determine the percentage of water absorbed by raisins, the following data was obtained
Mass of water taken in beaker = 50 g
Mass of raisins before soaking them in water = 5g
Mass of raisins after soaking in water for two hours = 8 g
The percentage of water absorbed by raisins would be **[CBSE AI 2007]**
(A) $\frac{8-5}{8}\times100$ (B) $\frac{8-3}{8}\times100$ (C) $\frac{8-5}{3}\times100$ (D) $\frac{8-5}{5}\times100$

Q.53 Which of the following sets of materials is required to set up an experiment to determine the percentage of water absorbed by raisins

(A) Raisins, beaker of water, blotting paper, weight box, balance

(B) Raisins, beaker of water, balance, weight box

(C) Raisins, beaker, balance, weight box

(D) Raisin, water, blotting paper, balance. **[CBSE Delhi 2007]**

Q.54 An experiment was set up to determine the percentage of water absorbed by raisins. If the mass of dry raisins was 40 g and mass of wet raisins was 45 g, then percent water asborbed would be

(A) $\frac{45}{40}\times100$ (B) $\frac{40}{45}\times100$ (C) $\frac{45-40}{40}\times100$ (D) $\frac{45-40}{45}\times100$

[CBSE Delhi 2007]

Q.55 A student soaked 5 raisins each of equal weight in three beakers a, b and c, each containing 100 ml of distilled water kept at room temperature. He removed raisins from beaker **a** after 10 minutes, beaker **b** after 20 minutes and **c** after one hour. He calculated the percentage of water absorption as Pa, Pb, Pc. What is true **[CBSE AI 2007]**

(A) Pa = Pb = Pc (B) Pa < Pb > Pc (C) Pa > Pb > Pc (D) Pa < Pb < Pc

Q.56 A student placed 5 raisins in three beaker, a, b and c each having 50 ml of distilled water kept at room temperature. Raisins were removed after 10 minutes from beaker **a**, 20 minutes from beaker **b** and one hour from beaker **c**. On calculating the percentage of water absorbed by the raisins, it was found that

(A) Maximum absorption of water was by raisins in beaker **c**.

(B) Maximum absorption of water by raisins was in beaker **b**.

(C) Maximum absorption of water by raisins in beaker **a**.

(D) Absorption of water was equal in raisins of all three beakers. **[CBSE Delhi 2008]**

Q.57 The following data was obtained on performing an experiment for determining the percentage of water absorbed by raisins

Mass of water in the beaker = 50 g

Mass of dry raisins = 20 g

Mass of raisins after soaking in water = 30 g

Mass of water left in the beaker after the experiment = 40 g

The percentage of water absorbed by raisins will be **[CBSE Delhi 2008]**

(A) 10% (B) 20% (C) 45% (D) 50%

Q.58 At the end of experiment to determine the percentage of water absorbed by raisins, the raisins were wiped just before weighing. This is to ensure that **[CBSE AI 2008]**

(A) Hands do not get wet (B) Raisins lose water before weighing

(C) Weighing scale does not get wet (D) Only water absorbed by raisins is weighed.

Q.59 A student soaked 5 g of raisins in beaker I containing 25 ml of ice-chilled water and another 5 g of raisins in beaker II containing 25 ml of tap water at room temperature. After one hour the student observed that

(A) Water absorbed by raisins in beaker I was more than that absorbed by raisins of beaker II.

(B) Wat absorbed by raisins in beaker II was more than that absorbed by raisins of beaker I.

(C) The amount of water absorbed by raisins of both the beakers was equal.

(D) No water was absorbed by raisins in either of beaker I and II. **[CBSE AI 2008]**

Q.60 In the experiment "to calculate the percentage of water absorbed by raisins", one of the precautions to be taken is

(A) Raisins should be wiped and wet before placing in water.

(B) Soaked raisins should be wiped before weighing them for calculating the amout of water absorbed

(C) Soaked raisins should be squeezed to remove the water absorbed before weighing them

(D) Raisins should be immersed only in distilled water. **[CBSE 2008]**

Q.61 Twenty dry raisins were soaked in 50 ml of water and kept for 1 hour at 50°C. What out of the following was the correct observation ? **[CBSE 2008]**

(A) 8 raisins absorbed water, 12 did not (B) 10 raisins absorbed water, 10 did not

(C) 15 raisins absorbed water, 5 did not (D) All the 20 raisins absorbed water.

Q.62 Raisins are soaked in water for determining the percentage of water absorbed by raisins. The formula used by the student for calculating the percentage of water absorbed is

[CBSE Delhi 2009]

(A) $\frac{\text{Initial weight} - \text{Final weight}}{\text{Initial weight}} \times 100$ (B) $\frac{\text{Final weight} - \text{Initial weight}}{\text{Initial weight}} \times 100$

(C) $\frac{\text{Final weight} - \text{Initial weight}}{\text{Final weight}} \times 100$ (D) $\frac{\text{Initial weight} - \text{Final weight}}{\text{Final weight}} \times 100$

SECTION - C

• **Assertion & Reason**

Instructions: In the following questions as Assertion (A) is given followed by a Reason (R). Mark your responses from the following options.

(A) Both Assertion and Reason are true and Reason is the correct explanation of 'Assertion'

(B) Both Assertion and Reason are true and Reason is not the correct explanation of 'Assertion'

(C) Assertion is true but Reason is false

(D) Assertion is false but Reason is true

Q.1 **Assertion:** Regions in Gangetic plains are very fertile.
Reason: It has mainly alluvial soil.

Q.2 **Assertion:** Every biological system resist a change and wants to remain in state of equilibrium.
Reason: Climax communities of an ecosystem are produced after several changes it has gone through succession.

Q.3 **Assertion:** Conservation of biological diversity under natural condition is in situ conservation.
Reason: Increase of Manipur deer from 17 animals to 150 in Calcutta and Delhi zone is one of an example of these.

SECTION - D

• **Match the following (one to one)**

Q.1

	Column I		**Column II**
(A)	Kulhs	(P)	Karnataka
(B)	Kattas	(Q)	Maharashtra
(C)	Tals	(R)	Rajasthan
(D)	Kadin	(S)	Himachal Pradesh

Q.2

	Column I		**Column II**
(A)	Environment problem	(P)	Public money swallowed
(B)	Economic problem	(Q)	Deforestation & loss of biodiversity
(C)	Social problem	(R)	Dispeaced present & tribal
(D)	Health problem	(S)	Malnutrition and Obesity

ANSWERS

CONCEPT APPLICATION LEVEL - II

SECTION - B

Q.1	B	Q.2	C	Q.3	D	Q.4	D	Q.5	A	Q.6	D	Q.7	D
Q.8	B	Q.9	B										

CONCEPT APPLICATION LEVEL - III

SECTION - A

1. Sustainable development
2. Conservation
3. Monoculture
4. Wild life conservation
5. Hug the tree movement
6. Convention on international trade in endangered species
7. Recharge the ground water
8. CO.
9. Efficiency of our machines
10. Sulphur & Nitrogen

SECTION - B

Q.1	B	Q.2	D	Q.3	B	Q.4	D	Q.5	D	Q.6	D	Q.7	A
Q.8	D	Q.9	B	Q.10	C	Q.11	A	Q.12	D	Q.13	C	Q.14	D
Q.15	C	Q.16	C	Q.17	A	Q.18	A	Q.19	A	Q.20	A	Q.21	D
Q.22	A	Q.23	A	Q.24	B	Q.25	B	Q.26	B	Q.27	A	Q.28	B
Q.29	D	Q.30	B	Q.31	D	Q.32	D	Q.33	D	Q.34	A	Q.35	D
Q.36	B	Q.37	A	Q.38	A	Q.39	C	Q.40	D	Q.41	C	Q.42	B
Q.43	D	Q.44	C	Q.45	D	Q.46	D	Q.47	B	Q.48	A	Q.49	C
Q.50	C	Q.51	B	Q.52	D	Q.53	A	Q.54	C	Q.55	D	Q.56	A
Q.57	D	Q.58	D	Q.59	B	Q.60	B	Q.61	D	Q.62	B		

SECTION - C

1.	A	2.	B	3.	C

SECTION - D

1. (A)-(S), (B)-(P), (C)-(Q), (D)-(R)
2. (A)-(Q), (B)-(P), (C)-(R), (D)-(S)

Printed by Libri Plureos GmbH in Hamburg,
Germany